ONE LITTLE LIFE

ONE LITTLE LIFE

A White Child and a Black Woman Struggle against Racism

Sarah L. Seymour-Winfield

"The lowly and invincible of the earth -
to endure and endure and then endure,
tomorrow and tomorrow and tomorrow."

William Faulkner
Tomorrow

In loving memory of
Mary,
who throughout my childhood
embodied for me that exalted state of immeasurable wealth
called
Poverty of Spirit

Dis 'lil light o'mine, I's gonna let it shine
Dis 'lil light o'mine, I's gonna let it shine
Dis 'lil light o'mine, I's gonna let it shine
Let it shine, let it shine, let it shine.

Let it shine 'til Jesus comes, I's gonna let it shine
Let it shine 'til Jesus comes, I's gonna let it shine
Let it shine 'til Jesus comes, I's gonna let it shine
Let it shine, let it shine, let it shine.

Ain't hidin' it undur no bushel, NO! I's gonna let it shine
Ain't hidin' it undur no bushel, NO! I's gonna let it shine
Ain't hidin' it undur no bushel, NO! I's gonna let it shine
Let it shine, let it shine, let it shine.

Let it shine over de whole wide world, I's gonna let it shine
Let it shine over de whole wide world, I's gonna let it shine
Let it shine over de whole wide world, I's gonna let it shine
Let it shine, let it shine, let it shine!

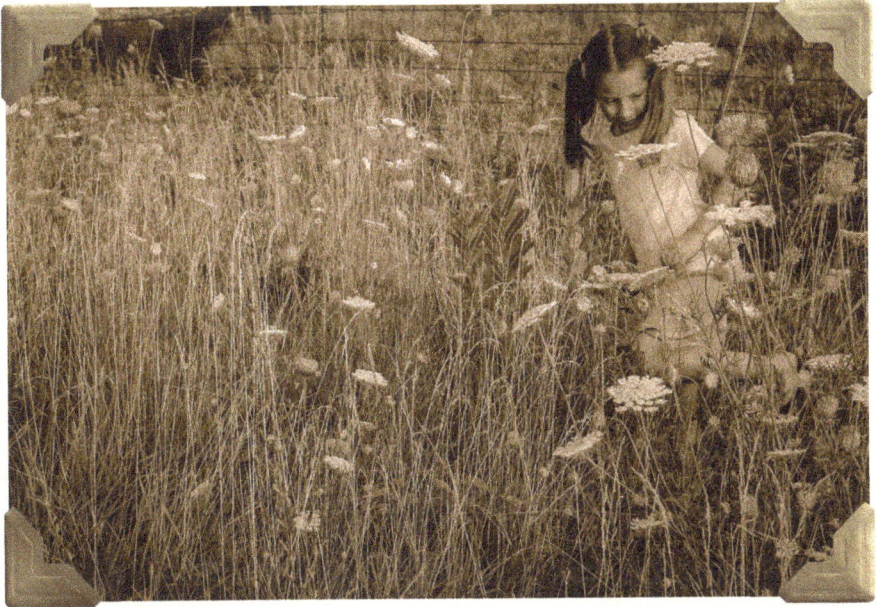

The author has been a life-long student of the Judeo-Christian mystical traditions, world literature, Greek and Roman mythology, and music. She lives a reclusive lifestyle in a wooded area of the Mid-West.

Printed in U.S.A.

ISBN 978-0-9971375-1-4

Braughler Books
braughlerbooks.com

TABLE OF CONTENTS

INTRODUCTION:
THE GARDEN

SLAVERY'S DRESS

INTRODUCTION TO RACISM

THE YELLOW BRICK ROAD TO DECISION

A CHILD'S NON-VIOLENT RESISTANCE

THE ETERNAL NOW

INTRODUCTION TO THE TRINITY

INTRODUCTION TO THE DEMONIC

THE CHRISTMAS LIGHT

THE FREEDOM TRAIN

COMPASSION

LOVE'S WEDDING DRESS

Dialect
Endnotes
Bibliography

A Letter to the Reader

Racism is the ugliest word in the English language, a prejudice which has cast over the American experience the longest shadow and left upon the Western world an indelible stain. Though the Emancipation Proclamation and the Thirteenth Amendment eradicated slavery forever, the roots of racism thrived throughout the twentieth century. Even at the opening of the twenty-first century, long after the Civil Right's Act, an elemental racism still flourishes in those northern and southern regions of America which remain steadfastly anchored in the failed Reconstruction Era.

As a child of the fifties and sixties growing up far above the Mason-Dixon Line, I witnessed a white family's racial antagonism addressed to their African-American servant and to their migrant workers. I also witnessed how those same servants dealt with this undying prejudice using elemental Christianity as their strength.

I realize now what a privileged childhood I was granted to see the dynamics of the antebellum South within my own history, and to mercifully witness the ultimate triumph of the love of Christ. It is my deepest hope that the relationship I cherished with the black woman on our farm will open ever wider the hearts of readers to empathy, compassion, and justice for all.

I am proud to introduce you to the woman who dared to cross the racial barrier to provide her *one little life* for the nourishment of my own. Welcome to our world – to Mary's and to mine.

Sarah Seymour -Winfield

THE GARDEN

Cain't you hear de hammer ringin'?
Cain't you hear de hammer ringin'?
Cain't you hear de hammer ringin'?
Shu'ly He died on -
Calvary

That ancient three-story farmhouse of Bessie and Clayton Clay was surrounded by a two acre garden which proliferated with the bounty of *nature's whole wealth,* a heaven on earth which God had seemingly planted long before humanity was driven forth to that harsh frontier east of Eden's guarded walls. Every conceivable flower and shrub flourished in that fertile earth made even more verdant by Miss Bessie's vigilant care. Throughout each summer of my childhood, that garden bloomed as the eternal high summer of a perpetual eternal spring.

On the northern border by Greyson's cow pasture, the garden was bounded by a simple fence which long ago had been rendered invisible by huge continuous mounds of ever-blooming pink fairy roses. On the southern border by Mr. Clay's potato field was another simple fence long ago made invisible by huge continuous mounds of fragrant honeysuckle, their scent simply overwhelming when I arrived in early June. Behind the barn to the east was a continuous row of blackberry bushes which scampered over their boundary fence in wild profusion and fantastic disarray, and to the west, near the single-lane country road by the little red country mailbox, stood a stiff, solemn row of proudly purple iris.

Roses bloomed everywhere. Roses clamored up the sides of the farmhouse to the second floor bedroom windows and up the sides of the barn till halted by the sudden heat of its sloping metal roof. Roses grew supported on old chipped wagon wheels and graciously offered their regal fragrance as they twined elegantly around every utility pole. The rose garden near the side porch was underplanted with pink petunias, whose spicy scent each evening was so strongly glorious when we sat on that side porch and watched those enchanting ethereal whirls called hummingbirds flash by. Roses bloomed continuously from the high promise of June through the high heat of September, providing a glorious rainbow of vivid and pastel hues among those thousand acres of green.

Throughout that garden flowed a wide gravel lane as that river once flowed through Eden. A smaller gravel tributary flowed beside the full length of that huge barn, and a narrower stream flowed east past the little red shed toward the blackberry bushes which flourished far away where the sun faithfully came up. Before that enormous barn and shed, that wide river and its smaller tributaries flowed into and gathered together as a large oval, pearl-colored lake. It was those imaginative waters which seemed to nourish all those roses and *Flowers worthy of Paradise,* where Mother Nature in that garden poured forth her splendors *profuse.* It was those same waters which seemed to sustain the trees of that garden, because near the shed, by the shore of that vast lake, an enormous weeping willow seemed to drink perpetually of its waters silver-grey.

A huge elm dominated the area behind the house, a gigantic tree which through two centuries had learned the wisdom of humility, because it graciously provided one of its massive arms as the support for my tire swing. Across the lane a mighty maple which had miraculously withstood a lightning strike arched proudly and resolutely over the gravel stream. Further down the lane, a lacy mimosa lent its ethereal grace among the shrub roses, daisies, and boxwood. But the trees which dominated that landscape, that *happy rural seat of various view,* were monumental pines, ancient towering pines, which zealously shielded the farmhouse from those wintry blasts which howled mercilessly across those fields. Among those pines, soaring upward beyond the roof, a tree so colossal it seemed to pierce the very height of God's heaven, was a blackish-green Douglas Fir beneath which a sea of ivy luxuriantly thrived.

That majestic tree grew directly outside my attic bedroom window. It dominated my vision for the first twenty summers of my life. It was the first tree I saw in the morning and the last I saw at night. They say that when a child is lost, that little one has been stolen by the spirit of the wood. Were those effulgent branches metaphors for the crossbeam of the cross, that tree soaring upward in this Eden as the cross once rose upon Golgotha?   Was that tree the Tree of Life *High eminent,* or was it the Tree of *Knowledge of good bought dear by knowing ill?*

Now I know it was all three.

SLAVERY'S DRESS

Our Fadder who is in Heav'n
W'ite man owe me 'leven bu' pay me seven
Dere kingdom come, dere will be done
But if I hadn't a'took dat, I wudn't a'had none.

I was supposed to call her *Colored Mary* the way everyone did, but even as a child that seemed wrong to me. My name was Sarah, but no one called me *Pinkish White*. I do remember two, maybe three times, when I must have been trying to please an adult, that I called her Colored Mary and felt miserable and ashamed of myself for days. Except for those few exceptions though, I steadfastly called her Mary, and I still often wonder if my steely determination contributed to at least some of the stresses in my early, little life.

Mary was the cook and house maid for that farm where I spent my childhood summers. Her cooking responsibilities though were so enormous that she rarely had time for any other room except the kitchen and its tyrannical stove. For ten hours each weekday, and often during harvest on Saturday too, Mary cooked and cleaned up after the equivalent of three Thanksgiving dinners a day, elaborate feasts with rolls and pies for us, Miss Bess and Mr. Clay, a sampling of their many adult children, and various men who helped with the animals and crops. After each meal was over, the tablecloth was shaken out, the floor was swept, and the blue-willow plates were washed, dried, and re-stacked neatly in the china cupboard, Mary was standing at the stove once again, and I was setting the table for the next meal. She was rewarded for all that drudgery during supper on Friday evening. Mary's husband, Leonard, would drive up the lane in his huge ancient car to take Mary home, as Mary stood patiently near Mr. Clay seated at the head of the table, meekly holding out her hand until he remembered to place into her weathered palm one solitary twenty dollar bill.

From the time I first became conscious of Mary until I saw her for the last time when I was a junior in college, she wore each and every day all summer long the same dirty sneakers and the same housedress, a beige-grey or gray-beige short-sleeved dress printed with a design which resembled dark swirling feathers. Over the years, I watched her sneakers and dress deteriorate and fade until the print, though still vividly imprinted upon my memory, nearly disappeared in reality, and eventually shoes, dress, as well as her many accompanying flowered aprons, were each held together by an increasingly abundant supply of dime-store safety pins. As an adult, I was shocked to learn that Mary was the same age as Miss Bess, which meant that when I was born, Mary was nearly fifty years old, but her slender, petite figure, her absolutely flat face with its shiny coal black skin, radiant eyes, and nearly constant hint of a smile, meant to me that Mary in her housedress of safety pins was not only young, she was ageless. To me, Mary was simply immortal...

except for those precious moments each summer when she and I would fanaticize what "purdy dresses we's gonna wear whin we grows up an' be de preacher's wife."

In the corner of the kitchen opposite the squeeeeky screen door, which led out to the side porch near the rose-petunia patch where the hummingbirds hovered each evening, were two narrow steps leading to a perpetually closed door. Behind the door was the narrowest of spiral stairways leading to two tiny bedrooms on the second and third floors. The first bedroom was no longer used, and the uppermost room I never saw, because I somehow thought that the rats in the cellar had a tunnel to the highest level of the house too, so I never went up there. Over that nearby window, a plank of raw plywood had been nailed which served as a humble shelf for the assortment of cacti which Mary grew in the almost total shade cast by that colossal backyard elm. It was upon the higher of those two steps where Mary and I would sit and look through the pages of the Montgomery Ward catalog, fantasizing what each of us would wear when we "grows up an' be de preacher's wife."

Mary sat down upon that top step in the corner before that perpetually closed door, wiped her hands on her safety-pin apron then sighed wearily –

"Chil', I got's t'sit down a minit. I got's t'catch my breath.
Jus' fu' a minit. Whut's you doin' undur de table?"

"Oh! I'm sweeping up some crumbs somebody dropped under here.
I'm almost done."

"Chil', I do t'ank you. Dat's mos' 'preciated.
Ain't you gittin' big, helpin' in de kitchen like you's all grow'd up.
Time sho' does fly. You's four year ol' alredy!
Jus' yestuhday you was a baby. Cain't b'lieve it.
Come on out frum undur dere, chil', an' sit by me fo' a spell.
Doan hit yo' head. Mind yo' head.
Gracious chil', how miny did we have fo' breakfast?"

"Two hands, and for lunch we had two hands plus one,
and Miss Bess said two hands for supper."

"No wonder I's tired. I's gonna sit righ' shere fo' a bit.
I jus' cain't face dat supper jus' now."

I placed my little broom and dust pan on a chair, then sat down
close beside her. Mary's dress always smelled of potato dust and potato
fields, and of whatever food she had been preparing. That day she
smelled of potato dust and fields, and tomatoes and corn. On washing
day next week, her scent would be potatoes, laundry soap, and bleach.

Snuggling close beside her, I said in strict imitation –

"Mary, I have to sit down just for a minute.
All those people and all those crumbs. No wonder I'm tired.
I have to catch my breath."

Mary chuckled her quiet chuckle
before her continuous litany began again –

7

"I got's t'start cookin' ag'in in a bit, chil'. Mistuh Clay, he wants rolls.
Miss Bess, she wants a sho'tcake, an' I got's t'wash dem ber'ies frum dis
mo'nin', an' den I got's t'cook dem chickins Laine done plucked.
We ain't gonna has no time t'make no beds.
I got's t'rest a bit, Sarh, just a bit."

I gazed up into her shiny black face and sighed wearily -
"Chickens and just a bit."

"O yung'in,
purdy chil', stay 'way frum dat shed, y'hear?
Such big brown eyes an' purdy hair.
Dem's fe'el hands down dere, Sarh. Dey ain't no house niggers,
dem's fe'el hands. You stay 'way frum dat shed."

"The grease and the tar."

"An' dem fe'el hands, Sarh! Is you list'nin'? Dem fe'el hands!"

"Fe'el hands!" I exclaimed with equal force
what I utterly lacked in comprehension.

Mary's voice grew soft once again -
"I got's a few minits, yung'in. Wanna –"

"– PLAY PREACHER'S WIFE!" I shrieked.

Mary laughed quietly.

· "I know y'likes - Lookee you, clappin' yo' 'lil hands.
Huny chil', whut's I do widou' shuu?"

Mary slowly shook her head as though she were saying 'No'
and gazed deeply into my eyes –
"Whut wuds I gonna do?"

Mary placed the new Montgomery Ward catalog in her lap
then carefully turned to the women's section.

"Yo' bandaid's a'floppin' on yo' knee, Sarh.
Lemme see undur dere. Lemme jus' lif' dat – Jus' lemme -
Look a'dat, Sarh! See dat? It's all heal'd.
Dat w'ite line, see dat w'ite line? Dat means it's all heal'd.
You kin pull dat bandaid off whin y'wants to."

"Will that hurt?"

"O chil', I ain't never seen such a scared 'lil t'ing.
Jus' stay close t'me, Sarh. I woan touch dat.
Dat dere bandaid's gonna fall off whin it wants to.
Doan shuu fret, yung'in. You's alrigh' by me."

I mashed my scrawny little body into Mary, wrapped my arms
around her as far as they could reach, and carefully kept my hands upon
the sleeve of her housedress. Bessie and Elaine had told me never to
touch Mary's skin.

"Chil', doan shuu fret none. You jus' stay righ' shere by me.
You 'member de rules 'bout Preacher's Wife?
Whut you's gonna wear whin we's de preacher's wife?"

"I can only choose one dress from each page."

"Only y'own page, Sarh, only y'own.
Only one dress frum y'own page.
An' d'odder rule? You 'member? You cain't..."

"What?"

Mary chuckled to herself -
"You cain't never..."

*"What? I cain't - Oh! I can't ever look back. Not ever.
I have to remember, because I can't look back."*

"Y'got's t'member, chil', 'cause y'cain't never look back."

I carefully removed my arms from around Mary's shoulders
and turned the page.

"Oh, look at this dress. I like this one."

"Dat's a purdy un, Sarh. Shu'ly is. All dem blue flowr's an' lace.
All dem people in dat church's gonna look a'shuu
whin you be de preacher's wife."

"I pick that blue one. Which one do you pick?"

"Dere ain't none on my page."

"But you could pick that pretty red one, Mary."

"I cain't wear dat un, Sarh. I's color'd, chil'.
I's gonna wear w'ite whin I's de preacher's wife.
W'ite dress, w'ite shoes, w'ite gloves, w'ite evyt'ing."

"You have to wear white?"

"No chil', I doan got's t'wear w'ite. I jus' wants to.
I's color'd, Sarh. I's gonna wear w'ite.
You's a w'ite, chil'. You kin wear color'd."

"Wh - What?"

"Jus' turn de page, Sarh."

"Oh Mary, look at this green one with pretty flowers
and such tiny buttons!"

"Dat's a purdy un, too. You's gonna look righ' purdy in dat.
Do y'alredy has a green one? Do you 'member?"

"Did I already choose a green one?"

"You's de one who got's t'member."

"I choose a blue one before, I remember. Which one do you pick?"

"Deys ain't no w'ite uns on dis here page nedder."

Mary turned to the nursing uniforms.
"Gracious, Sarh, look a'dat un!"

"Oh Mary, it has a little white hat and white shoes too.
You'll look so beautiful when you marry the preacher."

I turned back the page.
"This purple one is pretty, Mary. It has a collar that –"

"Why's dat cactus droopin'?"

"But I like this pink one too, with the little –"

"You kin only has one, de purple er de pink.
You cain't has both. Dat's de – An' why's dat cactus yelluh?"

"I like the pink one the best, with the little–"

"An' why's dat cactus lookin' sick?
Dey *all* looks sick."

"I don't know, Mary. I've been watering them."

"*WHUT?* You ben watuhin' my cactus?"

"Yeah. Sparkle buttons!"

"Whin you ben watuhin' dem?"

"Yesterday. I love sparkle buttons."

"An' b'fo' dat, whin you ben watuhin' dem?"

"Before yesterday."

"An' b'fo' dat?"

"Before what? Bows!"

"B'fo' yestuhday, whin you ben -?"

"Oh! I water them every day
after you leave with Leonard, if I remember."

"Well y'ain't 'memberin' no mo', girl,
you's fugitin'! All dem cactus is *dyin'*!"

"But they were so dry!"

"Deys *supposed* t'be dry, chil'! Dat's how dey breathe!
Dey got's t'breathe!
You watuh dem cactus whin it rains in Arizona."

"What? When it rains? In - ?"

"Whin it rains in Arizona you kin watuh dem cactus."

"W - What?"

"O gracious! Whin y'read in de papers, 'Is dat de truth? Well I'l be!
Tuhday it done rained in Arizona,' den you kin watuh dem cactus.
Whut's my gonna' do wid shuu? You leave my cactus 'lone."

"When - when it r-rains in the papers? then -?"

Mary chuckled again and sighed again
and shook her head from side to side as though she were saying 'No.'

"Huny chil', jus' leave'm be. Dey come back.
Dey be alright. Dey come back. I got's go, Sarh.
Miss Bess is comin' back frum Sloane's wid dat yeast,
an' I got's t'make dem rolls, an' fry up dem chickins,
an' fry up dem tatter patties.
You kin sit righ' shere an' look a'dem purdy dresses
er you kin run down de lane,
but y'cain't go nowhar near dat shed, y'hear?"

"Field hands and tar."

Dere's a Promise Land a'comin', I know it, I know it.
Dere's a Promise Land a'comin' just over dat hill.
Dere's a Promise Land a'comin', I know it, I know it.
I jus' got's t'hoe t'de top o'dat hill.

Though Mr. Clay devoted many acres to wheat for his cattle, and
grew one glorious acre of sweet corn solely for his family, and though he
practiced rotation farming with crops of alfalfa to improve the soil,

Bluebonnet was primarily a potato farm, a massive enterprise because each August, as many as six eighteen-wheelers lined the lane waiting for their potatoes to arrive off the conveyor belts processed by the migrant workers in that huge white shed. All summer long we ate a monotonous litany of potatoes, absolutely relentless, of boiled-fried-mashed-potato patties, followed by boiled-fried-mashed-potato patties. I always hoped we would arrive on the farm on a *mashed* day, because that was my favorite. We ate potatoes from the time they were the size of quarters to full size, just as we ate that sweet corn from the time when the kernels were barely discernable to the time they were so huge, we called it *horse corn*. Sometimes Mary walked down to the shed to gather the daily potatoes, but during most years when the field across the lane was not planted in alfalfa or wheat, she and I took the pitch fork and bushel basket and dug enough from that hedge row for that meal and the next.

Mary opened the screen door –

Squeeeek

SLAM!

walked across the porch to the two concrete steps
then shouted across the lane toward the chicken coop –

"Sarh? *Sarh!* Chil', is you hidin' in dat coop ag'in?
Has you snuck'd in dere t'terr'ize dem critters ag'in?
You ain't pickin' up dem ducks by dere necks, is you?
Sarh, I kin mos' feel y'in dere. Come on outta dere!
Ef'n you's in dere, come on outta -
Put dat duck down, right now! Sarh, put dat duck down!
Gracious, chil', dat ain't no handle. Dat's his neck!
You know dey got's t'breathe!"

"But I was only-"

"Run on over here! Ain't no tractors comin'.
Run on - Git on over here. Hur'y up now.
Durn flies. Shew! Flies al'ys buzzin'.
Careful on deez steps. Grab my dress. Yeah, be careful now.
Dirty yung'in certain. Mind dat floorboard."

"I was only-"

Squeeeek

"Hur'y on in dere. Watch dat bee. Shoe unfasn'd ag'in."

SLAM!

The kitchen table stood littered with bowls and flour,
the atmosphere filled with the spicy scent of freshly baked peach pies.

"Chil', whut's I gonna do wid shuu?
You cain't pick up dem ducks by dere necks! Dey got's ta -"

"I know. Dey got's t'breathe."

Mary chuckled her familiar chuckle -
"O my, chil'."

"Oh, your child."

"Gracious, look a'yo' dress! Whar's you ben? Down in dat shed?
Ain't I tol' you y'cain't -"

"No, Mary, I wasn't in the shed."

"Y'cain't go down dere. All dat grease an' tar. How miny times I got's
t'tell you? Dat's dirty dirt, girl. Cain't git dat out in no washin' 'sheen.
You stay 'way frum dat shed, y'hear?"

"But I wasn't in the –"

"Turn 'roun'. Lemme see. Jus' turn 'roun'. Jus' dirt an' mud,
jus' clean dirt. But girl, lookee here! Whut in tarnation?
Y'got's some chickin' doo here, but I reck'n I kin git dat out.
Dat kin come out. But you stay 'way frum dat shed, y'hear?"

"Grease and tar."

"An' y'ain't never gonna pick up dem ducks
by dere neck ag'in, y'hear? Dey got's t'breathe."

"Dey got's t'breathe."

"Now fast'n dat sandal shoe. Some stones in dat lane is sharp."

Mary leaned over, smiled, and whispered her secret -
"Sarh, I got's t'git some tatters. You wanna -"

"Can I carry the pitch fork?"

Mary chuckled again.

"Chil,' you know you cain't do no pitch fo'k. You's 'lil.
I know you's alredy four year ol', bu' 'lil girls ain't strong 'nough
t'car'y somet'ing dat heavy over such 'lil shoulders. Gracious!
You's ol' 'nough t'car'y one plate at a time t'ough, so you kin
set de table all by yuse'f, but y'cain't car'y dis big pitch fo'k jus' yit.
Someday whin you's great big,
you kin car'y it over yo' shoulder, an' den I's gonna car'y yo' basket.
Dat's my promise."

" I never get to carry the pitch fork! I always have to drag the basket!"

"You t'inks you's big, but y'ain't yit. Finish fas'nin' dat shoe, y'hear?
Buckle dat odder sandal shoe. Some stones in dat lane is sharp."

"We having mashed potatoes?"

"You know we's havin' boiled, plain boiled.
We had mashed d'odder day."

"I like mashed."

"Den you kin mash 'em up on y'own plate den. Look at dat dress.
Gracious! We ain't doin' no washin' fu' nudder week.
Dirty yung'in certain."

"When I'm five, can I could carry that pitch fork?"

"Whin you's great big you kin car'y dat pitch fo'k.
Now you drag dis basket. Jus' grab dis side righ' shere an' drag it.
Yeah, jus' drag it, like y'al'ys does."

Mary took the pitch fork leaning against the wall
and squeeeeked open the screen...

"Hur'y up, chil'. Drag yo' basket up over dis door sill.
Deez flies is al'ys buzzin'. Come on, girl. Watch dat bee!
Drag it up over dis – Dat's right, jus' -"

SLAM!

"Durn bugs al'ys buzzin'. All summer long deez durn bugs.
Miss Bess, she swats dem durn flies frum mo'nin' 'til -"

"Mary?"

"Uuu huu."

"Will there be snakes?"

"Chil', dere be snakes. Dere al'ys be snakes.
Snakes all over dem fe'els. Careful dat floorboard. Durn t'ing.
I's never know'd why Mistuh Clay doan nail dat durn t'ing down.
Somebody's gonna trip an' hurt demselves."

"Those little green snakes?"

"Chil', lemme git you down deez steps furst,
b'fo' we talk 'bout no snakes. Come on down deez two steps.
Drag yo' basket an' hang ontuh my dress real good.
Deez steps is so deep, I doan want y'fallin'.
My doan deez roses an' petunias smell good. Bet dey smell ev'n better
in de ev'nin'. Jus' drag dat down now – jus' slow, Sarh.
One mo' step t'go. You's mos' – careful now – you's mos' –
Dere. Dat's good. Dat tub o'pink portulaca has ben bloomin'
by dat ol' blue pump fo' es long es I kin 'member."

"Will there be snakes, Mary? Those little green snakes?"

"I reck'n, chil', bu' doan shuu mind, Sarh. Doan shuu mind.
Dey woan bodder us none ef we doan bodder dem.
Jus' hold ontuh my dress, chil'. Just hol' ontuh me, an' drag yo' basket.
Dat Rose o'Sharon sho' is big. Gracious! Clean up t'de top o'dat pole!"

*"I'm scared of those little green snakes, Mary.
I've never seen one at the orphanage."*

"I know you's scared, chil'. I know dat, bu' lemme tell you somet'ing.
Dooz 'lil green snakes live in dat tatter fe'el, 'cause dat's dere home.
Dey's 'posed t'be dere, chil', 'cause dat's whar God wants 'em t'live.
Truble is dem tatters b'long t'us. Our tatters is in dere home.
So we has t'share dat fe'el. It's dere home, bu' dem's our tatters,
so we got's t'share dat fe'el."

"Crayons!"

"Crayons? Whut's you talkin' 'bout, yung'in?"

"Oh! At the orphanage we don't have enough crayon boxes
for everybody, so three of us have to share.
Me and Kati and Mimi share one box."

"Den, yeah. We got's t'share de tatter fe'el
like y'share yo' crayons wid yo' friends.
Mary an' Sarh an' dem 'lil green snakes got's t'share dis fe'el.
Now we's come t'dat 'lil place 'tween de honeysuckles whar dat sho't
path is intuh de tatter fe'el. Hold ontuh me while I hol' back deez
branches. We doan want none snappin' yo' 'lil face.
Careful now, jus' drag yo' basket thruu here 'til we git intuh de fe'el.
Yeah, we's mos' dere. Doan deez flowr's smell like heav'n.
Gracious, flowr's all 'round us.
Makes me wanna eat de air! It's nice I doan see no bees nowhar.
We's mos'- mos'- mos'- Dere! We made it!
An' no branches hit shuu. Dat's good."

Before us lay a vast field which stretched beyond Baxter's hog
farm, past the road to Jamestown, then on to the horizon where the two
woods came together. Great long rows of potato plants converged into a
point far away.

"Crayons, Mary! Looks like crayons!"

"You's right, Sarh. Ain't dat somet'ing. I ain't never seen dat b'fo!
Dat fe'el sho' does look like a big ol' box o'green an' brown crayons.
Sho' do. Like God jus' laid 'em out side by side His own Se'f,
den color'd de whole sky yelluh an' blue."

"Share the crayon box."

"Dat's right. Dat's 'xactly right.
Sarh an' Mary an' all dem 'lil green snakes is gonna share dis fe'el
in peace tuhday. Dey woan bodder us none ef we doan bodder dem.
So whut's you gonna do whin y'see one?"

"Jump and get cold."

Mary chuckled.

"I 'spect so, Sarh, but whut's you gonna t'ink t'yuse'f?"

"Oh! Dey woan bodder us none ef we doan bodder dem."

"Dat's right. Dat's good. Now let's git some tatters."

"Can we have mashed?"

"You know it's a boiled day, plain boiled."

"Then I'll mash 'em up on my own plate then."

Mary looked down at me as I looked up at her -

"O my, chil'."

"Oh, your child."

O, whut's y'gonna eat, gonna eat, 'lil chil'n?
Whut's y'gonna eat way up in dat Heav'n o'God?
O, whut's y'gonna eat, gonna eat, 'lil chil'n?
'Milk an' honey at dat table o'God!'

Frank and Elaine were the sort of relatives referred to as *shirttail,* or sometimes *twice removed.* As a child, I never understood exactly what their relationship was to me, and after their passing, I lost the interest to inquire. My only concern was that the first day of every June, they drove me from the orphanage to the farm to spend three months in the presence of Mary. After interminable hours in an unair-conditioned car, the winds howling with hurricane force through every opened window, the atmosphere smelling so strongly of exhaust that my fingernails turned blue in the Allegany tunnels, we at long last turned left onto the single-lane country road near Ike Porter's outdoor summer market by Sanford's wispy asparagus farm. Rural Route 2 had a narrow lane of gravel along one side which enabled cars and pickups to pass slow moving tractors and combines. It led past several other farms set far back from the road toward the potato farm owned by Mr. and Mrs. Clay.

"Looks like Blackwells had another baby, Frank,"
Elaine always commented.
"Fresh diapers on their line again.
All those children, and now another."

"Rabbits," was all Frank said.

I leaned as far as I could into the front seat, thinking my effort would push the car faster so that soon, I would be once again, for one whole summer, close to Mary. After driving about ten miles past several farms with their pastures and fields, so eager with anticipation that my shoulders hurt from leaning so hard into the seat, I saw Greyson's farm with the backyard beauty shop, the farm which momentarily hid our farm from view. When we passed Greyson's, I suddenly saw on the horizon our flat-roofed, three-story white farmhouse, and that pain in my chest burst into joy.

"Oh look, Frank. Look at that.
Farm looks the same, Frank. Looks the very same."

The house was obscured by those various trees and dark pines and all those flowering shrubs I knew so well. An enormous barn where the cows were kept was set far back from the house, and an even more enormous shed where the tractors, combines, and the potato conveyor belts were stored, was barely visible on the opposite side of the barn. The chicken coup and other tiny outbuildings were not apparent this far away, but as Frank drove closer, the whole configuration of buildings and vegetation came increasingly into view. At the eastern edge of that property, at the far end of that long lane, near the gravel which led back to the split-rail fence where the blackberries scrambled and their brambles forever hummed with bees, stood that small, leaning dark red shed, it's finality at the edge of that property serving as a lopsided punctuation mark. That was where the echo-bird lived.

"Must have rained last night again, Frank.
That creek back there is swollen, by Wilson's."

Frank drove slower now, the wind through the windows

a

slow

lazy

stream.

It's too late for Mary to be there, I thought
but did she remember my cake?
Did she remember my birthday cake?

"Trees there on Greyson's hedge row look washed, dirt dark.
Rain must have come through here long.
Crops look good, though. No damage.
Bess said it'd been comin' down nice and steady this spring.
Farm looks the same, Frank. Looks the very -"

" - same," was all Frank said.

"The hay smells so good, and even the manure smells sweet."

"Sweet?" was all Frank said.

I hope she remembered vanilla.
Mary said she always has a bottle of vanilla in the pantry.

"Remember last year about this time? It had just rained too.
Seems like we always come here after a rain.
And all those cows dead? Remember?"

Will it have chocolate frosting? Mary promised to remember.

"When lightning struck that stream, Malcolm's place.
Thirty cows? Was it thirty? Thirty cows I believe.
All struck dead from lightning drinking from that stream.
County officials all over that field, remember, and those cows just —"

" - stiff," was all Frank said.

"It's about seven. I told Bess we'd be here about seven."

If she remembered chocolate frosting, did she remember those little flowers? I like those pink flowers, all round the side.

That fear and self-doubt tightening in my chest...

She doesn't have to remember those flowers,
but will she remember my cake?
What does it mean that Mary remembers?

While still leaning hard into the seat,
that tightness made it even more difficult to breathe.

What if Mary forgets? What if she forgets my cake?
Does that mean she forgets me?
If she has forgotten me, then will anyone be my mother?

With that thought, my feelings solidifying into terror, we turned into the lane and drove slowly toward the little leaning red barn where the echo-bird lived.

Whenever Frank and Elaine were about to leave the farm at the end of the summer to take me back to the orphanage, Mary promised that next June, she would make me another vanilla birthday cake with chocolate frosting and put it under the silver cake-saver on top the tall cupboard in the pantry.

"Y'know I make you dat cake, Sarh.
I know how much you like yo' cake."

"Can it be vanilla again, Mary? That's my favorite."

"Lookee you, clappin' yo' 'lil hands.
Chil', you know dat's yo' cake. You know dat's a promise."

"But what if you don't have enough vanilla?"

Mary leaned over, smiled and whispered –

"Chil', I al'ys got's 'nough 'nella fu' dat cake, so dat cake al'ys be w'ite,
but I be sho' t'save 'nough choclit fu' dat frostin'.
Dat frostin' be dark. You can count on dat frostin' bein' dark."

*"I like chocolate frosting. We can't have chocolate at the orphanage.
The Nuns call it x – x- cessive."*

"Dat frostin' be dark, Sarh. I know y'like dat."

"Can you put those little pink flowers around the sides like last year?"

"I doan know 'bout next year, Sarh, 'bout dem flowr's.
I doan al'ys has dem flowr's, chil'. Miss Bess buys 'em at Sloane's
in town, an' niggers ain't 'lowed in dere."

"But chocolate frosting on vanilla cake?"

"Yeah, an' ef I ain't' got's no pink flowr's, it's gonna all be dark."

"It will all be dark. Then you'll put it under the cake-saver?"

Mary chuckled again and smiled.

"Whut's I gonna do wid shuu, Sarh?
Y'know I will. Dat's my promise. Y'know dat.
An' ef I's gone whin y'all comes, you know dat cake be dere."

She never broke that promise, but because I was so accustomed to emotional abandonment on that farm, I always expected she would. On the turnpike each summer, I always wondered if she remembered me at all, since I seemed to be so easily forgettable, and my stream of consciousness was always the same – *What will it mean if she remembers, and what will it mean if she forgets?* We usually arrived in the evening after Mary had left. Bessie without fail was waiting for us, rocking on the side porch in her favorite chair, her grey hair piled up in a perennial bun on top her head. After unknotting my legs and unlocking my knees, and after giving Bessie nothing more than a polite kiss, I stood at the screen door on the side porch near the rose-petunia patch, my nose pressed into the dirty screen, the wooden crossbar through the middle of the screen pressed into my forehead. I peered through the kitchen toward the silver cake-saver in the pantry and felt that anxiety which is a mixture of hope and dread, because if Mary had forgotten not only the cake, but also me, I would truly be alone in this world.

"We made good time, Bessie. Seventeen hours again.
Did it storm here?"

"Last night, through the night, Laine, and through this morning.
Nice slow rain, though. No run-off. No run-off."

"Frank and I were remembering all those dead cows
last year."

"When lightning struck that stream? Terrible!
But they had insurance, and you know those Malcolms are well off.
Massie comes from money. Oh yeah!
Her father left her that whole farm!"

28

While the women endlessly gossiped,

I slowly

hesitantly

pulled open that squeeeeky screen door.

There before me was the large farmhouse kitchen which would be the stage for some of the most painful and lovingly memorable moments of my childhood, the room where I would learn the most fundamental lessons of the Christian life. I quietly closed the door.

To my right, was Mr. Clay's enormous wooden desk upon which piles of farm papers were sometimes neatly stacked but were usually scattered in utter disarray. Next on that wall was an un-curtained window around which Mary twined a scraggly philodendron supported on bare nails. In that corner, a huge carved rocking chair stood next to Mr. Clay's filing cabinet, which housed insurance papers and legal documents in its three drawers. The connecting wall was more brick than wood, because there was the enormous cavern of the fireplace which, because I visited there in the summer, I would see only once in use. In the corner opposite me were the two steps leading to that perpetually closed door near the window with Mary's cacti, and next to that window was the china cupboard which was soon to have such significance for me. On the wall to my left was the sink in the far corner with the stove nearest me, and to my immediate left was the doorless entrance to the short hallway which led past the back stairway to the dining room and the center hall. In the center of the room was an enormous wooden table which could comfortably seat ten, but often was required to seat a dozen, and in front of the fireplace was the old wood stove, used by then only for burning papers. But directly across from me was the entrance to the pantry where the refrigerator was kept, and where the tall cupboard stood with its silver cake-saver on top.

Though I always wanted to run toward the pantry, I always walked very slowly, like a child approaching a treasured grave, that silver dome and its contents holding such desperate meaning for me. I'd pull over that rickety, old, partially painted chair, stand on it on rigid tip-toe, and push the dome up timidly with my index finger. There, in that sliver of evening light between the plate and the silver dome, I saw the dark swirls of chocolate frosting on my birthday cake, and sometimes I saw a row of those little sugar flowers from Sloane's. Then I breathed again, and my knees stopped quivering, and all my fear evaporated away.

The strange thing is that as a child, I never remember taking that cake down, even when I was tall enough to reach it easily, and even though I loved Mary's cakes *from scratch*. It was enough for me just to know that it was there, and if it had remained there all summer, that would have been fine with me, because the cake itself meant that Mary remembered me, and the chocolate frosting with it's little sugar flowers was her pledge that she loved me.

Then I ran.

I jumped off the chair, ran through the kitchen, rounded the bend by the stove, ran down the short hall past the back stairway and up those two steps into the dining room, and ran until I came to that grand entrance hall where I pressed my nose into one of the cut-glass panels on either side of that massive front door. There, in one of those tiny octagonal facets of glittering glass was the blackish-green hallucinogenic image of my fir tree underplanted with a sea of ivy, each tiny heart-shaped leaf glistening in the early evening light. When I turned around, there was that grand wooden staircase spiraling upward three stories, its walnut banister terminating before me in one huge coiled wooden knot. The walls, upright piano, and staircase were illuminated by slanting shafts of light piercing those deep green boughs, casting hundreds of tiny rainbows of hope upon those steps and walls. I opened the front door, walked across the porch with its tall white columns, stepped down toward the blue hydrangas into that magical Eden, and turned left toward the clump of tall purples, daisies, and little mounds of little yellows. When I drew near the rose-petunia patch by the side porch, I heard Miss Bess still endlessly gossiping –

"Oh yeah, Laine.
Massie's father was sick a long, long time, in that new hospital down
in Jamestown. Well, it's not new now, but it was then.
Two days before he died, he called in a lawyer, and cut his own son
right out of his will. Oh yeah, he was in sound mind and all!
I don't rightly remember what that family feud was all about,
but land sakes! - that court case went –"

" - on and on," was all Frank said.

INTRODUCTION TO RACISM

He be shuckin' an' javin'
Lookin' fo' a place t'take a nap
Only t'ing, all animals hate dem niggers.
Prob'ly de only bird a nigger attracts
Is a buzzard t'peck out his eyes, his eyes,
Is a buzzard t'peck out his eyes.

When Mr. Clay stood on the side porch, he was the same height as the screen door, which meant he had to remove his work hat and bow a bit when he stepped over the threshold into Mary's kitchen. Everything about Clayton Clay was larger than life. He was too tall, his shoulders too wide, his neck too brown, his voice too deep, his hands too large, and his work boots too long. Of all the bib overalls which gathered around that table, his were the dirtiest, the most stained with that "dirty dirt" from the shed impossible to "git out" in Mary's "washin' 'sheen."

He took a bath once a week, a hallowed ritual to which everyone gladly contributed by using no hot water that entire afternoon. After dinner on Saturday evening, after the grand oblution occurred, Mr. Clay stepped out of that tiny second floor bathroom clean shaven, smelling of Old Spice, wearing a fresh pair of jeans, a clean denim shirt, a brown leather belt with a huge staghorn buckle, and one of his hideously garish ties printed with a matador or a national monument, an Arizona sunset or a naked woman. He then put on his *weekend* hat, a fedora which he kept carefully wrapped in cellophane on top Bessie's cedar closet, then drove out the lane in his huge Buick, straw and oats stuck in both fenders and blowing out the tail pipe.

No one knew exactly what Clayton did on his evening out. Perhaps he went into Maysville to talk with the other farmers, leaning back on those straight-backed chairs beneath the revolving barber pole, bragging about his crops or lamenting about the weather. Perhaps he went to a movie in that tiny theater then ordered a soda like everyone else in the corner drugstore with the diagonal door across the street. He owned a bar in Jackson, so perhaps he visited there, questioning how sales had been that week and inquiring about any rowdies. But this last possibility was the most likely - Miss Bess often complained that Clayton visited *"that damn woman in that trailer down in Jamestown,"* and there was even talk on the side porch after supper, as the evening air grew heavy and the hummingbirds flashed by, that Clayton and Bessie's own sister were *"carryin' on."* Whatever he did on his evening out, he always returned in the wee hours and slept late on Sunday morning right through the milking chores.

When their children were young, Bessie and Clayton owned that tomato farm appropriately called *The Lowlands*, because the soil in that notorious region never seemed to dry. After three summers of abnormally abundant rainfall, the tomatoes rotted in the fields, and their young family during the Great Depression nearly starved. Several photos still remain from that time, the parents and four of their nine children standing shoeless in a pig stye, their clothing hanging about them as rags. When *Bluebonnet* became available, the family moved to notably higher ground, and after changing his cash crop from the precarious tomato to the more adaptable and resilient potato, Mr. Clay's farming success was assured. This transition was evident in my little life, because in the storeroom across the hall from my attic bedroom stood two tall stacks of magazines, *The Tomato Farmer,* and the even taller stack, *The Potato Farmer.* It was of this farm that Mr. Clay was so enormously proud.

Several evenings each week, Clayton drove his Buick slowly down each and every country road which interfaced with his fields, noting what areas of what hedge rows needed trimming, and what stray seedlings from other fields had sprouted among that field's dominant crop. Stray sunflowers from seeds which birds had carried in, as well as wild mustard which blew in from that infamous wild mustard farm thirty miles away, were recorded in a little notebook which he kept in the glove compartment of his car. His findings were reported to his sons the following day. As a result of these observations and his workers' vigilant care, his immaculate rows of crops and the dirt ruts between them appeared as green and brown crayons in an orderly crayon box. The border strips were as beautiful as his fields. The only weed Mr.

Clay not only tolerated, but actually nurtured, was the Bluebonnet. Though no seedlings were allowed between the rows of any fields, a large clump flourished at the corner of the last field before Anderson's dairy farm. Since those flowers seemed to proclaim the name of Mr. Clay's domain, that solitary clump was actually encouraged to thrive.

Though he took great care of his fields, and took great pride in his appearance on Saturday night, he cared nothing about the farmhouse itself. That apparently was the realm of the women, and about their world and their unique needs he simply did not care. One morning, a long black snake was coiled next to a bed, having slithered down the chimney, because there were no chimney guards. The electrical system was so hopelessly antiquated that the walls were often hot to the touch. The plumbing was bad, the toilet often backed up all summer, and no one ever called a plumber. The dirt-floor cellar was home to generations of rats, and at night, the kitchen swarmed with armies of mice, their tiny nervous clawings and mysterious presence suddenly vanishing when I switched on the light. As long as banquets of food were on his table, his farm was thriving, his fields were immaculate, the top drawer of his kitchen desk was stuffed with fifty and one hundred dollar bills, and his Saturday evening ritual of bath and socializing remained intact, Clayton Clay was enormously content with his world and his life. Compassion for others, at least during my childhood, was notably lacking in his character.

One evening on the side porch, when the fireflies were setting aglow the alfalfa across the lane, the entire field shimmering under the phases of the moon, Mr. Clay described in graphic detail how he and his brother one rainy Saturday afternoon long ago had cut up the family dog and hung the bleeding pieces from the ceiling of their own side porch to play butcher shop. When his children were young, he brought home one pint of ice cream on Friday night, took half for himself and left the remaining cup to be fought over by his nine children. I'd heard that he, overcome by a blind rage, had once thrown a pitch fork at one of his sons, and that he had made his daughters plow fields and milk cows before they could catch the bus to their little one-room schoolhouse. I had seen him drape the tails of young colts over the electric fence to see

how fast they could bolt, those terrified creatures darting across Donald MacPhearson's paddock as fast as their wobbly legs could run. I was horrified the day the young, inexperienced farm insurance representative came to speak with the owner of Bluebonnet. Since he had rehearsed his speech by addressing an imaginary *Mr. Smith*, he several times referred to Mr. Clay with this innocent mistake. But when Clayton had had enough of his inexpertise, he ordered Mary to bring out a bowl of the peach ice cream she had just hand-cranked. Since that young man had never eaten home-made ice cream, he bolted down a bowlful with gracious gratitude as Clayton waited and watched. Suddenly that young man grabbed his temples with both hands and doubled over when the ice cream headache hit, and Mr. Clay laughed with pure delight at "this city boy!"

Though all the above behaviors were sufficient to progressively teach me that from Mr. Clay I should keep my distance, it was the behavior of his grown daughters who visited the farm which made me more and more suspicious of him as I grew older. They exhibited toward him a strangely unnatural and stiff respect far beyond what his presenting behaviors or even their relationship to him merited. The inflection of their voices when calling him "*Daddy*" sounded familiar yet cautious, as though that word ended in a perpetual question mark. Though his daughters gossiped and joked in that kitchen with what appeared to be an easy fellowship, their eyes on close inspection were as hard as steel, each woman's eyes a duplicate of her sisters', and their laughter was so forced that their combined gaiety was notably aggressive. During their visits, the atmosphere in Mary's kitchen was contrived and synthetic, his daughters' adapted behaviors displaying a duplicity which even as a young child unnerved me.

It wasn't until I was much older that I slowly realized the dark secrets lurking within the shadows of that family. One afternoon, I overheard two of his daughters crying, whispering about years long ago when "*Daddy*" had kicked them repeatedly in the ribs as they writhed upon the floor, recalling anguished scenes at night on that remote farm which caused my knees to quiver. I saw only the results of the brutality and abuse which apparently had been expressed toward his children on those isolated one thousand acres during those ink-black country nights illuminated only by stars, but I plainly witnessed the dark side of his character in relation to anyone whose skin was obviously of another race. Mr. Clay was an enigmatic blend of evil and good, cruelty and charm, an archetypal figure which had been placed alongside Mary on the center-stage of my life for three months each year. Those two characters dominated this Eden of geraniums and roses, wickedness and snakes, and one almighty fir tree.

The stressor on that farm which was to me then and is to me now as enigmatic as the sound of one hand clapping was the racism directed toward Mary and the black migrants upon whom Mr. Clay's farming success did utterly depend. During the summers when migrants came up from Mexico, gracing the fields with all their colorful clothing like brushstrokes of paint on a canvas of green, the tensions on the farm were not so rigid, but during the summers when black workers came up from the Deep South, tension on that farm, far north of the Mason-Dixon Line, was severe. Though it tormented me to witness the abuses directed toward the migrants, it was the abuses directed toward Mary herself which so threatened me that I forced myself as a child in sheer desperation into the domain of the mystical. Most of those abuses took place in that infamous farmhouse kitchen, that same room where she and I played *Preacher's Wife,* abuses based upon the supposedly irrefutable truth that Mary was somehow inherently less than we.

Though I was allowed to address Mary by her given name, I somehow knew it was mandatory that I privately think of her as *nothing but a filthy nigger.* Mary referred to herself as *a nigger,* and always said, "I'd rather be a nigger den po' w'ite trash," an expression which even then bent my little mind to the breaking, because I knew what trash was. With all the meanness on that farm and all the dirt, the toilet backed up for months with no one seeming to care, the endless swearing, Mr. Clay's women and bars and drinking, and people getting beat up with broken collar bones and thrown out of the back seats of cars into ditches, and Mary receiving only twenty dollars a week for her incessant work, weren't we the *poor white trash?* Weren't we the *filthy niggers?* Maybe what she said was true, maybe it would be better to be Mary than to be us! Yet for all the derogatory remarks about her, Mary appeared to be Bessie's friend, both women having raised nine children together, with Mary herself even serving as the midwife for one of those births. Though she and Bessie spent many hours of most days together, there were several times every summer which I did profoundly dread.

In the corner of the kitchen opposite the two stairs leading to that perpetually closed door, on the other side of the old wood stove where Mary sat on a stool to eat all her meals, was a recess large enough to hold an enormous carved wooden rocking chair near that uncurtained window around which Mary twined a spindly philodrenden supported on bare nails. It was in that chair where Bessie sat most mornings, endlessly gossiping and telling Mary what to do as Miss Bess swatted against any hard surface endlessly renewable generations of flies.

> "Oh yeah, old man Kitchner,
>
> he said his granddaddy came home from Maysville one snowy night –
>
> well he was *trying* to get home, but he fell down in a snow bank
>
> and froze to death. Oh yeah, they didn't find him for weeks!
>
> We're having twelve today, Colored Mary,
>
> and I 'spect Clayton will want some more of those lemon pies.
>
> All those kids and their daddy frozen solid in a snow bank.
>
> I'm gonna have to get me some new fly swatters.
>
> See if the Rag and Ware Man has a couple in his truck
>
> when he comes. This one is about done in."

Suddenly an invisible racial curtain fell, a sudden stiffness in the air somewhere between Bessie sitting in her rocking chair and Mary standing at the sink! Without warning, Mary regressed from being a friend to being a *filthy nigger*, a *colored woman* who had somehow trespassed into our *white* kitchen, and I never knew why. In my childhood mind, I thought on the days when Bessie sat at the *table* swatting flies, that if I sat in her rocking chair in the corner by the philodendron, I could predict when that curtain was about to fall and somehow prevent it. But after years of concentrated attention, I never did hear or see that moment coming. It was always a shock for me, a sudden horrible pain in my heart that Mary would now be the object of verbal abuse until that interval passed, and a sudden horrible shame in myself that I wasn't *colored*, but *white*.

Since I didn't want to add to Mary's shame by her seeing yet another white face in that dreadful kitchen, I always jumped up to run, hearing the verbal abuse beginning behind me, and run, and run, and run up the spiral stairway to the attic where I'd fall down breathless between those tall stacks of magazines in the storeroom-bedroom across the hall from mine, and stare, and stare, and stare into the air, waiting for that moment to come, begging for it to come, when the room would disappear, nothing visible at all, no sound at all, and I'd stare into that emptiness and feel holy awe.

When I intuited that Mary's abuse was about to be more severe than usual, when that curtain descended with Miss Bess simultaneously rising from her chair, I'd run down the lane to be even farther from the violence, past the rose-petunia patch, past the towering height of the lavender Rose of Sharon, past the spirea and forthysia bushes, past the mimosa tree, all those assorted perennials, and all those rose bushes supported on old wagon wheels, down to the iris at the very end of the land. In sheer desperation, my heart hammering, my mind a panic, I'd look out breathless across the fields or across Mr. Zellner's strawberry patch, and stare, and stare, and stare, and stare, waiting for that moment to come, begging for it to come, waiting until that white-out appeared again, that holy vastness where there were no blacks or whites, no suffering or pain, and even little me disappeared into the ocean of God. Though that avenue into wordless adoration was available to me when I was able to run away, those summers provided many situations when I was unable to escape and was totally at the mercy of the ignorance of the adults.

In my little mind during my little life, I could not fathom the disparity between what I was learning about the compassion of Christ from Mr. Slain at the orphanage versus the indifference and cruelty which white people directed toward those who inherently possessed skin tones different from theirs. This disparity intensified into extreme cognative dissonance, because I knew the entire Clay family was Christian. I could sometimes articulate a scriptural verse which clearly articulating the evil of this disparity, but often when I observed this graphic and painful discrepancy, my mind simply went blank, a dumbness which in my own mind apparently reflected the dumbness of the people inflicting the abuse. There was no articulation of English words which could adequately express my shock that people who often sang in triumphant tones at the piano in the central hallway the somber tune of *The Old Rugged Cross*, could so utterly fail to address that mercy and charity to human beings with the very same needs and wants as they. Once I had even passed by Mr. Clay's bedroom and seen him stark naked praying on his knees by the side of the bed when the potato plants were dying from drought, petitioning his worries to the same God as Mary prayed to at her little Baptist Church. Trying to reconcile these diametrically opposed world views produced in me all the mental stress of a Zen koan. Since I knew that Jesus not only would have disapproved, but also would have spoken aloud about the abuses He saw, I attempted to say words and exhibit behaviors which would indicate that I as a little girl disapproved too. I did not know though that the commandments of racism were carved on a mountain every bit as formidable as Sinai. Scenes of graphic cruelty are branded forever on my mind.

Sunday was the day when Mary rarely worked. Sunday mornings on the farm were sheer bliss for me, an introduction to Heaven. Frank and Elaine drove into Maysville early to do whatever Frank and Elaine did in Maysville early, and Mr. Clay, the only person I've ever known to observe the Sabbath perfectly, remained in bed or very near it until almost noon. The migrants were down on Clifford's farm, the mice which swarmed the kitchen at night were now asleep, and no eighteen-wheelers crowded the lane waiting for their potatoes. All the chaos and racket of the week dissolved on the Sabbath into peace. I'd sit in that rocking chair in the corner of the kitchen and hear nothing, glorious nothing, a symphony of nothing. When I read as an adult that an alternate translation of the Hebrew *still small voice* was the *sound of utter silence*, I knew that was what I had heard during those few transcendental hours, *the sound of utter silence.*

Sometimes, I walked round the front garden, feeling *the cool of the day*, smelling the roses and observing their dew, watching the shadows shorten as the sun became more firmly established in the sky. Most of those hours though I spent in the kitchen looking out that side window where Mary's philodendron twined endlessly supported on bare nails, listening to silence and feeling that life was just too beautiful to bear.

I didn't know the word *brunch*, so I thought Sunday dinner was just a weird mixture of food because Mary wasn't there, of scrambled eggs plus green beans, or scrambled eggs plus corn. Supper though was usually eaten at fancy restaurants, which must have been exquisitely expensive because fifty years ago, I remember Mr. Clay flashing out of his wallet, with a great deal of embarrassing fanfare, one hundred dollar bills and leaving ten dollar tips. This scene though took place in the evening at a more humble restaurant, where Miss Bess liked to order clams, and since the ride there passed a clearing where I almost always spotted one or two deer, I loved to go there. We arrived before the dinner crowd, about four o'clock, and the Clays, Frank, Elaine, and I were given the center table in an otherwise unoccupied room. I faced a beautiful double window through which I saw fields and woods and the warm glow of the late afternoon sun.

"What are you getting, Bessie?"

"Oh Laine, I think I'll have those clams."

*"You're ordering them again? You order them every time!
I don't see how you can eat those rubbery old things.
Sarah, what are you getting?"*

I twirled a lock of hair with my forefinger
as I smoothed the yellow ruffle on my best dress.

"Dreaming again. Always dreaming. Sarah!"

"I love this pretty ruffle.
When I'm the preacher's wife -"

"Sarah, I'm asking you what you want to eat."

"Oh! Mashed potatoes."

"Laine, that girl would live on mashed potatoes if we'd let her."

"Mashed potatoes and what else, Sarah?"

I continued to admire my ruffle,
then pulled up my sagging sock by its lace trim.

"Butter."

"Sarah, you need to order something else.
What else do you want?"

"There's a hole in my lace. I'll get a -"

"What else do you want?"

"Oh! Macaroni.
I'll get a safety pin from Mary. She has lots of safety -"

"Sarah, for a five year old, you can't think at all!
Do white girls wear safety pins?"

"But Mary's dress is full of -"

"Protein," was all Frank said.

"Did you hear that? Frank's right. You need protein.
Do you want chicken or fish?"

"Do I have to?"

"Yes, make up your mind. Chicken or fish?"

"But I like mashed potatoes."

"Sarah, are you listening?"

"Vacant," was all Frank said.

"Chicken or fish?
Tell the waitress, she's waiting for -"

"Oh! Chicken, please.
I love this ruffle."

"It is very pretty, Miss, and I think I heard you say
you wanted mashed potatoes too?"

"Oh yes, please, and vanilla cake with chocolate -"

"Sarah! You have to eat your dinner first before you -"

"The trials of Job," was all Frank said.

We were eating dessert when a young black couple with a little girl my age were led to the booth directly opposite me by that large double window, the husband on the right, his wife on the left, with the little girl seated behind her mother. I remember being very surprised at their daughter, thinking that all *Negros* were destitute, because she was wearing the same yellow dress with the wide yellow ruffle identical to mine. As soon as they were seated, racial hatred erupted.

I heard from the other end of our table what sounded like the hissing of two giant snakes, long continuous ugly hissings which were punctuated periodically only by Bessie's or Clayton's need to breathe. Both adults had turned and were glaring toward that window, apparently assuming that their horrid hissing sounds and hateful facial expressions would drive that little family away. As that young couple continued to peacefully study their menus as though nothing at all out of the ordinary were happening, both Bessie and Clayton escalated their hatred from hissing to spitting loudly in their direction. As Mr. Clay grew increasingly agitated and angry at the couple's refusal to acknowledge his and his wife's graphic disdain, he quickly escalated his spitting to verbal epithets, muttering words I couldn't understand under his breath. He loudly punctuating his mutterings with "nigger!" and "filth," then continued his sentence with more syllables I couldn't hear before punctuating that mumbling with "scumb" and "swine." As Bessie continued to spit toward the window, loudly questioning, *"How can a restaurant like this serve such –"* that couple looked up from their menus and gazed intently at each other. When that little girl hopped up and stared toward our table, wild-eyed with fear, her mother's left arm shot straight out to the side to keep her child in the booth.

I assumed the adults at our table didn't understand that that family was like us, because that child was wearing the same yellow dress as mine. My favorite yellow dress with that same pretty ruffle around the hem must have been her favorite dress too. So I shouted out, *"Why is Bessie —"* and Frank kicked my knee so hard I cried out, those horrible hissings and hateful words continuing from our table. Despite that pain, I tried again to understand what simply could not be comprehended by calling out even louder, pointing toward that couple, *"Why is Mr. Clay—"* and Elaine slapped my hand down hard against the table.

My mind was a chaos of panic as though the room were spinning. I wanted desperately to run again, run up to the attic to fall down breathless between the two tall stacks of magazines, or run down to the end of the lane to stare out over Mr. Zellner's strawberry patch until that white-out mercifully appeared again, but there was no place I could go. The hissing of snakes continued all around me, echoing throughout that empty room. But through all the confusion and through all those hateful sounds, I watched as that couple leaned closer and closer toward each other until their faces almost touched, gazing deeply into each other's eyes, giving each other strength, their profiles etched forever in my memory, the late afternoon sun glowing iridescent behind them.

That same waitress ran into the room her eyes wide with fear, her hands flapping up and down like the wings of a bird, shouting over and over in a voice of near panic, *"You have to leave! You have to leave!"* Apparently Bessie and Clayton assumed she was addressing that black couple, but when they realized the waitress was insisting that *we* leave, the Clays became incensed! Those horrible words and hateful expressions exploded more visciously then, directed toward the window as we got up to leave. That little girl looked at me so scared and confused, and I looked at her equally scared and confused, and I wanted to say goodby and tell her I liked her dress, but I was afraid I'd be hit again. Frank and Elaine pushed me out of the restaurant toward the car, my legs unable to bend, feeling such confusion and such terror that I felt physically sick and faint.

"Get in the car, for Christ's sake! *SARAH!* Get in the -"
"*Legs locked like some stupid thing, stupid as those nigg -* "
"Why in God's name do you bring her here? Leave her at the —"
"*My God, Sarah, bend your knees!*"
"Looking like a bug again, all bug-eyed, *SARAH!*
Mouth catching flies, *SARAH!* Get in that car, NOW!
My God, such a stupid – FOR CHRIST'S SAKE, *MOVE!*"

I remember nothing about that ride back to the farm, neither the deer nor what I'm assuming was very loud talking in our car. I must have been in that place of awe again, that transcendental realm far beyond this terrible world, because my shame of being *white* had been so profound, I simply wanted to die.

Somebody's knockin' at yo' do'
Somebody's knockin' at yo' do'
O sinner, why doan shuu answer?
Somebody's knockin' at yo' do'.

Maybe it's Jesus
Somebody's knockin' at yo' do'
Maybe it's Jesus
Somebody's knockin' at yo' do'
O sinner, why doan shuu answer?
Somebody's knockin' at yo' do'

On the wall of the side porch near the screen door hung a silver dinner bell next to the large bridle which had been worn long ago by Mr. Clay's original plow horse. Each weekday and sometimes during harvest on Saturday too, Mary would squeeeek open the screen "just a bit," reach around so she wouldn't admit too many flies, then clang that clanger several times until she was sure the men in the outbuildings had heard that dinner was ready and it was "time t'git washin' up!" In the grass near the narrow sidewalk by the side porch stood an antique wrought iron boot scraper, which Miss Bess vehemently insisted each farm worker must faithfully use. Though each worker was careful to scrape his boots each and every time he entered the house, the kitchen floor nevertheless was constantly in need of "a good scrubbin'." No matter how many times Mary crawled around on that battered linoleum dragging her slop bucket, fresh dirt was always deposited the very next day.

"Dis floor is gittin' so old, Sarh, I do b'lieve I cain't tell no mo'
de diffunce 'tween de good floor an' de bad dirt.
Gracious! You 'mind me de next time de Rag an' Ware Man comes
dat I's a'needin' a new knee pad. Dis un is 'bout done in,
'cause I kin hear my knees 'plainin' just a bit."

I liked to watch out the philodrendon window as the men approached the house, seeing their heads one by one pass just above the window ledge. Then when the door burst open and the men and the flies burst in, pandemomium burst upon the peace of Mary's kitchen.

"Clayton? You been driving that Buick
out in those fields again?" Bessie shrieked.

"No, no, Bess. That's just oats from the barn and –"

"You have so! Land sakes, you have so!
I can see with my own eyes plain as day.
There's potato leaves wound 'round the –"

"No, no, Bess, that's just –"

"Clayton? Clayton!
You keep driving that Buick over those ruts,
that battery shaft – or that axel box –
or whatever that thing is called -
is gonna fall right out in a ditch somewhere,
then where will we –"

"Clifford," Clayton bellowed,
"last night I saw a sunflower poking up in –"
"Clayton? Are you listening to -"
"- that field by Anderson's.
You cut that "Clayton?" down after "Clayton!" dinner,
won't you?"

Bessie scowled then continued her tyraid directly to Mary,
though just loud enough for Clayton to hear -

"If he doesn't stop that foolishness,
that crank axel, or that shaft tank, or whatever that thing is called,
is gonna fall right out in a ditch somewhere! Then where will we be?
Nothing to drive to Sloane's but tractors and combines.
And with all those springs out in that old pickup,
that driver's seat's like the back of a buckin' bronco!"

Two young farm workers whispered in the corner
waiting for the other workers to finish washing up,
waiting for an opportune time to grab the soap.

"Tonight I'm gonna bag her."

"Who?"

"Florencie, after the square dance in Jackson."

"Not with them doggies you ain't! Henry, you smell like a –"

"And Clifford?" Clayton bellowed again -

"Sir?"

" - On the hedge row near that last field before MacPhearson's,
there's more of that wild mustard clumping up near the road."

"I saw that myself this morning coming in.
When I finish ploughing near Anderson's, I'll dig that up and -"

"*My goodness, Bessie, it's hot in here!*"

"Needin' another towel over here!"

"*Not as hot as last winter, Laine. Oh yeah.*
Clayton put logs in the fireplace the size of tree trunks,
and I was sure he was gonna burn this whole house down!
We didn't know if we were eating roast, or we were being roasted!"

"Clifford, just leave off the ploughing until that clump's dug up.
That damn stuff worries me. What are we having today, Bess?
I'll take both pitchers of lemonade."

"*Well, fried chicken, but you can smell that, and fried potatoes,*
more corn and rolls, some nice beans
from Porter's stand. Oh yeah, his son's back from the hospital."

And this morning I went down to Sanford's to pick up my Avon, and Delsie gave me these nice cucumbers."

"Any more lemon pies?"

"No, we ate the last of them last night, but Colored Mary made cornstarch pudding this morning."

The new farm workers now took their place at the sink and continued their conversation about a *bag.*

"Tonight, after the square dance. Tonight's -"

"You devil! That fiery little red-head?"

"Yep, tonight's the night!"

Mercifully I was sent out into the pantry to retrieve the last one pound block of butter from the refrigerator. As I opened the dairy drawer, I wondered if it were possible, *hoped* that it were possible, for that army of mice to pry open the door and nibble away all the obnoxious cheeses Mr. Clay stored there.

Then I heard a faint tapping at the pantry door.

The sound surprised me, and a vague apprehension rose in my chest, because no one had ever knocked there before. The Rag and Ware Man, the vet, and the insurance salesmen always came to the side porch near the lane. Since the entire family was assembled in the kitchen, I didn't know who was knocking at my door.

After a moment, I dared to peek around the refrigerator. There standing near the screen in the dense shade cast by that colossal elm, was a migrant worker -

Dem's fe'el hands, Sarh.
You stay 'way frum dat shed, y'hear? Dem's -

                holding his work hat over his heart,
turning the brim slowly round and round, inch by inch, as he gazed
directly at me.
"Ma'am?"
he whispered hesitantly from the shadows -
"Ef – uhhh - Ef'n y'pardun me, Ma'am?"

When our eyes locked, he backed slowly

down

the three concrete steps

and stood anxiously in the grass.

My knees went rigid!

My hands dropped the butter!

Our eyes were fastened upon each other!

Dey ain't no house niggers, Sarh. Dem's fe'el hands.
Purdy 'lil chil', you stay 'way frum –

"Ma'am?"
he whispered, his face now lowered,
alternately looking at the ground and glancing up at me -
"Ma'am – Miss – Ah ain't no gempmum,
bu' ain't Ah mo' 'n jist wuthless swamp trash?
Ah ain't had nuff'n t'eat fo' t'ree days,
an' Ah's pow'ful hongry affah all dat wu'k.
Ev'n swamp trash needs mo' 'n watah t'wu'k.

Ah ain't meanin' t'bodder y'none, Ah ain't meanin' t'be no truble.
Ah's jist a'wunderin', Ma'me."

He continued to turn his hat round and round in the shadows, his glance moving down then up, his voice so hesitant –

"Dis mawnin' heah, Ah wuz sk'yerd Ah wuz dyin',
sk'yerd an' feelin' hongry an' sik wid no' mo' 'n watah
an' kuz Ah's all wore ou' wid wu'k. Ah's dyin'. Ah knows dat.
Ah's sik an' dyin', an' Ah doan k'yer no'mo'
whut ol' Massah Clay duz t'me. Er hiz Missus.
Ah doan k'yer whut hiz fambly duz t'me. Ah's gwyne tek dat chanst.
'Whut's de wustest t'in' dat kin happ'n' at de big 'ouse?' I t'ougt.
Ain't Ah's 'redy has de wustest t'in'? Ah's dyin' enyhow.
Dey's gwyne lay me soon 'neaf dat willah enyhow."

In sheer terror, my mind became a cloud... my consciousness floating...as though I were staring out over Zellner's into that great mental white-out...but instead I was staring not at fields, but at this field hand.

"I – I'm so sorry, but – but I don't understand anything except hungry? and sick? and – and dying?"

As I slowly...quietly...closed the refrigerator door,

he cautiously

hesitantly

stepped up onto the

bottom

step.

Into that mental vacancy and blank staring I always assumed whenever my constant fear intensified to the unbearable, the voice of my Sunday School teacher, Mr. Slain, mercifully intruded -

"Sarah, are you – Sarah?
Dreaming is inappropriate for Sunday School Class. Are you -"

"Oh! I was just -"

"Do you remember what Jesus said?
Did you memorize that verse that I –"

"Oh! He said, "If - if you see somebody who's hungry,
well - that's me! because -"

"Well, Sarah, He actually said - but - but that's good enough."

The migrant's voice was so low in contrast to the deafening din in that kitchen, and his pain and fear so obvious that I dared to step even closer to the screen.

Once again, he cautiously

hesitantly

stepped up onto

the

second

step,

his gaze now direct and unwavering.

"Wud y'hap'n t'has enyt'in' t'et?
Nemmine t'aint possum an' greens. Nemmine t'aint korn pone.
Ev'n ef Ah has t'ast 'm twice, Ah's gwyne tak' dat chanst.
Ev'n ef deez is de las' wuds out'a m' mouf, Ah's gwyne tak' dat chanst,
else Ah be dyin' in dem fe'els t'day."

Mr. Slain's persisent questioning continued -
"Do you recall anything else, Sarah?"

*Yes! I do, I do. He said, "If - if you take care of the sick,
well - that's me too! because-"*

From the shadow beneath the elm tree, that faltering voice continued –

"Miss, Ah's mo' 'n swamp trash,
bu' ev'n trash needs sumfn' t'et.
Y'all's 'bout t'et yo'se'f, 'cuz Ah kin heah dat.
Ah's no diffunt, Miss, no diffunt. Ah's mos' ez gud."

Two conflicting tides from two mighty rivers from two rival worlds collided in my mind and swirled into one devouring vortex - the unknown terrors of the shed, my established fear of field hands, and the deep humility of those dark eyes in that dark face gazing so respectfully into mine. Mary's voice and voices from Sunday school continuously clashed in mighty competion. But the command which overpowered all the oppositions, the command which swept through my mind with irresistible force was –

Love your neighbor, Sarah, as you love yourself.

Then I heard his voice again as from a distance far away -

"Jist enyt'in' 'il do, Ma'am, jist enyt'in'."

With those words, we both stepped directly up to the screen.

He looked down at me, his hands endlessly circling,
and I looked up at him and whispered –

"I- I'm so sorry you feel sick.
I don't like to be sick. I never like to be sick.
We have – um - Well - Do you like green beans?"

His voice more confident now, his eyes fastened on mine -
"Enyt'in' y'kin spare, Ma'am, jist enyt'in'."

"And Sarah? What did Jesus say about strangers? Are you listening?"

"Oh, Yes!
Jesus said, 'I was a stranger and you welcomed me!'"

"That time was perfect, Sarah. Thank you."

This is Jesus! I realized in utter astonishment.
This is Jesus come to our farm!
Then my psychic cloud and mental vacancy vanished away.

This man so meekly standing before me was not only a child of
God just like me, but was Christ Himself disguised as a migrant, whose
pierced palms and bloodied fingers were endlessly circling over His heart
the rim of His own crown of thorns.

Strengthened by the memory of the Gospels,
I announced with firm resolution –

"I'm sorry you're sick, but I'm so glad you're hungry,
because Mary has just made a big dinner."

Then I threw open the door and said -

"Come on in!"

Then began one of the most confusing moments of my life, because everything was happening simultaneously. Instead of coming in, the man backed hurriedly down the steps, shoving his hat onto his head as he retreated, staring at me with huge eyes, backing away even farther toward the far edge of the house. On his face was a mixture of feelings I couldn't read, so though I was still smiling at him, I thought he was mad at me, because I had said *green beans* instead of *corn* or had done something terribly wrong. Then someone hissing *"Jesus Christ"* hit me from behind, the full force of someone's level forearm striking me across my back, slamming me over against the blue-willow china cupboard and knocking the wind out of me. Then I heard erupting all around me that same awful hissing sound, like a million *z's*, like the hissing of swarms of snakes. Everyone's voices were loud and angry –

"Jesus Christ! What's he doing here? Frank?" *"Clayton?"*

"Good God Almight- !" *"Frank!"* "Get out of here!"

"Go away, you filthy –" "What's he doing so close to -"

"Go away, you son of a bitch!" **"My *GOD!*"**

My knees locked! My spine went rigid! I couldn't breathe! I wanted to run, but all the adults were hemming me in by the wall. *If you do this to the least of these my brothers,* I silently screamed – so terrified that I would be hurt again. I stood there frozen with fear, stiff and rigid against the wall. *If you give a cup of cold water in my name!* – hearing the hissing of snakes all around me. Then I stared wild-eyed as two chicken wings and two pieces of white bread were thrown onto a blue-willow plate and that plate shoved around the door before the screen was closed with a bang and locked with the latch!

I was horrified! – feeling that frantic, panicked desire to run away to the last cliff of the world, the word "nigger" and "filth" shouted all around me, so scared that that man and I would be hurt even more by all those selfish people.

"Sarah, what the Hell did you think you were doin'?
Good God, Sarah, you can't let those filthy –"

"Her legs are locked again, Frank. All stiff.
Just pull her away from that wall. Yeah, that's right.
She goes so rigid, you'll have to force her. Yeah, just yank her.
Just pull her over here.
You'll have to push her too. Yeah, just push her down into her chair.
Bend your legs! Sarah, do we have to go through this
every damn day? Good Lord, what an ordeal."

"I think you've got a simpleton on your hands, Laine.
Look at her, lookin' like a bug – all bug-eyed.
Pass that chicken, won't you? Touched in the head is what I think.
Yesterday, when I was driving the cultivator back,
I seen her standin' like a statue at the far end of the lane.
Just starin' out over Zellner's like she's got no sense.
Now I'll need some of those fried spuds. "

"At the orphanage they say she's a smart little girl,
but I don't see any evidence of that."

"Start that corn goin' 'round, Clifford."

"Maybe her head's like a furnace, Laine –
kicks on in the winter and kicks off in the summer.
I'll need about six of those rolls."

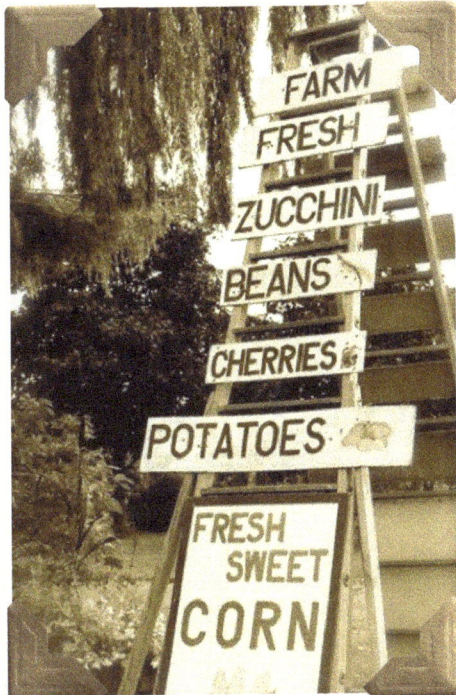

FARM
FRESH
ZUCCHINI
BEANS
CHERRIES
POTATOES
FRESH
SWEET
CORN

Who hit me? Who hit me?
Was it you? I silently screamed.

"Sarah, Marvin is passing you the potatoes.
Can you take – Sarah! Are you here at all?"

Was it – was it you?

"Here we go again," was all Frank said.

I won't eat anything! You can't make me! That man just has two –

"I don't know if she'll eat anything when she gets like this,
but Frank, put some food on her plate, will you?
I don't know – just some potatoes, she'll probably eat those,
and one corn, and a few of – yeah, and one roll, and just a little –"

STOP TALKING ABOUT FOOD! STOP IT!
HE CAN HEAR YOU THROUGH THE CACTUS WIN –"

"Remember, Sarah, no cornstarch pudding
until you eat all your dinner."

"Even bug-eyed bugs have to eat, Sarah, even them.
I think Clifford's right. She's just a stupid kid."

I sat through lunch wide-eyed, feeling a cold numbness alternating with impotent rage, with Mary sitting silently on her stool behind me. My back was hurting from striking the corner of the china cupboard, and my mind was screaming, "Do unto others!" I ate a little of what was placed before me, but I said absolutely nothing, because I thought that if I didn't say a word, that man would think I wasn't there, wasn't eating all the food he wasn't allowed to have.

"Colored Mary? We need more lemonade here.
I could drink a whole pitcher myself."

"Marvin? After dinner, drive over to the road near Glacie's
and dig up that clump of Pennsylvania smartweed
right there by the road."

"Yes Sir."

"And if you happen to see Ben Glacie,
ask what he thinks of his new irrigation system."

I worried about that migrant all through dinner, that man being not more than fifteen feet away and there being absolutely nothing I could do.

Sick people need bathrooms too. When I'm, sick I need bathrooms.
But there's nothing outside that cactus window but an old chicken c –

"Is smartweed good for anything, Bessie?"

"I heard it was good for poison ivy. Massie used it once."

"I know the jewelweed at Baxter's is good for that."

"Look at Daddy eating corn off the cob."

"I do believe these old chompers will last me another year!"

Sick people need water too.
Sister Angela says sick people need to drink lots of water.

There's no water there!
The spigot is by the rose-petunia patch
on the other side of the house.

"Laine, your girl is lookin' like she's about to burst."

"What a strange kid your kid is, Laine.
Always starin' or cuttin' ugly roses. Pass those green beans."

I ate only the food which had been given me, and I spoke not a word. I wanted to leave as soon as possible to see if that man was feeling better, not knowing what I could do if he wasn't. I left quietly by the side porch door, so I wouldn't attract attention, but instead of turning right to run down the lane, I turned left, ducked beneath the philodendron window, then rounded the first corner of the house. When I came to the far corner, I hesitated for a moment, imagining I would find him vomiting on the steps or dead. But gathering up all my courage, I dared to peek around the house…

and there he was, sitting on that top step, leaning against the kitchen drain pipe sound asleep, nothing on his blue-willow plate but a few small bones sucked absolutely clean, just like Mary's.

I stood there staring, unable to move, experiencing emotions so colossal, it was as though I were in them rather than their being in me, some mixture of love and outrage swamping me like a tidal wave would swamp an infant. I wanted to scream and throw things, and hit people and destroy, because I knew that man and I were right! Absolutely right! Down to the bottom of my soul, I knew we were right! And those hateful people in that house were absolutely wrong! I don't remember what happened next, but I do remember that I was embarrassed to watch him sleep, so I have no doubt that I ran once again down to the iris at the end of the lane to get as far away as I possibly could from all those people who were nothing at all, *nothing at all!* like Mr. Slain's Jesus.

THE YELLOW BRICK ROAD TO DECISION

Las' night I was a'dreamin' 'bout de Promised Land
But de dream I lives tuhday is jus' too hard, too hard
Las' night I warn't no nigger, I was just a man
But de dream I lives tuhday is jus' too hard

That must have been a merz. That was just another merz.
My face is wet, my pillow is on the floor, and my sheet is in a knot.
It must have been a merz.

All the girls at the orphanage have merzs at night, and we all cry.
The girls sleep in St. Clare's Hall, and the boys sleep in St. Francis.
I don't know if the boys have merzs too, but all the girls do.

Our beds are lined up along the walls in the Night Room, that long
room with two tall windows at each end. My bed is No. 23. My
friend, Mimi, sleeps in bed 24, and we love to put our faces on the iron
posts in the hot weather, because that metal always feels cool. Even
on hot fall days, that iron feels cool. When Mimi has a night merz,
Sister Catherine takes care of her. Sister lays her little book with the
pretty ribbons down on her tiny desk in the far corner, presses her
beads into her skirts so they won't make any sound, picks up her
little candlestick with its candle shining always in the night,
and tiptoes over to sit between Mimi and me.

I'm sorry Mimi has such terrible merz. Her father did something
awful to her that she doesn't ever talk about, and now she has to see the
doctor every other month, and she doesn't talk about that either. So
she wakes up many times every week crying and shaking. Sister
Catherine's little candle makes a huge circle on that high ceiling, a
huge glow that looks just like the high sun over Mr. Clay's potato

fields. Their voices are so quiet, such low whispers, that I never hear what they are saying, but soon Mimi stops crying and shaking and soon falls asleep again. Sister Catherine tiptoes back to her corner pressing her beads again into her skirts, carefully carrying her candlestick back to its place on that tiny desk. She looks around the room, her eyes moving from bed to bed, and when she is sure we are all right, she picks up her little book with the pretty ribbons, and looks down again. She sits there till the bell rings at seven. All night she just sits there with that little book and her beads, walking back and forth with her candle if anyone has a merz.
I don't ever see her at any other time.

When I have a merz, she sits on a little chair between my bed and Katy's bed, No, 22. Then I can see her face. Mary's face is flat and black, and her nose doesn't stick out at all, but Sister Catherine's face is white with a nose that pokes out just like mine. She wears a white thing over most of her face, but I can see her eyes at night when she talks to me with that huge glow on the ceiling above us. She always whispers to me, "It was an asksident, Sarah, just an asksident," Then she tells me that they are with God now. She always tells me, "Now they are with God." She takes a tissue and wipes my cheek, because in almost every merz, I've been crying, then she smooths my pillow and smooths my sheet and blanket, and tells me to "drift off again."
I don't know what that means, but I soon fall asleep. The next morning, I see her still sitting at her little desk, then she disappears again until the next night. This must have been a merz. I hate them, because they are always so real, as though they are really happening! But this one couldn't have happened. It just couldn't.

It seemed like I was sitting in the corner of the kitchen in that huge rocking chair. Miss Bess was sitting at the table swatting flies, complaining that the Rag and Ware Man should bring her some new fly swatters, because these "are plum worn out." Mary was standing

at the sink peeling tomatoes, when suddenly, Miss Bess got up from the table, stomped over to that sink, raised her forearm over her head and struck Mary's back near her shoulders, just like somebody struck me the day I opened the door to that field hand. Mary bent over the sink but made no sound, and I got up and ran! It seemed like I got up out of that rocking chair and ran! It seemed like I threw open the screen door, and as I was running across the porch, it seemed like I tripped on that little floorboard that Mary always called "dat durn t'ing." She always says, "Somebody's gonna trip an' hurt demselves." It seemed like I got up, jumped down the two concrete steps, then ran down the lane, past the rose-petunia patch and past the Rose of Sharon and past all the roses propped up on all those wagon wheels, and when I got to the end of the lane, it seemed like I hid behind the spirea. It all seemed so real. I even felt scratchy grass on my knees. I even saw some ants. My arm is even hurting, because it seemed so real! Somebody hit me,
but Bessie wouldn't dare hit Mary.
Would Bessie hit Mary? She was just peeling tomatoes while she was talking to Bessie swatting flies.
Bessie couldn't have hit Mary.

That was just a merz, another merz like at the orphanage. I wish Sister Catherine was here. She would tell me, "Hush now, Sarah. You're safe now Sarah," and then she would say, then she would tell me to "drift off" again. That didn't really happen. That couldn't have happened. That was just another night merz. I wish they didn't happen to me or to Mimi or to Katie. They are scary,
and I don't like them at all.

I sat up in my attic bed and wiped my cheek on my knotted sheet. When I reached down to retrieve my pillow, I saw the moonlight streaming through the fir tree window, casting an enormous white circle on the braided rug near Palmer's old childhood train, which lay always on my floor. The moonlight shimmered beneath me now, just as Sister Catherine's light from her candlestick glowed above me, and that familiar image was comforting as I wiped my ear too on my sheet. Then I noticed a bruise on my left arm, a hurting place, a throbbing place, a dark patch which reflected no light in the night. That bruise wasn't there yesterday, was it? Where did that come from? I remembered I had bumped my arm on the screen door when I carried out the scraps to the dog, but had I bumped it that hard? Had I really tripped over that raised floorboard on the porch, that "durn t'ing" Mr. Clay never remembered to nail down? Had that merz been real?

Somebody struck me, but no one would hit Mary.
No one would strike her as they struck me.
I must have hurt my arm on the screen door.
That must have been just a merz.

Temptation, hidden snares sometime take us unaware
An' our hearts are made t'bleed fo' a t'oughtless word er deed
An' we wonders why de test whin we tries t'do our best
But we'l understand it by an' by.

The next morning, the farm workers trudged into the kitchen for breakfast after their milking chores, their heads filing one by one just above the sill of the philodendron window. Mr. Clay as usual gave each worker his instructions for that day, reporting what weeds he had seen the previous evening growing inappropriately here and there. After breakfast, I fed the dog our scraps as I always did and carried Mary's perennially burnt toast out to that abominable compost heap. That morning as usual, Frank held a piece of black toast up to Elaine, his eyes seeming to say - Why don't they just buy a toaster? Elaine's eyes as usual seemed to respond - They've always made toast under the broiler, Frank. That will never change. Mary as usual sat on her stool patiently waiting for leftovers, but responding immediately to any additional needs of anyone at the big table. That was the morning when Miss Bess announced –

"Clayton, you'll never guess who called me this morning on the party line. She got right through, because no one was on the party line then. Well - Dotty Hendricks in Scranton! She's coming up this weekend to see her new grandbaby in Maysville, and said she'd like to drop by for a nice long visit. I said, 'Drop by for a visit? Why sure, Dotty! Sure you can drop by for a nice long visit.' How many years has it been? I would guess about five or six. Colored Mary, I want her to see my new antique sofa in that front parlor, so you'll be needing to give that room a good cleaning and a good airing out. I don't believe those windows have been opened since last summer."

Mary said simply, "Yes'm."

The remainder of that morning, Mary continued to say only "Yes'm" or "No'm." Since Mary seemed to be lost in her own thoughts, somehow unapproachable and distant, I ran down the lane, sat under the mimosa tree, and talked to Greyson's cows through the wall of pink fairy roses. When the cows walked away to graze farther from the fence, I ran back to the kitchen and found that the situation had not changed. There was Miss Bessie sitting at the table endlessly gossiping about "old man Lemsford" and "old Miss Manswell," swatting as always endlessly renewable generations of flies. But while Mary made yet another trio of lemon pies, she answered Bessie with nothing more than "Yes'm" and "No'm."

So I carefully climbed up the back stairway to the attic and looked at the pictures in *Moby Dick*.

I wish I could read more than sounds, because I'd love to read Moby Dick. I bet Sister Bernadette has read it. Librarians read everything. I wonder what those pokey things are sticking out of the whale's back. Looks like arrows. Why do sailers shoot arrows at whales? Where are their bows? Oh no! Their little boat is overturning into the ocean! That whale is turning that little boat right over into the waves! I bet he's mad with all those arrows stuck into him. I would be too if someone shot a bow and arrow at me! Whales must be afraid all the time, swimming way down in the dark water, with hunters far above them. I sure wouldn't like to be a whale. In science class we learned that whales don't hurt people. Then why do people hurt them?

When I returned to the kitchen, it was time to set the table again as the men appeared one by one above the window sill. As everyone was eating, Bessie addressed Mary -

"Looks like we'll have enough of this roast for dinner and enough of that macaroni salad Ida Mae Anderson gave us. Doesn't she make the best macaroni salad. For the church pot luck, does it every year, but she said she had plenty left over. So Colored Mary, all you'll need to make is lemonade for supper, so you can clean that front parlor all this afternoon. Those windows haven't been opened since last year, so that room will need a good airing out. I sure want to show Dottie my new antique sofa. She will think that dark red is so pretty. I'm going down to that Sears store in Jackson this afternoon to buy a real nice new something for that new baby."

Mary nodded and quietly said, "Yes'm." That was all she said.

After the dinner dishes were washed, dried, and put away again in the blue-willow china cupboard, and I had shaken out the tablecloth over the side of the porch for the second time that day, Mary and I silently left the kitchen carrying the broom and several cloths, stepped up the two steps into the dining room, crossed the center hall, then opened the door to the front parlor. Hot air smelling stale and dusty blasted from that room. First Mary threw open all the windows, and in rushed a breeze and the sounds of Greyson's cow pasture. For a moment, she and I stood silently by the window and just breathed in the fragrance of the fields.

She dragged the carpet out onto the front porch by the fir tree and beat, and beat, and beat it with the broom as great clouds of dust swirled upward from the flowered tapestry. Then she swept, and swept, and swept that rug until it once again appeared as new. Then she shook, and shook, and shook the curtains until the dust made us both sneeze, then she handed me a cloth and made a sweeping motion which told me that I was to dust every surface which was low enough for me to reach.

For the remainder of that afternoon until very nearly suppertime, we silently cleaned and dusted and swept until that parlor looked prettier than any room I had ever seen pictured in either *The Potato Farmer* or *The Farm Journal*. The pleats in the curtains hung perfectly aligned, and every fiber of that tapestry carpet had been swept to lay in the same direction. I was convinced that the only thing missing was a bouquet of flowers. I wondered if I should ask Miss Bess if I could make her a bouquet of real folded roses in a real vase, rather than the bouquets of the open, flat roses I arranged in mason jars.

When Mary was satisfied that the parlor was as beautiful as Miss Bess had requested, she sat down on the polished floor and sighed. Then she finally spoke to me like the Mary I had always known –

"O chil', I got's t'sit down a spell. I got's t'catch my breath. We's ben a'wurkin' so hard dat I's needin' t'rest a bit."

"My bones are aching too, Mary, and my knees are 'plainin' just a bit."

"I's a'memberin', we has 'nough o'dat roast cold fo' supper,
an' we's still got's some o'dat salad frum dat church.
An' dere's still a pie left frum las' night,
so looks like all I got's t'do is slice
some mo' o'dem madders an' make mo' lemonade.
We still has t'ree lemons frum dooz pies,
an' t'ree make 'nough fo' supper.
Gracious, my bones is tired. I's a'wunderin' Sarh,
kud you run intuh dat kitchen an' git me a nice, tall glass o'watuh?
Doan ev'n need no ice. Just watuh 'ud be nice.
Den I kud just sit on dis here floor an' rest a bit."

*"Mary, can I make the lemonade?
You showed me how to use the paring knife for lemons.
You hold it this way – like – like this - and slice like –
and be careful to – and be careful not to - like this.
Could I bring you lemonade, and I could put an ice cube in it?
Could I? I'm five now, I'm big,
so I can reach the freezer from my chair now too."*

Mary mopped her forehead with her dusty cloth.

"Well...?"
she said slowly as she studied her hands -
"Well...?"
she wondered again as she gazed out the fir tree window -
"I 'pose if y'hold de knife –"

"- like this!"

"Yeah, an' den hold dem lemons wid –"

"- like this!"

"Yeah, an' de sugar tin is –"

"– on the floor behind the washin' 'sheen. Can I? Please? Can I?"

"Well Sarh, I'd sho' 'preciate y'bringin' me
some o'y'own lemonade. Dat sho' wud be nice.
Den I's kin jus' sit an' –"

"– rest a bit, 'cause your knees is 'plainin' just a bit."

As Mary instinctively wiped her hands upon her flowered apron, her safety pins gleaming in the late afternoon light, I left the woman I had always known and ran out of the room and into the kitchen.

From out of the blue-willow cupboard I took one coffee cup, and from out of the bottom drawer of the refrigerator I took the lemons. Holding the paring knife just as Mary had taught me, I carefully cut in half the last three lemons. Then I squeezed their juice into the cup and with a teaspoon removed all the seeds. Then I ran into the pantry and scooped up one cup of sugar from the green tin on the floor and added that sugar to the lemon juice. I wondered why my combination had made only one cup of lemonade, but I thought maybe that was because I was a little girl, that grown-ups made big pitchers of lemonade, but children made only a little. Then I carefully wiped the table, carefully added one ice cube so the cup wouldn't overflow, and carefully carried it into the front parlor and proudly presented it to Mary.

"O my, doan I t'ank ya. Dat's real nice, Sarh. Real nice."

Then Mary drank from that cup, grimaced violently, stood up, and began shouting at me, her face contorted, her arms gesturing as I had never seen before.

"Girl, whut's you done? Whut on earth has you done?
Dat ain't how you's 'posed t'make no lemonade.
Dat's *syrup*, girl! Dat ain't nut'ing nobody kin drink. Whut was you –"

"Oh Mary! The water! I forgot to add the –"

"How kud you be so - so -
Dem's de only lemons I has left.
Dem's de only ones I got's! Now you's ruined evyt'ing,
an' Miss Bess 'il have my hide! She'l have my hide, she will.
She's gonna come down on me so hard, 'cause you was so –"

"Oh Mary! I'm so sorry!
Please don't be angry at me. Please don't be.
I just forgot to add the water!
We could just pour that cup into the big pitcher, then add –"

"Now I ain't got's no mo' lemons,
an' I ain't got's no time t'make ice tea nedder.
Mistuh Clay doan like tea aftuh it's jus' ben made.
It has t'sit in de cold thruu de night. O how kud you be so *dumb!*
Dey's gonna come down on me so - so – Dey's gonna –"

"Mary! Let's pour that little bit in the pitcher, then just add –"

"Girl, whin's you gonna wake up?
Wake up, Sarh! *Wake up!*
**A *nigger* jus' drank frum dat dere cup.
Ain't no w'ite foks gonna drink aftuh no filthy *nigger!***
Whut was you –"

"Oh please! Mary, please! Your eyes are so -
I promise I won't tell them!
Miss Bess and Mr. Clay will never know that you –
I WON'T TELL! I WON'T BECAUSE –"

"Stop yo' cryin'! Jus' stop dat right now!
I's in 'nough truble widout shuu cryin'.

Whut's dey gonna do whin dey sees only ice watuh on dat supper table?
O glory, O glory. **Stop dat cryin' right now!**–
O God, I's in deep truble now! No mo' lemons
"MARY, PLEASE!"
an' niggers ain't 'lowed in Sloane's.
O glory. O GRACIOUS! *O LORDEE!*
Dey's gonna come down on me!"

*"Mary? Mary! Please – please don't – please don't be so mad at me.
I'm so sorry! Can't we just – please just –"*

"Git outta here right now!"

*"But Mary! I said I was sorry.
Please, I'm just a little girl! I just forgot!"*

"Get out! Go on!" *"Mary? "* **"I SAID *GET OUT!*"**

"BUT MARY – PLEASE! I JUST –"

**"AN' TAKE YO' CRYIN' WID SHUU!
I'S IN A PECK O'TRUBLE ALL 'CAUSE O'YOU.
A HEAP OF TRUBLE ALL 'CAUSE O'YOU.**
Whut's I gonna do? O *God,* whut's I gonna do?
I cain't t'inks o'nut'ing. O Lord, have mercy!
Whut's I gonna do?"

I ran from that room, tore across the front porch, raced down the lane, and hid in desperation behind the iris near the mailbox. I had lost the only person who loved me, and once again I wanted to die. If I could have dug my own little grave, I would have gladly crawled in, so profoundly did I want to die.

I remember nothing else. I don't remember setting the table, and I don't remember seeing the pitcher of ice water where the lemonade was supposed to be. I must have hid outside for the remainder of that terrible day, snuck inside after the fireflies came, then hid under my quilts on my bed and covered my bruise with my hand.

Whar shall I go? Whar shall I go?
Whar shall I go fo' t'ease my trubl'd mind?
I went t'dat rock fo' t'hide my face,
De rock cried out 'no hidin' place.'
Whar shall I go? Whar shall I go?
Whar shall I go fo' t'ease my trubl'd mind?

Early the next morning, I tiptoed down the front stairway, crept out of the house and hid behind the holly bushes near the fir tree. By the time the sun was firmly established in the sky, I was cold. I had been crying since I passed the front parlor where Mary had sent me away. My shirt was wet with tears, and I had forgotten to bring any tissues and forgotten to bring a quilt. I sat beside the ivy sea shivering slightly, my legs straight out, my hands folded in my lap, watching whatever bug crawled into view. I felt utterly desolate, because Mary no longer wanted me. I had no mother, would never have a mother, and now Mary herself didn't want me.

I didn't understand, couldn't possibly understand why she had been so angry at me. In my little consciousness, she had sent me away because I had made one mistake. I thought I had done such a good job making that lemonade. I had used the paring knife correctly, just like she taught me, and had carefully lifted out the lemon seeds, just like she taught me, and had even wiped the table after I put in the sugar so the ants wouldn't come. But Mary didn't like what I had done. She was angry at me because I made one mistake – I had forgotten the water. I guessed that was the worst sin anyone could commit. At the orphanage, lying was a child's worst offence, but on Bluebonnet, forgetting to add water to lemonade was the worst thing anyone could do.

I watched through the holly as the men arrived then left again after breakfast, and I watched the men come back from the fields and leave again after lunch. I watched Bessie drive out the lane in her Buick, and a little while later, I watched Frank and Elaine drive out the lane too. Everyone had eaten three meals since I had made that mistake, and I hadn't eaten anything. I was hungry and cold and miserable.

When I realized that Mary must be the only person left in that farmhouse, my stomach tightened that she would find me in the garden and be angry at me again. Then I heard the screen door open –

Squeeeek

SLAM!

then I saw her walk across the lane to the chicken coop and peek inside. Then she turned around and looked toward the tire swing. I wondered, with a confusing blend of relief and dread, if she was looking for me! She walked around the tall purples, daiseys, and little mounds of little yellows, then stepped up onto the front porch. Expecting the very worst, but hoping for the best, I had no idea that our conversation that afternoon would be one of the most enlightening of my life.

"Sarh? Sarh! I knows you's out dere hidin' somewhar!
I kin feel y'out dere like I knows my own se'f is a'standin' righ' shere
on dis here porch. I jus' now checked dis whole durn house fu' you.
You ain't ev'n hidin' 'hind de chair in – 'cause I –
Sarh? *Sarh!* **Whar's you at?"**

Mary wiped her hands upon her safety-pin apron
while listening attentively, turning her head to the side
to hopefully hear me call to her from the garden…

but a heavy solemn silence reigned in Eden.

"I kin 'most hear y'listenin', chil'.
I's ben wor'ied 'bout you, yung'in. I ain't seen you since yestuhday,
an' I knows you's awful hongry. Kin you hear me?
You warn't at supper las' night, an' you warn't at breakfast dis mo'nin',
an' now y'ain't at dinner nedder."

I heard a tractor sputter slowly down Rural Route 2,
then I heard a car carefully pass alongside on the gravel strip.

"Chil', I's a'wantin' you t'know dat all dem men is back in dem fe'els,
an' Miss Bess done left in her Buick fu' Porter's,
'cause Maybelle's roses is bein' 'tacked by dem beetles jus' like ours is,
an' Frank an' Laine went down t'dat Sears store in Jackson
t'git dat part. Dat 'veyor belt done slipped ag'in,
an' Mistuh Clay has had it wid dat 'sheen.
He like t'had a fit dis mo'nin', cussin' a blue streak whin dat –
Sarh, I's a'*callin'* you! I doan has much time!
I got's t'clean up b'fo' dey all gits back,
so I needs t'talk t'you righ' quick.
I made choclit an' 'nella puddin' frum dat cornstarch box,
'cause I knows y'likes dat,
an' I used an extra egg, 'cause y'ain't had nut'ing t'eat,
an' I's a'savin' a big bowl jus' fo' you, 'cause –"

I whispered cautiously from a world far away -
"Mary?"

Mary sighed deeply…then clasped both her hands over her heart.
"O Sarh," she whispered, "O Sarh, dat's my chil'.
Yung'in, you's soundin' close by.
Which way is you?"

I whispered timidly from the shrubbery -

"The - the holly,"

"- near the –"

"- fir-"

"- tree.
O chil', I's ben so wor'ied 'bout you.
You was a'scarin' me."

Mary walked slowly toward the holly bushes, peeked around those
berried shrubs, and saw me sitting on the grass beside the ivy sea
which beneath that towering tree luxuriantly thrived.
I abruptly dropped my gaze to study a tiny bluish-green bug crawling
across the buckle of my left sandal shoe.

Mary paused a moment...
then knelt quietly in the grass some distance away.

A minute of respectful silence.

Then Mary spoke slowly

softly

solemnly –

"Sarh, I – I's a'wantin' t'tell you somet'ing.
I's wantin' you - I wants you t'hear it real good."

I continued to examine the tiny wings of the bug, then observed it fly
from the buckle of my left shoe to the buckle on my right.

Mary was silent…
until she found exactly the right words -

"Chil', listen t'me.
I know you's deep down in yo'se'f right now,
real deep, deep down – bu' – bu' -
I seen y'run, Sarh, an' I hear'd y'fall."

The little bug was crawling now around the full perimeter of my buckle.

"I seen y'arm yestuhday too, chil'. I seen dat bruisin' just a'startin',
an' I seen dat yo' skin ain't broke, so I's glad."

That little bug hesitated for a moment…
then flew away.

I whispered, my voice so tiny from the grass -
"It's purple and – and blue,"
as I placed my hand over my bruise and lightly stroked my arm.

"O chil', whin I hear'd you fallin', Sarh,
my heart jus' hurt fu' – O Sarh! I jus' ached fu' –
O chil, I wisht I had fall'd myse'f, just fall'd myse'f.
You's such a 'lil t'ing t'be fallin' 'cause – 'cause o'dat.
I wisht I'd be fallin' myse'f.
It's alrigh', Sarh. It'l be alright.
We kin put a bandaid over dat, ef'n y'wants to,
so's nobody kin see dat.
O *chil'*, I's ben so wor'ied 'bout you."

Two squirrels scampered down the fir tree
and hid beneath the blue hydrangeas.

After a pause,
Mary smiled and said –

"I cain't b'lieve it. I jus' cain't.
Is – is I a'seein' whut I t'inks I's a'seein'?"

I nodded my head shyly -
"Yeah."

"Is I right? Is I seein' yo' eyes?"

"Yeah."

"Such purdy eyes. I like's lookin' at dem."

"Yeah."

Mary brushed away a fly then once again stroked her safety-pin apron,
trying to find the exact words –

"Sarh, chil' –
dere – dere's 'most nut'ing in dis' world dat's as it otta be.
Dere's mos' nut'ing, mos' nut'ing dat's right.
I know dat's righ' hard fo' a yung'in t'know –
but dat sho' is de Gospel truth. Dat sho' is de raw truth.
You kin look at it dis way. Dat holly dere? Y'see dat?
Purdy wid all dem berries? So purdy wid all o'dem?
Ev'n dat, Sarh – ev'n dat.
Dey say dem soldiers took dem leaves an' made Jesus' crown o'thorns.
So ev'n dat holly is – Well it – it -
Dere's just nut'ing in dis world, Sarh, dat's as it otta be."

I frowned, trying to imagine a scene from long ago,
then watched as the blooms on the hydrangeas shook
as those squirrels played below.

"Dey say dat at my church. Dat's whut dey say.
Dat dis world ain't as it otta be, an' dat's why we got's t'be patient."

Mary brushed away that same fly.
"An' y'know whut else dey say?"

"What?"

"Dey says at my church -
my pastor – he tol' me dat de fir tree means patience."

"A tree?"

"Yeah. He said dat tree dere means patience.
He says 'cause it grows so tall an' lives so long, it's patient.
Dat's whut he says."

"P - Pay chence? What's that?"

"Patience?...

Patience?...

Patience."

Mary was incredulous for a moment,
as she pondered the meaning of a virtue which she so perfectly embodied
that she had never thought of its meaning before.

"Y'know, Sarh, I – I doan rightly know whut dat wurd means.
I ain't never t'ought 'bout it b'fo'.
I know I knows it, bu' I doan know whut I know."

Mary stroked one of her safety pins with a far-away look in her eyes.

"I guess it means - Patience? I – I guess it means -
sufferin' bad widout complainin'.
Is dat right? Is I t'inking 'bout dat right?

Yeah, dat sounds 'bout right. Yeah, dat's right.
Jus' sufferin' widout complainin'. Dat's whut it means.
Jus' sufferin' bad, bu' not grumblin' 'bout it."

"Just suffering?"

"No! No, Sarh! No, not jus' sufferin', chil'.
Gracious, evybody gots t'suffer in dis world whar nut'ing's right.
Evybody's sufferin' bad 'bout somet'ing,
bu' mos' fo'ks sho' doan does it right.
No, no, I ain't talkin' 'bout jus' sufferin'. No.
I's talkin' 'bout sufferin' widout grumblin' none."

*"Suffering without grumbing?
How can anybody suffer without - without -"*

Mary crept a little closer, leaned forward,
and stared even more deeply into my eyes,
her voice so hushed, her words barely audible -

"You an' me, Sarh? You an' me? Is you hearin' me?"

"Yeah?"

"You an' me, Sarh, dat's whut we's gotta do, suffer widout grumbin'.
Dat's whut we has gotta do, chil'. Dat's whut we got's t'do.
Dis world ain't fittin', Sarh. You an' me knows dat.
Dat's whut makes our life so hard. We knows it.
You an' me's just a'knowin' it all de time!
Dis world just ain't fittin', bu' mos' foks sho' doan know dat.
Bu' we do, Sarh. We know. We knows t'ain't fittin'.
Someday it's gonna be diffunt.
Way down deep in my heart, chil', I know dat real plain.
But t'ain't fittin' righ' now, an' dat's why we got's t'be patient.
We jus' got's t'be patient."

"Suffer, but not grumble about –"

"Dat's right. Suffer widout 'plainin' none.
Doin' de righ' t'ing, Sarh, doin' whut we knows is right,
al'ys doin' whut is de righ' t'ing, 'cause dat's de mos' 'potant t'ing,
bu' not grumblin' none whin dat righ' t'ing gits us whut it gits.
O chil', such a 'lil t'ing you is.
You jus' keep yo' 'lil heart anchor'd in de Lord, Sarh,
an' doan 'plain none whin dat gits you whut dat gits."

The squirrels scampered up onto the porch,
sat on their hind legs, and gazed at Mary and me.

"Just do the right thing, and not complain when we –"

"Yeah. Do de t'ing we knows is fittin',
bu' not 'plain none whin we gits whut we gits."

I pondered as a child the deepest truth of non-violent resistance,
then spoke as a child from my own experience –
"Mary, is – is that like clean dirt?"

Mary suddenly sat up, folded her arms across her chest,
and resumed her far-away expression
as she pondered once again something she had never thought before.

"Clean dirt? Is dat like clean dirt?
Y'know, Sarh, I ain't never t'ought o'dat b'fo',
bu' dat *is* like clean dirt!
Sufferin' widout 'plainin' is like clean dirt.
An' den I reckon sufferin' an' grumblin' 'bout it is like –"

"Dirty dirt?"

"Well I'l be. Ain't dat somet'ing. Sho' is, Sarh. Sho' is."

"Cain't git dat out in no washin' 'sheen?"

Mary chuckled, uncrossed her arms,
and shook her head from side to side as though she were saying 'No.'

"Out o'de mouths o'babes. Cain't git dat out in no washin' 'sheen."

Mary and I sat motionless for a time, listening to the breeze
and the chirping of the birds, two iconic figures beneath that ancient tree.

Mary gazed up through those mighty boughs.

"I's also hear'd dat fir trees is good mamas.
Dey's so tall, Sarh. Jus' look how high dis un is. Gracious!
It's so big, it jus' stands dere an' purtects all de 'lil trees.
It doan do nut'ing bu' jus' stands dere.
It jus' stands by dem 'lil uns, bu' it doan overshadow dem none.
It purtects dem frum dem winter winds,
bu' dey still lives in de light."

I looked up through the boughs and saw a little bird perched on a branch.
A pair of cows mooed behind the fairy roses,
and those squirrels scampered off the porch and raced back up the tree.
Mary spoke almost inaudibly again,
as though she were talking to herself -

"Look how dat ivy loves dat tree. Look how it loves it so.
Dat ivy all's a'clingin', just all's a'clingin'.
It ain't never lettin' go o'dat tree, Sarh. Dat ivy ain't never lettin' go.
All dem 'lil heart leaves. O my, jus' look at dem.
All dem leaves jus' lovin' dat tree.
Al'ys a'clingin', just al'ys a'clingin'."

Mary sighed again, and we looked at one another.
Then as though by intuitive understanding, we simultaneously rose.

"I got's t'git back t'dat clean-up, chil'.
We got's t'earn our bread by de sweat o'our brows.
Dat's whut de Good Book says. Dat's whut my preacher says.
An' you got's t'git somet'ing t'eat. You mus' be pow'ful hongry."

"Yeah."

"Is you wantin' some o'dat –"

"Yeah."

"Nella?"

"Yeah."

"An' choclit too?"

"Yeah."

"'Nella an' choclit jus' fo' you. You come on in dere wid me, Sarh.
We kin change yo' shirt, an' warm you up.
You kin eat while I's a'washin' up, an' we kin jus' be tuhgether."

"W – We can just be together? Like – like before?"

"Yeah, chil', yeah. Jus' like b'fo', Sarh. Just like b'fo.
You kin sit on dat step by dem cactus, an' we kin jus' be tuhgether,
jus' like b'fo."

Mary placed one hand on my back as I took hold of her dress.
As we passed the holly bushes, I imagined the berries to be drops of
blood. We walked past the tall purples, daisies, and little mounds of little
yellows, then rounded the corner of the house by the rose-petunia patch.

87

All night, all day,
Angels watchin' over me, my Lord,
All night, all day
Angels watchin' over me.

That night I made an altar *unto the Lord,* and prayed for His protection. It was a cardboard box turned upside down and placed in the center of the floor near Palmer's train. That box worried me. I knew from studying Mt. Sinai with Mr. Slain, that since God didn't like smooth stones, He certainly wouldn't like smooth cardboard either. So I found a small jagged pebble in the lane that I was sure He would like and placed it on the box. I assured myself that since Jesus said that little children who suffered could *come unto Him,* my altar of cardboard and one rough stone would be accepted. I also placed on it a jelly jar without water which held one petunia, one marigold, and one outdated rose. In the attic storeroom across the hall, I had found an abridged pocket Bible with a green cover which I opened to Psalm Twenty-Three, since I knew that was God's favorite. Near the binding I pressed one four-leaf clover for good luck, one sprig from the large patch of mutant clovers which grew near the side porch by the tub of pink portulaca and the old blue pump.

I knew the Lord's Prayer and the Gloria Patri, and all the children at the orphanage, even my friends who weren't Catholic, knew the Hail Mary. I felt anxious about that last prayer for several reasons, the primary one being that it included *the hour of our death,* exactly the thing I was praying for protection to avoid! That prayer was supposed to be accompanied by that necklace-y thing with a cross on the end. I could never remember the name of that thing, but I didn't have one of those anyway.

I knelt before that box and bowed to it, my hands reverently folded, facing due west toward the fir tree window, completely forgetting that altars faced the opposite direction. I said those three prayers, asked Jesus to keep me safe through the night, and tried to sound the Psalm while wondering why so many words ended in *eth.* So armed with these prayers, that Psalm, my four-leaf clover, three wilted flowers, and one tiny jagged nugget upon an altar of cardboard, I faced another night of troubled sleep in that beastly-hot attic with the screech owl in the fir tree nearby. I comforted myself that the circle of moonlight on the rug was actually Sister Catherine's circle of candlelight, and I imagined her sitting all night on the little chair by the fir tree window, reading her little book with the pretty ribbons, and playing with her necklace-y thing with the cross on the end.

Then I put my altar away, each part in a different section of the room, so no one would suspect, and climbed into bed, piling upon myself both my quilts, so that if anyone tried to hurt me during the night, their hands couldn't reach my skin.

During the night I awoke to the hard driving metallic sound of rain hammering on the tin roof of the side porch. I thought vaguely, *It's only 3:30. Guess Mr. Clay was wrong*, and fell back to sleep.

I woke again at seven to a strange grey light, and such a damp chill that it seemed to be raining in my room. The entire farm was enveloped in a great fog bank so dense that looking out that front window, I saw nothing but one tip of one bough of the fir tree. I placed my Nine Patch quilt on my little chair by the window where I imagined Sister Catherine had prayed throughout the previous night, sat down, then wrapped my Monkey Wrench quilt round me and gazed in amazement out the window into that immense ocean of cloud.

I can't see anything. Nothing! There's no ground, no fields, and no sky either. I can't even see the lane! The holly's disappeared. There's no fairy roses. I can't see anything but the tip of that little branch right here. It's like there's no farm at all! I can't even hear any sounds either. Can't even hear Greyson's cows! But maybe they're still in the barn.

I shivered then pulled my quilt up over my head
and around my face.

Seems like everything has disappeared. Seems like this farm is
floating on a sea. This farmhouse is floating on a white sea.
That's funny. I guess Mary was right.
'Dere's jus' nut'ing in dis world dat's as it otta be.
Dere's jus' nut'ing in dis world dat's right.'

I sneezed, said 'Pardon me,'
then wiped my nose on the finger.

How did those soldiers know to come here for that holly?
I thought That Lantic Ocean was awfully wide.
Maybe everyone who knew Jesus knew how to walk on water.
There were an awful lot of miracles back then!

I rubbed my arms under my quilt
and rubbed my cold toes together.

Mary said,
'Jus' keep yo' 'lil heart anchored in de Lord, Sarh.
Jus' anchored in de Lord.'
Mr. Slain says that too, except he calls me 'Sarah,' not 'Sarh.' That's
what the disciples did. They kept their 'lil hearts anchored in the Lord.
Just stayed with Jesus all the time.

My toes were still cold,
so I drew up my knees and tucked the quilt under my feet.

I wonder...
If I had been born in Bethlehem, would I have been a disciple?
No, silly, Herod would have killed me. That was so mean!

I wonder...
If I had been born in Nazareth, would I have been a disciple?

90

I don't know. Jesus and I would have walked to school together,
but I don't know if we would have been in the same class.

I wonder...
If I had been big, like that big fisherman on that Jesus lake,
would I have been a disciple? If Jesus had called me, 'Sarah,'
would I have said, 'Sure'? I think I would have said –
Yeah, I would have said 'Sure.' I would have said that.

I sneezed again and wiped my nose on my hand.

I wonder if there are disciples now.
No, silly. They all died. Herod probably killed them.
He was such a nasty man! But Mr. Slain said that in Scranton,
there's a church called 'Disciples of Christ,'
so there must be some somewhere.
If Sister Henrietta let me join that church, could I be a disciple?
Mr. Slain said there are all sorts of disciples. They're even some who
don't believe in Jesus! Mother Agnes doesn't like it when he says that,
but Mr. Slain says that's true. All those disciples knew what
Mary said. They all knew 'dis world ain't as it otta be,
just ain't as it otta be.' Even if they didn't believe in Jesus,
they knew that 'sho' is de Gospel truth. Dat sho' is de raw truth.'

David knew that Goliath man wasn't fittin', just ain't fittin',
so he threw a stone and killed that giant.
How could a boy throw a stone that heavy?

Gandhi knew that Indian place wasn't fittin', just ain't fittin',
so he tossed a paper into a basket and shook the world. How could
a paper shake the world? I didn't know paper could get that heavy.
That's heavier than Mr. Clay's whole filing cabinet.
Heavier than his whole desk!

Gandhi suffered bad without 'plainin' none.
He didn't grumble when he got what he got.
He kept his 'lil heart anchor'd in de Lord,
and didn't complain none when that got him what it got.

Where do these adults find things so heavy?
I wish I was big. I could carry the pitch fork, and then I could pick up
Bessie and throw her down the well for being so mean to Mary. And I
wouldn't complain none when dat gits me whut dat gits. Oh! I
almost forgot. And I'd throw her lemons in after her, and I'd never
drink lemonade again! And then I'd throw in Sloane's too for not
letting Mary in there. She can't even buy those little sugar flowers,
because she's not allowed in there. Oh! And I'd pick up Mr. Clay and
throw him in too for paying Mary such a teeny bit of money when he
remembers, and for working her so hard. She can't even buy a purdy
dress in the Monkey Ward catalog! How will she ever be the preacher's
wife? And she has to sit on that stool and wait for leftovers while we
eat. Oh! And then I'd throw in this whole farm for calling her
'colored.' I'd even throw in the roses. Maybe that's what God is doing
right now, because I can't even see this farm.
Maybe He's thrown it all down the well for being so mean
to Mary.

I wish I could throw a heavy stone and kill a giant, or carry heavy
paper and shake the world. David was a boy when he killed that nasty
man, but I'm just a little girl. Mary won't let me carry heavy things.
I can't even lift Miss Bessie's fancy brush, because she says it's too
heavy. I can't even pass the mashed potatoes, because the bowl
is too heavy.

The only heavy thing Mary lets me carry is one plate.

At that moment a strange inexplicable light appeared in the fog, a huge glowing quivering place in that cloud like candelight on the Night Room ceiling. Gradually I discerned it was the headlights of Leonard's car slowly driving Mary to work on Rural Route 2.

I watched as those approaching lights moved cautiously through that dense solemn silence with that last thought thundering in my mind –

The only heavy thing Mary lets me carry is one plate.

The headlights crept up the lane, past the invisible shrubs, past the invisible wagon wheels, past the invisible Rose of Sharon, then disappeared from view near the side porch of the house.

Is one plate heavy enough to shake the world?
Is one plate heavy enough to kill the giant?

Dis world ain't fittin', Sarh. You an' me knows dat.
Dat's whut makes our life so hard. We knows it.
You an' me is just a 'knowin' it all de time!
Al'ys doin' whut is de righ' t'ing, 'cause dat's de most 'potant t'ing,
bu' not grumblin' none whin dat righ' t'ing gits us whut it gits.

What if I put one heavy plate on our – next to – and then said –
Will it be heavy enough to shake the world?

The rest of that morning, I sat on the top step in the attic, listening for the right moment to enter that kitchen. I heard breakfast sounds, and after the men had returned to the fog, I heard Miss Bess faintly gossiping endlessly as Mary washed up. When the fog began to lift as the sun became little by little more firmly established in the sky, I began to hear outdoor sounds too, and could tell that Greyson's cows were once again grazing in the pasture behind the wall of pink fairy roses. I heard a tractor sputter down the lane, and I heard the pickup which Miss Bess said felt like a "buckin' bronco." When I was sure I was hearing the sounds of dinner preparation, I wondered if everyone would say - *Why didn't we think of this sooner? This is so fun!* or *Yeah, it is! This is sure fun!* But maybe they won't like it at all, and I'll have to do that "sufferin' widout grumblin' t'ing", that "clean dirt." When I was sure it was time for me to set the table,

I

stood

up.

A Child's Non-Violent Resistance

Daniel saw de stone, hewn out de mountain
Daniel saw de stone, hewn out de mountain
Daniel saw de stone, hewn out de mountain
Tearin' down de kingdom o'dis world.

Has you seen dat stone, hewn out de mountain?
Has you seen dat stone, hewn out de mountain?
Has you seen dat stone, hewn out de mountain?
Tearin' down de kingdom o'dis world.

I walked into the kitchen and rounded the corner by the stove where Mary was stirring gravy in a frying pan with a wooden spoon. Bessie was making that grand characteristic sweeping gesture with the checkered tablecloth which drifted down so elegantly onto that table as though having learned perfection through long consistent practice.

"Sarah, where have you been?
It's almost time for the men to come in,
and this table isn't set. Get busy, right now.
Up in the attic all morning doing who knows what.
We're having ten today. Clifford, Marvin, Palmer, and Winston,
and Marvin is bringing his brother back from that fancy agricultural
college in Madison. Clayton could teach that fancy school a thing
or two. Why I remember last evening, Clayton said, 'Bessie?
The ring around the moon is telling me that it will rain tonight
by four o'clock.' Sure enough, it began a little before.
He's always right, you know. Something in his blood

about that rain, just looking at the ring around the moon.
Bet that school could learn a thing or two about farming from him.
Sarah, get busy. Just standing there like a statue again.
What a day-dreamer you are.
Laine and Frank will be back too right quick, so get moving."

I walked over to the blue-willow china cupboard and retrieved one plate. *Mr. Clay* I thought, and put it down at the far end of the table. Then I walked back to the blue-willow china cupboard and retrieved another plate. *Clifford* I thought, and placed it down at the near end by the cupboard. Walking back and forth with one place a time, and walking back and forth between the table and the silverware drawer, I set the table for ten people. Then as Mary continued to stir her gravy, and Bessie distributed around the table various platters of steaming food, I walked back to the cupboard, picked up one extra place, and wedged it between the four others on the side by the old wood stove.

Before every meal, it was Bessie's custom to point to each individual plate and list a corresponding name to each blue-willow. But today, when she arrived at the last plate with no corresponding name, she looked up at me and asked with a dark energy in her voice -

"Who's that for?"

It was then that I announced loudly and proudly -

"Mary is sitting there by me!"

Mary dropped her wooden spoon in the gravy and grabbed with both hands the door handle of the stove! Bessie's face contorted into rage, glaring at me with that hatred I had seen at the restaurant! She grabbed that last plate and almost *threw* it back into the china cupboard. Then she grabbed that place setting of silverware and threw it into the sink, that fork, knife, and spoon striking the pans soaking there and splashing water onto the ragged dirty cellophane on the wall. Mary stood frozen, still grasping the stove, the gravy bubbling around the wooden spoon.

"I said ten!," Bessie roared! "Ten! That's all!
Land sakes! No nigger's gonna be sitting next to me.
Not in my own house is any filthy – Ten plates are all we need.
When I say ten, I mean ten!"

I ate my dinner within a strong determined silence sitting absolutely straight in my chair, with Mary sitting silently behind me. While she waited patiently for leftovers, I thought -

This just ain't fittin', Mary. It just ain't fittin'.
That's the Gospel truth.
That sho' is the raw truth.

The next morning I waited at the top of the attic steps, listening once again for the time when I should set the table. When I rounded the bend by the stove, Mary was coming into the kitchen from the pantry. She gave me a stern scowl and slightly shook her head from side to side as though she were saying 'No.' Bessie once again was making that grand characteristic sweeping gesture as the tablecloth fluttered down onto the table with elegant simplicity.

"Sarah, we've been waiting for you again.
This is becoming a habit. We're having nine today.
Marvin's brother went back to that fancy farming school,
so there's only nine today."

Once again I walked back and forth from the blue-willow china cupboard to the table and back and forth from the silverware drawer to each plate. Once again, I solemnly placed an extra plate on the side next to the old wood stove. When Bessie found yet another plate with no corresponding name, she shrieked -

"I won't have this in my own home!
What's this world coming to when kids tell me what to do!
Bad enough niggers are in restaurants now,
but they're not eating at my table. Do you hear me, Sarah?
Do you hear me? No nigger is eating next to me at my table.
I don't care who they are, they aren't eating with me at my table!"

The next day, Bessie watched me through narrowed eyes as I walked back and forth between the china cupboard, the silverware drawer, and the table. When she intuited that I was about to add one unnecessary plate, she exploded for the last time -

"You will never, and I mean never, set this table again!
Ever! This world is going to Hell in a handbasket,
just going to rack and ruin.
Whites feeding niggers, and niggers marrying whites.
You will never, ever set this table again!"

I sat once again and ate my dinner within a strong determined silence as Mary quietly waited for leftovers behind me. That was the day I knew I had become a disciple. My plate had shaken the world. And I didn't complain at all that I got what I got.

Though I obviously couldn't control where Mary ate, I thought that since I ate at the large table, I could at least assume the responsibility of providing her with more food. Each of my strategies though, ended over and over, day after day, in failure. Corn was Mary's favorite food, other than fried green tomatoes, a skillet I wouldn't touch if my life depended on it, because those slices in their brownish-red juice gave me the *creeps*, looking for all the world like tomatoes in blood. So my campaign to provide her with more food began with an attempt to acquire for her whole ears of corn, so she would never again have to nibble isolated kernels from the ends of two dozen ears to equal the kernels on one, though she could continue to suck the cobs if she wanted.

That morning, Miss Bess was scheduled to have that blue rinse put on her hair down at Greyson's backyard trailer beauty shop, so she wasn't able to set the table. Since the workers were farming beyond the sound of the dinner bell, Elaine had driven into those southern acres to gather up the men. The only person left who could set the table was me.

Mary thought for a moment…
pondered for a moment…
then looked at me.

She held up ten fingers then one and said in a loud clear voice -
"Ten plus one, Sarh. Is you seein' dis?
Dis is ten, an' dis is one.
Dat's 'leven, Sarh, jus' 'leven,
an' doan shuu be plannin' t'set no mo'."

Pandamonium burst upon Mary's kitchen when everyone arrived once again from the fields, jostled once again at the sink, and complained once again about the heat. I could tell that, because it had rained the day before, Mary's kitchen floor, despite the faithful use of the wrought iron boot scraper, would require yet "'nudder good scrubbin'."

I wondered once again at Mr. Clay's ability to predict the weather, because though he had said it would begin to rain at five a.m., the storm had actually begun ten minutes before. Everyone thought he was always right, but I knew he was always wrong.

Everyone gathered at the table and began to pass around the steaming blue-willow platters when suddenly, Miss Bess burst unto the scene.

SLAM!

"Clayton!
Wait till you hear what I just —
Oh I could see that coming a mile away. A whole mile away.
Sure as I know the sun's gonna rise tomorrow behind the barn.
A country mile away, I could see that one comin'."

"Oh Bessie, stop your fussing and sit down. Pass the roast."

"Clayton, I just drove up to Greyson's backyard beauty shop
to have that rinse put on my hair,
and there was a big ol' padlock on that trailer.
And I thought to myself, 'What the devil is going on?'
That's what I thought. So I —"

"Oh stop your stompin', Bessie. My plate's rattling. Pass the potatoes, Winston. I guess it's a plain boiled day."

"That means fried tomorrow, Mr. -"

"Is anybody listening?
So I went to the back door, and her nigger girl let me in,
and there was Grace Greyson piled up in a chair

lookin' like a heap of clothes waitin' for the ironing board,
crying her eyes out with tissues falling every which a'way
and that. Just bawling her eyes out, just bawling she was.
Oh that daughter of hers. When I see her next time,
I'm gonna give that tramp a good tongue lashing!
Oh I could see that coming. Oh yeah.
I knew that was coming. Poor Grace! That poor woman!
Her little red-head daughter parading all over Maysville
in those scimpy shorts with half her business hangin' out.
Like a walkin' advertisement, she was.
Oh yeah. I saw that girl traipsing this summer with her –"

"**Bessie!** Will you *stop* this and –
Clifford, that hedge row near Anderson's still needs –"

"Clayton, that square dance in Jackson is as good as a hayride!
Every summer some trollop from the High School gets –
And this summer it was Grace's own daughter.
The disgrace! Such a disgrace!"

The two new farm workers were sitting opposite me.
Suddenly one turned toward the other,
his fork in mid-air, and whispered -

"Florencie? Florencie *Greyson*? Did you – Did she -?
Good God, Henry! Her father's gonna skin your *ass* when he –"

"Whoever it is better marry her. He better marry her for sure. She'll be ruined if he doesn't. Just ruined! That's all I have to say. That's all I've got to – That's just all I've -"

"And we'll all be most grateful, Bessie. Now sit down!"

When Elaine passed that platter of steaming yellow-gold to me, I took six ears, four for Mary and two for me. But before I could place the last ear on my rising pyramid, I heard someone shout, *"Girl?* What do you think you're doin'?" before Elaine whisked away the top four ears, leaving me only two.

"Why on earth do you bring her here? There's something we have to deal with every damn day!"

"I know! At the orphanage they say she's smart, but I don't see any evidence of that."

Since I was quickly learning that a dramatic display didn't help my cause at all, I didn't try that strategy again.

On another day, thinking that no one seemed to notice my taking two ears, I took a pair from the pile, planning to eat one but secretly planning to save the other for Mary. The question then dominating my consciousness was - *Should I butter hers or not?* After weighing all the pros and cons of hot versus cold butter on hot versus cold corn, I decided to butter both ears. On that particular day though, dinner was terribly long, because Mr. Clay told stories, as he did at least once every summer, about his trips to Cuba when he was a young man, always the same stories about the same women and the same taxi drivers.

"That scraggly plant Colored Mary twines round that window there?
In Cuba that stuff grows wild. Looks like grass would look here.
Just everywhere. Climbing up trees and *everywhere*.
Even when that taxi driver, can never remember his name,
was driving like a maniac up and down those winding back dirt roads,
me hanging onto the front seat for dear life, I could see that stuff growing
everywhere. He thought nothin' of goin' eighty or ninety miles an hour,
with me hangin' on for dear life! He'd destroy a tractor in one afternoon.
Would hate to see him try to pump up a combine!
Can never remember his name."

But there was one name Mr. Clay would never forget.

Mr. Clay sure loves to talk about Adelina. She was
the Spanish lady he visited in Havanna every year before he met
Bessie. Adelina lived on a back street with all her sisters,
because he says there were always a lot of women in her house.
She had a piano in her front parlor that a man,
maybe that was her brother, was always playing,
and everyone was drinking something with a worm in it.
How could anyone drink something with a worm in it!
I'd hate to find a worm in Mary's iced tea.
I wish I could have seen Adelina's garden,
because Mr. Clay says she had two huge watermelons.
He says that he would "nestle like a bird between" – but whenever he
gets to that part of the story, Miss Bess always shouts "Clayton!"
before he finishes his sentence.
I guess birds like watermelons too, because when I go out to the compost
heap with the scraps the dog doesn't want,
I notice birds pecking away at the rinds.
The other strange thing was that it seemed like every time
Mr. Clay went there, there was an earthquake! He kept talking about
"the earth moving." That's another sentence Bessie keeps interrupting.
I don't know why he kept going back to Havanna if there were

so many earthquakes! And when he says
that Adelina weighed three hundred pounds and
"that old girl didn't need any pillow under her –"
both Bessie and Elaine always shout, "Enough! Enough!"
I wish I could go to Havanna to talk to Adelina
without somebody interrupting. She sounds like a nice lady.
I bet the gardeners at the orphanage would love to see
her watermelons.

Mr. Clay could be a mean man, but when he recounted his Cuban memories, his face changed, the same wrinkles which could convey such hatred now radiating an impish charm. Though he was wearing the same overalls permanently stained with the same tractor grease and the same farm dirt, he was a different man.

On any other day, I would have gladly observed this extraordinary transformation, but that day, I observed the transformation of Mary's solitary ear of corn as it regressed from golden and steaming to pale and cold, the butter surrounding it congealing into a little frozen pond. I don't remember Mr. Clay's monologue terminating, but I do remember that, as I was leaving the table, Bessie leaned back slightly to whisper to Mary, who was munching on those horrid pickled pigs' feet which she kept in a jar in the pantry -

"You know what this means, Colored Mary? It means that
tomorrow morning, Clayton will give those field hands their orders
for the whole day, then he'll put on that hat and that big buckle
and drive that Buick down to Jackson and spend all day
at the burlesque shows and his damn bar.
The whole durn day at those burlesque shows! I just know it.
I know it like I know my own name.

I know that as sure as I know that tomorrow
the sun's gonna rise over the barn."

After breakfast the following morning, Clayton instructed the farm workers then drove out the lane in his Buick, straw and oats stuck in both fenders and blowing out the tail pipe.

⚬────⊃

Though all my strategies thus far were abysmal failures, I remained resolute, determined that if I couldn't provide Mary's second favorite vegetable, I could at least provide her with a wide variety of foods by taking onto my plate more than I could ever eat. One pork chop/mashed potato day (those two days luckily seeming to always coincide), I took an ordinary amount of food, one chop, a few spoons of the omnipresent potatoes, some tomatoes which Mary grew in the shade near the old chicken coop, and a sea of the ubiquitous applesauce, and proceeded to devour it all. Then I loaded my plate with everything on the table, eating only a little, secretly saving the remainder for Mary.

"Laine," Bessie asked, "since you're going to Sloane's after dinner,
could you pick up seven or eight boxes
of those cherry flavored cough drops? I'm feeling a cold coming on.
Oh yeah. I knew it this morning.
I said to myself, 'What the devil? Is this a cold comin' on?'
So pick up about eight boxes, won't you?
Because if I chew on those cough drops for about a week or so,
the cold always goes away. Works every time."

"Bessie," Clayton asked, "where's Henry?
He didn't show up in that south field this morning,

and now he's not here for dinner either."

The fork of that young farm worker
stopped again in mid air.

"Oh I forgot to tell you, Clayton.
he called early on the party line. He got through right away,
because no one else was using it that early.
Guess I was thinking about this durn cold coming on
and Elaine buying those cough drops.
I learned a long time ago that if I just chew on –"

"Bessie, what did Henry say?"

"Well Clayton, it seems like his family
is suddenly just plum falling apart!
Seems his father is dying, his mother's just come down with TB,
and his sister apparently had an accident
and has to have both her legs chopped off,
and his brother is filing bankruptcy!
I forget all the others. So he went home.
Seems like the plagues of Egypt if you ask me.
That family is just falling apart at the seams."

"That's a shame, Bess, a real shame, because I –"

"Oh yeah. A real crying shame, Clayton.
Why I remember just the other night you were saying

that – What exactly did you say? –
'That Henry must have dirt in his blood.'
That you didn't think he was going to be a field hand very long,
that he was headed real quick to have his own farm
and be a farmer himself."

"A real shame. A real –"

"Elaine, while you're at Sloane's, pick up some tissues too.
My nose is already – already – already - *Ah Chuuu!*
Land sakes!"

"Guess that means Tom, you and Clifford, and Palmer and Marvin
will have to double up a bit till we can find someone else in Maysv -
"Ah Chuuu!"
and after dinner, that hedge row near Glacie's needs some work.
I saw that last night. That damn wild mustard farm is far too close for –"

"Ah Chuuu! Glory! I'm 'bout to burst a lung.
Good thing I have two."

"Sarah, you're about to eat us out of house and home.
Eating as much as a farm hand."

"Well Palmer, I've been running around down the lane
and by the barn cutting roses, and am really, *really* hungry."

"I don't know why you like to do that. You only pick the ugly ones.
Big bouquet of ugly roses over there by the cactus."

"I'm not allowed to pick the pretty ones, Palmer, just the flat ones."

"Well boys," thundered Mr. Clay, "it's about time to be getting back.
It's supposed to storm tonight or tomorrow, so we need to get
that wheat field bailed up. I'll know for sure if the moon is out tonight.
Henry was supposed to do that, so Palmer? Marvin?
Elaine, pick up some more of that Limburger cheese at Sloane's,
won't you? We're running low.
And see if they still have some of those cheeries."

As I was leaving, I saw Mary reach for my plate and remembered that stray dog in the backyard that ate our scraps. That poor little black dog. Half his coat was missing, because his previous owner had beaten him with a chain. Though his broken bones had healed, they had never been set. His walk was permanently crooked, his head hanging down so pathetic in an attitude of perpetual obeisance. When I gave him his scraps, I always wore my yellow playclothes so he would recognize me, but even then, he ran away with that crooked run down to the barn, peering over his shoulder the whole time to see if I would hurt him. By the end of that first summer though, when he came to live on Bluebonnet, he had learned that the girl in the yellow flowered shorts and faded yellow shirt meant him no harm.

I realized with a shock that the only difference between the scraps that dog ate and my scraps intended for Mary was the plate on which they were served, the dog eating from a pie pan and Mary from blue-willow. With that shock came that shame, a shame now as familiar to me as that awe, that I who didn't call Mary *colored,* and who didn't think of her as *nothing but a filthy nigger*, was nevertheless treating her as I treated that poor scared little creature who begged at the back door.

Those days were filled with lessons I never wanted to learn, that Mary's dignity was more important to me than even the food she needed to sustain her life, but the hardest lesson involved Jesus' "Judge not." I thought that if Mary was no longer able to eat off my plate, somehow the superior *white* and inferior *colored* would be eliminated forever from our relationship. So from then on, I cleaned my plate and sucked all the bones, and nibbled away all the kernels off both ears of corn, so that she would never again feel the humiliation of eating what I didn't want, and I would never again feel the humiliation of treating her like a dog.

The wheels of racism had rolled round full circle, and she and I were back to where we had begun, with me at the big table and Mary waiting patiently on her stool. Though she remained thin, she never starved. There were always acres of potatoes and leftover bones, scraps of corn and bread, and when necessary she ate those horrid pigs' feet. But nothing at all came from my own plate. I had learned that the most generous of behaviors could be viewed by others as the most selfish. That that was why Mr. Slain had taught me that Jesus commanded us to "Judge not."

THE ETERNAL NOW

God is a God. God doan never change!
God is a God. An' He always will be God!
He made de sun t'shine by day,
He made de sun t'show de way.
He made de stars t'show dere light,
He made de moon t'shine by night.
God is a God. God doan never change!
God is a God. An' He always will be God!

Clayton Clay knelt in the potato field across the lane, clawed up a fist full of dirt then tightly squeezed his fingers. He remained in place for about a minute, looking up and down his immaculate rows, then slowly loosened his grip. He observed how particles of soil fell from between his fingers and observed the degree of disintegration in the original clump. Then he stood up, tossed down the dirt, squinted up at the enamel blue sky and mumbled, "We sure do need rain."

The next morning, it began to mercifully sprinkle which Bessie grumbled to Mary *"isn't enough to settle the dust,"* but that shower continued until after supper. It continued long into the evening as Clayton and Bessie sat on the side porch, listening to its patter upon the tin roof, speaking to each other a refrain which punctuated my little life like the subject of a Bach fugue -

"Nice rain, Bessie."

"Nice and slow."

"No run off."

"No run off."

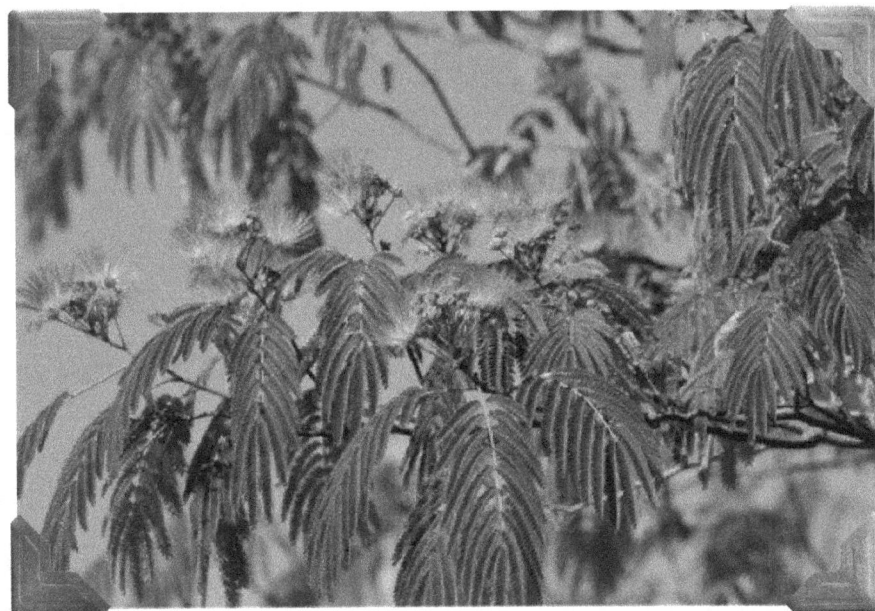

That slow gentle shower continued throughout that night and on into the next day, and everyone who gathered round that kitchen table was enormously relieved. But when it continued into the third day and on into the fourth evening, Clayton became worried.

After dinner the fifth day, he ventured once again out into that potato field wearing his work hat against the rain and scooped up a handful of mud. Once again he squinted up toward the sky as the drops beat onto his face and mumbled, "We're gettin' too much now. This is just too much."

Rain or the lack of it, or welcomed rain intensifying into an agricultural deluge, was one of the persistent topics of discussion and concern as well as the impetus for many sleepless nights on those one thousand acres. Sometimes cold spring rains continued too long, and fields had to be sown later, which meant that a few times, we drove past barren acres when we passed the row of honeysuckle on the first of June. Sometimes hard driving spring rains washed away the seed, so fields needed to be replanted. Sometimes it rained late in August and ruined the wheat. But during most years, rainfall was adequate, sometimes perfect, and the refrain punctuating my memory like the recurring subject of a Bach fugue was -

"Nice rain, Bessie."

"Nice and slow."

"No run off."

"No run off."

During the despair of the Depression and those three failed harvests when his young family nearly starved, it never occurred to Clayton to seek another means of livelihood. He was a farmer and would always be a farmer, the descendent of a lineage of farmers which stretched across the Atlantic back to Germany and receded into the dimmest recesses of history back toward the dawn of time. Soil, dirt, and mud seemed to flow in his very bloodstream. To subtract farming from Clayton's existence would have been to destroy his very DNA. In the dim origins of some ancient German dialects, the word *farm* means simply and essentially *life*. It was that ancient understanding which was so powerfully represented in the modern existence of Clayton Clay. Bluebonnet was his life, his essence, his wife, his mother, and his lover. Long before I knew about mythological gods and goddesses, I understood why primitive man worshiped the earth.

Though a farm is technically a portion of earth devoted to the production of food, the domain of Clayton Clay was the stage where the grandest elements of the human psyche, from the most exalted to the most depraved, were presented each year as classic drama. Every summer I regularly attended the performance of *Bluebonnet* which I had attended the previous year. I knew the characters, the plot, the conflict, the staging, and the costumes. The same actors wore the same overalls, and one female actress always wore a housedress of safety pins. I knew which shrubs would be blooming as the curtain rose in June, and which flowers would be fading as the curtain descended each fall. The sound effects were always the same, the lighting consistently consistent, and with rare exceptions, notable exceptions, the extras were always mute. The only difference between and among those twenty summers was the depth of consciousness and understanding I brought to Bluebonnet as an evolving soul.

Though subtle variations of artistic presentation inevitably occurred, some welcomed, others viewed with sheer horror, that farm seemed to be suspended in that Eternal Now which the greatest dramatists have explored, from the ancient Greeks and their trilogies and masterpieces to the simple majesty of Thorton Wilder's *Our Town*. That scene of Clayton observing his handful of dirt crumbling between his fingers could have easily been immortalized in the royal rhythms of Homer or Aeschylus. On that stage of vast expanses of potato fields and one stool by one old wood stove, I witnessed the greatest conflicts which have tormented our entire species since twilight last descended on Eden, of Man versus Nature, Man versus man, Man versus himself, and Man versus God. As a little girl, I witnessed the darkest recesses of the human heart immortalized in the plays of Eugene O'Neill, the most ridiculous and banal aspects of Greek comedy, and I daily witnessed the fundamental principles of Aristotle's *pity and fear* leading to the evolution of *compassion.* I participated in my own suspension of disbelief, observed the worst of all tragic flaws, and saw those dramatic reversals of fortune from abundance to destitution, and from destitution to abundance.

But fundamentally, I was a miniature, diminutive Antigone, struggling with the knowledge that Christianity's most noble and most supernatural values clashed violently with the most hateful and deeply rooted of all accepted social norms. Bluebonnet was essentially the stage of the eternal conflict of life in dynamic tension with death, of love versus the raw energy of hate, of hope struggling against all odds against despair, all dramatized on a simple and plain stage and set of roses and fireflies, potatoes and petunias, and one almighty fir tree. As our car passed Greyson's farm for the first time the first week of every June, it was no accident that Elaine always exclaimed -

"Farm looks the same, Frank. Looks the very same."

All my trubles 'il soon be overwid,
Soon be overwid, soon be overwid.
All my trubles 'il soon be overwid,
All over dis world.
All over dis world, all over dis world.
All my trubles 'il soon be overwid,
All over dis world.

One afternoon while Mary was washing out the "clean dirt" in the pantry "washin''sheen," and Frank was working under the sink with a wrench, muttering more words under his breath than he ever spoke aloud, and Bessie and Elaine were formulating a lengthy list for Sloane's, I was allowed to water the cacti because yesterday apparently, at long last, it had finally "done rained in Arizona." With the small amount of water still remaining in my little sprinkling can, I watered the philodrendon twining around the chipped window frame and noticed Mr. Clay slowly approaching the house carrying a bushel basket. He was arched backward by the burden of his load, and when he stomped up the two steps onto the side porch, he called out –

"SOMBODY OPEN THIS DOOR!"

Squeeeek

"Clayton, what on earth is -"

Slam!

Thud,
as he dropped the basket.

Everyone including Mary gathered round that bushel, peering down toward a contents they had never seen before.

"Land sakes! What the devil is –"

"I've never seen anything like –"

"Huge!" was all Frank said.

"I've never seen the likes of –"

"THEY LOOK LIKE THREE BROWN WATERMELONS!" I blurted out.

"Oh Clayton, surely they're not – Are they? How could –"

"Yep, they are! These are three watermelons spuds!"

"Potatoes?"

"Yep, that's what this farm grows,
and this year, this farm produced these whoppers!"

"Three potatoes to fill one basket?"

"Yep!"

"But how could – How did –"

"Well Bess,
you remember I used a new seed potato this year,
and a new brand of fertilizer,
and then we've had perfect rainfall too."

"Lord have mercy!"
exclaimed Mary, as she wiped her hands
upon her safety-pin apron.
"Evy tatter kud serve 'bout twenty fo'ks! O Lordee!"

As everyone marveled and laughed at the farm's incredible yield,
Mr. Clay sat down at his huge desk and called his broker -

"'Gracie Lynn?...Put me through to John Jeffers, won't you?
This is Clayon Clay...Yeah, John Jeffers...
That's right over in Scranton.'
Bessie, I can't wait till John hears about this.
Oh I can't wait to hear what he will have to say about –
'John?...Yeah this is Clayton in Maysville. Clayton Clay...
That's right...Oh yeah. It's been a great summer. Just perfect...
Six trucks, you say?...That sounds about right...
Beginning when?...Next Monday?...Yeah. We'll be needing them!
We started harvesting today, those bottom acres near MacPhearson's,
and well John, you'll never believe this, but I have a bushel basket
on the floor next to me filled to the brim with only three potatoes!...
Yep! That's what I said. Three fill the whole damn basket...
Well, I used a new seed potato and a new fertilizer,
and like you were saying, we've had a perfect spring and summer,
and now this! You should see that field, John. Rut after rut of brown
watermelons just baking out under this sun. I've worried those doozies
are gonna' bend my conveyor belt again!...
All total, about nine hundred, a little over nine hundred.
Nine hundred acres full of watermelons. ...
What's that you say? I didn't quite...This phone must be..."

Suddenly Mr. Clay's animated upper body came to a complete
standstill, and his deep resonate voice was heard no more. For several
minutes, we waited in a tense silence before Clayton spoke, almost in a
whisper –

"All - all right, John.
I'll…ah…I'll be waiting for your call tomorrow."

"Clayton, what's the matter?
You look – Hang up the phone and tell – Clayton!
Hang up the phone. What did John say?
You look so – so – what did he say?"

"Bessie –"

"Clayton, what did he say?"

"He - he said -"

"What? Clayton tell me!"

"Oh Bessie. Oh no.
He said they – said they - "

"What?"

"He said they won't sell, 'cause they're just too big.
Nine hundred acres left to rot, 'cause they're just too big."

Throughout that afternoon and throughout dinner, the farm fell strangely quiet. That evening after Mary had left, when the spicy scent from the rose-petunia patch was overpowering and the hummingbirds darted by, the Clays, Frank and Elaine, and I gathered on that little side porch, but for the first time, no one gossiped. Even Bessie, who chattered throughout each and every day, was silent. Memories of the despair they had felt during the Great Depression and during those three ruined tomato harvests when their four children at The Lowlands nearly starved, must have tortured the souls of Clayton and Bessie that evening, memories so crushing, so haunting, and so indelible that none needed to be verbally articulated.   Though all thoughts were riveted on the tremendous loss of yet another failed harvest, all eyes were focused upon the great clouds of fireflies swirling above the alfalfa field across the lane under the regal majesty of a cresent moon.

Farm life resumed somewhat normally the next morning with renewed hope about what the broker might say. That call came during dinner. Ring!...Ring!...Ring!...Ring!...Everyone nervously waited to see if the fifth ring on the party line meant the call was for Baxter's hog farm. But when no ring followed number four, Mr. Clay swung around from his position at the head of the table, and grabbed the phone -

"John?...Yeah, Clayton here."

That tense silence fell on the room again,
everyone holding his fork poised in mid air.

"They what?...*What?*...You don't say!...I'll be damned!
Aren't I fit to be tied! Never in a million years would I have…
Oh you bet, John, we'll be needin' those trucks...Oh, yeah! Oh, sure!
Sure will!...Yeah, sounds about right. We'll be needing all six,
and possibly a new conveyor belt too!...
You bet. Be talking to you Monday morning
bright and early."

Mr. Clay hung up the phone, swung around, and slapped both his thighs.

"Bessie, you'll never guess!
Restaurant chains all over the country
are begging for my potatoes
for – for
french fries!"

Joyous pandemonium erupted in Mary's kitchen. After lunch, Bessie drove down to the Sears and Roebuck store in Jackson to buy Mary two deep fryers.

"Sarh, I ain't never used no deep-fryer b'fo',
but I 'spect I's gonna has t'cut dem whoppers in thurds,
or dere ain't no way dey's all gonna fit in no durn pot."

Frank and Elaine discussed how they were going to buy a deep fryer for their own kitchen.

Next Monday, two eighteen-wheelers sat in the lane waiting for their bags of potatoes, as I carried glasses of iced tea and lemonade to the drivers waiting in the shade of that maple. On Wednesday, another two eighteen-wheelers arrived, as I carried glasses of iced tea and lemonade to the drivers waiting in the shade of that maple. On Friday, two more eighteen-wheelers arrived, as I carried glasses of iced tea and lemonade to the drivers waiting in the shade of that maple. When I asked Elaine if I should carry lunch to them too, she said, "*No!*"

The next week, I was taken back to the orphanage with six fifty-pound bags of brown watermelons in Frank's trunk, Frank muttering under his breath more words than he ever spoke aloud whenever we hit a bump. When we arrived back at the orphanage on September 2, Mother Agnes thought those watermelon spuds would make great mashed potatoes, since "*Each potato will nicely serve several tables of children.*" All that fall and well into spring, I finally had all the mashed potatoes I could ever want.

Sometimes I feel like a mudderless chil'
Sometimes I feel like a mudderless chil'
Sometimes I feel like a mudderless chil'
Far, far ways frum home
A long, long ways frum home

Sometimes I feel like I's almos' gone
Sometimes I feel like I's almos' gone
Sometimes I feel like I's almos' gone
Far, far ways frum home
A long, long ways frum home

Loneliness was my constant companion during the months I spent on that farm. How much I missed my friends at the orphanage and the Sisters' vigilant care. Though the Clay grandchildren sometimes briefly visited, none ever stayed. Loneliness was so pervasive during those languid summer days that it seemed to have taken root in my very DNA. Out of necessity I was forced to invent little rituals to occupy myself, because on many days, Mary was simply too busy to spend time with me.

I daily shook one of the three massive spirea shrubs and down rained over me the last of the tiny white fragilities. I curled my little hands tightly around one mimosa leaf to watch it curl as though it were night. I stood on the wooden gate by the pasture behind the barn and watched Mr. Clay's cows grazing near the stone chimney which stood there in majestic isolation. I did not like it at all though when the bull jumped up on a cow's back, and I liked it even less when Palmer or Winston or Clifford slapped him down. But when the loneliness was so oppressive that I needed to be close to Mary laboring at her chores, I'd sit on that side porch and watch it raining down at MacPhearson's.

Mary stood slaving at her tyrannical stove
as I sat on the side porch staring
out over the potato field.

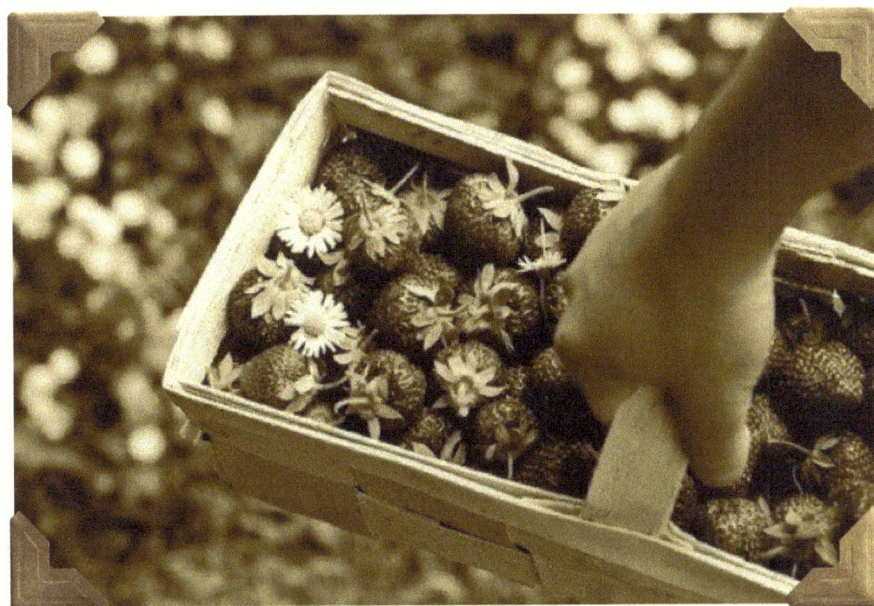

"Mary?"

"Uuu huu."

"Mary, why is it –"

"Uuu huu."

"Mary, can you come and –"

"Chil', ef'n you want me, you's gonna has t'come in here.
I's got's too much a'goin' on ta-"

Squeeeek –

"Mary, it's raining down at –"

"Shut dat door, girl!"

"Why is it –"

"SHUT DAT DOOR!"

SLAM!

"Durn flies al'ys buzzin'.
Miss Bess' ben swattin' flies all mo'nin'. Whut's you want, Sarh?
Miss Bess wants dis mess o'beets fo' supper,
an' I got's grease a'fryin' an' bread a'bakin'.
I ain't got's no time ta –"

"It's raining down at MacPhearson's again.
I see it raining there every day. It's always raining!"

"O chil', whut's you foolin' 'bout? T'ain't rained fu' days.
Doan you come nowhar's near dis stove, y'hear? Durn grease.
Dat sky, dat sky is hard, chil'. T'ain't rainin' noplace."

"But It's raining down at MacPhearson's.
It's always raining near that woods. Come see!"

"O chil', whut's my gonna' do wid shuu?"

Mary sighed wearily, mumbled to herself,
then walked toward the door.

"I jus' 'membered, I got's t'bring up dat ice cream, too.
Durn freezer door al'ys stuck. Hard es a brick evytime.
Mistuh Clay, he be –"

Squeeeek

"Durn flies. *Shew!*
Why God made flies, I never know'd."

SLAM!

"Durn hole in dat screen. Mistuh Clay he be -"

"See, Mary? Look! It's raining down there.
See those woods down there? See the rain?"

"It's rainin' whar? Whar's y'seein' it rainin'?"

"There! See there?"

"You's talkin' 'bout dere?
Whar dem two woods comes tuhgether?
Dat's whut you's talkin' 'bout? Dere?"

"See it raining?"

Mary's urgency

suddenly

slowing,

the emergence of a smile.

"O, huny chil', whut's I do widou' shuu?
It jus' looks like it's a'rainin', Sarh.
It jus' looks like it is, but it ain't."

"It's not raining?"

"No, chil'. It jus' looks like it is 'cause o'dis heat."

"What?"

Mary chuckled that old familiar chuckle.

"Dis heat makes de air t'shake, so it looks like it's a'rainin'.
De air in dis heat, it's a'shakin'.
I fugit whut dat's called. Long time 'go I hear'd it wunst.
I ust t'know, bu' t'ain't comin' t'my mind jus' now.
Dat's jus' somet'ing dat looks like it is, but it ain't."

"It is? And it ain't?"

Mary shook her head as though she were saying 'No' -
"O chil, you is a light. You sho' is."

A breeze brought the scent of roses and petunias
from the rose-petunia patch.

"I ain't got's much book learnin', Sarh.
Y'has t'ask yo' school teacher.
All's I know is dat t'ing is somet'ing dat looks like it is,
but it ain't."

"It is, but it ain't?"

"It ain't real, but it's real. Dat's all I know.
I got's t'git back t'dem chops, chil'. Dey's fryin' in dat -"

Mary turned to leave,

then paused...

"Chil', look at me."

Waiting...

"Look up at me, Sarh."

Waiting...

"Sarh, look up at me now, y'hear?"

A bee buzzed by.

"O Sarh, has you ben hurtin' yuse'f ag'in?
O my, yu' lip all swelled an' black!
O chil', why y'do dat t'yuse'f? It's raw, an' dare it's a'bleedin'.
You got's t'stop hurtin' yuse'f. You just got's to!
T'ain't fittin' fu' no w'ite chil', a purdy 'lil girl like you.
Y'got's t'stop dat, y'hear?
O my, chil'."

"Oh, your child."

"Such a scared 'lil t'ing you is. An' now y'got's tears in yo' eyes.
O Sarh, you's gonna be fine. You be's –"

"Clifford said –"

"Clifford said whut, Sarh? Whut'd dat Clifford say, yung'in'?
Whut'd he tell you?"

"He said – he said –"

"Whut, Sarh?"

"He said, 'Get away from me! You look like a filthy nigger.'"

"O *Gracious!* O Mercy! Lord have mercy. Have mercy Lord.
Gracious me! Why's he sayin' dat? O Glory!
You ain't no nigger, Sarh. Gracious chil', I's de nigger!
You ain't no – Glory me! You ain't no -
You's a purdy 'lil w'ite chil', so scared all de time.
O Sarh, you's a purdy 'lil w'ite chil'. You ain't no nigger!"

A shift in the breeze brought the scent of hay from the barn.
Mary leaned close, face to face, and whispered –

"Come on in dis here kitchen, Sarh, an' lemme talk t'you."

Squeeeek

"Go on in dere, Sarh. Watch dat bee.
Seems like dat bee jus' lives on dis door."

The table stood littered with bowls and flour,
the atmosphere filled with the aroma of baking bread.
Mary silently closed the screen.

"Let's go over t'dem steps by dem cactus.
No, not dat way, Sarh! Stay 'way frum dat stove.
Dat grease's a'flyin' tuhday evy which a'way fu' some reason.
Dat way ain't safe. Just go – dat's right.
Go by de wood stove."

Mary turned down the flame under the skillet,
then she and I sat down upon that top step.
I looked up at Mary, as Mary looked down at me.

"O chil', dat sad 'lil face. O Sarh, dem big eyes is breakin' my heart.
Dat sad 'lil face is – An' now you's cryin'. O Sarh. Now you's –
Dat's alright, Sarh. Dem tears kin fall all dey wants to.
Ain't nobody here but us. Dat's righ', Sarh, you just cry all you want.
Jus' cry yo' 'lil fill, righ' shere t'supper time, ef'n you wants to."

I cried wracking sobs into Mary's dress as she wrapped one arm
around my shoulders. She swayed us slightly from side to side
and softly hummed for a time in her characteristic way.

"Sarh? Kin y'hear me?"

Through muffled sobs -
"Yeah?"

"Sarh, listen t'me.
Dat car - dat driver, he din' mean t'hurt nobody.
He was doin' de best he kud in dat pourin' rain.
He din' mean t'hurt 'em. It was an accident."

*"That's what Sister Catherine says.
She – she – she always says it was an asksident."*

"Yeah, po' baby. Yeah, Sarh, it was an asksident.
An' yo' mama, she tried so hard t'stay livin',

'cause she wanted so bad t'stay wid shuu,
an' yo' daddy, he tried so hard t'stay livin',
'cause he wanted so bad t'be wid shuu,
an' dem doctors, dey tried so hard t'keep 'em both livin',
an' dem nurses was helpin' dem doctors an' wurkin' so hard,
evybody wurkin', an' wurkin' so hard,
bu' Sarh, yu' mamma an' daddy was hurt too bad,
an' dem doctors kudn't fix 'em.
Dey wanted to, Sarh. Dem doctors an' nurses was wurkin' to.
Dey tried, an' dey tried, an' yo' mama tried, an' yo' daddy tried,
an' dem doctors tried, bu' dey jus' kudn't do no mo', chil'.
Evybody jus' got tired, so tired, an' nobody kud do no mo'.
Evybody jus' got tired, chil', so evybody had t'rest.
Dey wanted t'stay livin', an' dem doctors wanted 'em t'stay livin',
bu' dey all got so tired, dat evybody jus' had t'rest, jus' rest."

Mary rocked me gently to and fro by the cacti,
with my hands folded in Mary's lap.

"They were too tired."

"Dat's right. Dey wanted t'stay wid shuu, bu' dey was so tir'd, Sarh,
dey jus' had t'rest. Dey both was so tir'd, dey jus' had t'rest."

"They were so tired, they just had to rest."

Mary rolled the corner of her apron to conceal the safety pin
near the hem, then patted my face with the cloth.

"It was an asksident, Mary."

"Yeah, Sarh, dat was an asksident.
Nobody knows why, chil'. It jus' happened."

"It just happened. Nobody knows why. It was just an asksident."

Mary whispered softly -
"I know dat place in yo' 'lil heart is real sore now, Sarh.
I knows it. I feel it too. It's gonna be sore fu' some time,
but all you can do is bear dat sore place an' love 'em.
Dat's all you kin do. Just bear dat sore place an' love 'em."

"Just love them."

"Yeah, dat's all you kin do. It's gonna be sore fu' some time,
but all you kin do is bear it an' love 'em. Dat's all you kin do, chil'.
Just bear dat sore place an' love 'em."

"That's all I can do."

Mary and I stopped swaying and sat in silence for a time.

"Sarh, did you know deres two odder foks dat sit 'round dat table
whose hearts is achin' too?"

"There are?"

"O yeah, two o'dem."

"Who?"

"De man y'see evyday.
He's al'ys here, bu' he doan talk much. He doan say –"

"Frank?"

"Yeah, Frank! Ain't dat somet'ing?
His mamma died whin he was just a 'lil bitty boy."

"Was it an asksident?"

"No, chil'. She got real sick wid dat fever.
Dem doctors t'ought Frank was gonna die too, bu' he got better.
He got's a sore place too, 'cause y'know why?"

"Why?"

"'Cause sometimes he says he smells a flow'r an' it 'minds him
o'somet'ing, bu' he doan know whut it 'minds him of.
He knows he's 'memberin' somet'ing dat he doan 'member no mo',
an' dat keeps his heart real sore all de time.
Miss Bessie's roses an' all deez purdy flowr's keeps
'mindin' him o'his mama, so smellin' 'em makes him feel better too.
He's feelin' bad bu' feelin' good at de same time here, jus' like you.
I 'spect dat's why he doan talk much.
Dat's why he's so quiet. An' you know who else?"

"Elaine?"

"Dat's right. Laine too! She ain't so sad es mad all de time,
'cause her daddy run'd 'way whin she was 'bout yo' age,
an' he never come'd back. He jus' left, an' never come'd back.
Jus' left his yung'ins an' never see'd 'em ag'in.
Laine knows he's out dere somewhars, bu' she knows he doan want her,
so dat's why she's jus' mad all de time.
She knows her daddy doan want her, an' dat makes her mad.
Dat's why she doan has much patience wid shuu, Sarh.
You 'mind her o'somet'ing bad dat happened t'her,
an' dat's why she's so mad all de time wid shuu."

I pondered Mary thoughts for a moment –
"Frank's suffering is like clean dirt.
Suffering without complaining."

"Sufferin' widou' 'plainin' none. Dat's right.
Dat's whut you an' me got's t'do too."

"Clean dirt."

"Clean sufferin'. Dat's whut we's gonna do."

Mary looked down at me, as I looked up at her.

"Y'know whut, Sarh?"

"What?"

"Do y'know whut yo' mamma an' daddy wants fu' you?"

"What?"

"Dey's wantin' you t'be happy.
Dey want you t'has dem purdy dresses an' –"

" – be the preacher's wife?"

"Sho', you kin marry dat preacher.
An' dey want you t'has –"

" – bows?"

"Sho', you kin has bows in yo' hair ef'n y'want to, an' –"

"– sparkle buttons?"

"An' ev'n dem purdy sparkle buttons. An' dey want you t'git dat book
learnin', an' be a school teacher ef'n you want to,
an' learn why dat air shakes whin –"

" – it is but it ain't?"

"Sho', yeah. Why dat hot air makes it look like it's —"

"— always raining at MacPhearson's?"

"Yeah, why it's al'ys rainin' down at 'Fearson's."

Mary rolled the hem of her apron again and patted my eyes.

"Ain't dat nice. You's feelin' better, yung'in. I kin tell."

"Yeah."

"An'…An'…Is my eyes seein' whut dey t'inks dey's a'seein'?"

"Yeah."

"Is…is dat a smile?"

"Yeah."

"I do b'lieve dat's a purdy smile."

"Yeah."

"I'd like t'see mo' o'dem purdy smiles."

"Yeah."

"Now Sarh, deres somet'ing I want you t'do fo' me."

"What?"

"Y'know dat wagon wheel wid dem yelluh roses down de lane?"

"Yeah?"

"Dere's some tall weeds growin' dere
wid real purdy flowr's. I seen 'em whin I come'd dis mo'nin'.
I want you t'go pick – Wait, Sarh! I – I ain't finished.
Y'jumped up like a 'lil jack rabbit, but I warn't done.
I want you t'pick dem flowr's, dem weed flowr's,
an' we kin put 'em in a nice mason jar on dis cactus shelf jus' fo' us, an'-
Wait, Sarh! You's jus' wantin' t'run, ain't ya?
I's so glad. You's feelin' better. I kin tell dat real good.
You bring me dem purdy weeds, an' whin you's comin' back,
you kin stop an' pick dat one las' daisy by dem tall purples.
I want you t'has dat flow'r jus' fo' you."

As Mary spoke her last words, I jumped up, threw open the screen,
SLAM!
jumped over the tilted floorboard and ran down the lane.

I never knew when my profound sense of abandonment would erupt. My routine at the orphanage was so firmly established that my sense of loss did not overwhelm except in nightmares. On the farm however, where all routine was lacking and where indifference and neglect dominated my little life, those eruptions took me by surprise. Mercifully, for nine months each year, I had Sister Catherine's reassurance during the night, and during each summer day, I had Mary's love.

Just before supper that afternoon, as Mary clanged the bell,
I slipped onto Frank's plate one solitary marigold.

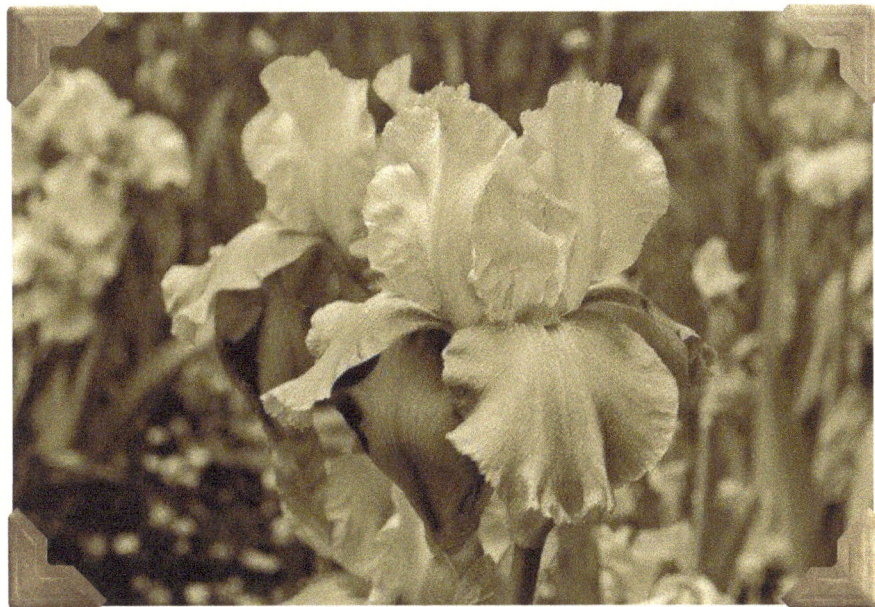

Lord, I's bearin' heavy burdens, tryin' t'git home
Lord, I's bearin' heavy burdens, tryin' t'git home
Lord, I's bearin' heavy burdens, Lord, I's bearin' heavy burdens,
Lord, I's bearin' heavy burdens, tryin' t'git home

Lord, I's standin' such hard trials, tryin' t'git home
Lord, I's standin' such hard trials, tryin' t'git home
Lord, I's standin' such hard trials, Lord, I's standin' such hard trials,
Lord, I's standin' such hard trials, tryin' t'git home

My life at the orphanage was managed with benevolent military discipline, not solely to cope with such a large number of children, but also to provide the stability of the routine itself as a modest substitute for the security of parents now lost. The schedule was regimented each day by the tolling of the monastic bell, the meaning of each number of bells as well known to me as the number of rings on the party line. Every bulletin board in every room displayed three sheets of letterhead paper upon which *The Rules of Christian Conduct* were written in Mother Agnes' most elegant hand. Expectations were clearly defined, standards were clearly set, and childish deviations addressed with benign sternness. Those expectations, the tolling of those bells, and the routines of the school rarely varied, molding the character of us children as unvarying tides mold the sands upon the shore. Except for the terror of nightmares which no imposed system had the power to banish, fear for all of us had been compassionately eliminated, allowing us to evolve and mature in an atmosphere of respect, support, and peace.

How strikingly different were my summers on that farm, where except for meals, routine was non-existent. I clung to the small rituals I had invented for myself and clung to those precious moments which Mary afforded, but my little life was basically in free-fall for three months each year. The bonding of the Nuns to their children was replaced by emotional indifference, that ambiguous bonding which has driven some unfortunate children insane. Structure was replaced by uncertainity, and security replaced by fear. I was stranded between a mother I would never know and a black woman whom I couldn't touch, and except in the interior lives of Mary and me, Mother Agnes' *Rules of Christian Conduct* simply did not apply. At the orphanage, Mary would have been referred to as *Mrs.*, but on the farm she was *colored.*

The orphanage was a soothing cocoon of warmth and security which was replaced each summer by an environment of anxiety and fear. That anxiety was all the more profound because I never knew when an experience of terror would arise. That ever-present possibility was dramatically enacted in the innocent scene of the echo-bird.

The little leaning red barn which stood so meekly at the far end of the lane, announcing the termination of the gravel river as a lopsided punctuation mark, was always a source of wonder for me. That structure was so old and so weather-beaten that shifting slants of light were visible between its battered boards. I loved to study those moving shadows and wondered what would appear if I were older and could lift that long horizontal wooden bar across those ancient peeling doors and discover what treasures were hidden inside. I always thought of it as simply a barn, until that morning when, while picking more dying roses and assembling yet another weed bouquet, Marvin explained to me that that dilapidated structure was actually the home of the echo-bird.

Squeeeek

SLAM!

"Chil', whar's you ben? I's ben a'callin' –"

*"Down by the barn talking to the echo –
Where is everybody? Why are you making sandwiches
when it's almost –"*

"Dey ain't comin' t'supper tuhday.
I got's t'finish all deez by de time Miss Bess gits back.
Run intuh dat pantry an' fetch me some mo' mustard.

I's done cleaned out dis -"

"Where is it?"

"On dat bottom shelf."

"WHERE?"

"ON DAT BOTTOM SHELF NEAR DE –"

"NEAR DE – OH! THE SOAP. I SEE IT."

"Y'GOT IT?"

"YEAH. WHAT HAPPENED?"

"MISS BESS WAS FUSSIN' WID DEM PURPLE ROSES
BY DEM HOLLYHOCKS, AN' WHIN –
I do t'ank ya – an' whin she stood up 'cause her back was a'hurtin',
she seen smoke."

"Smoke? Oh no! Where?"

"At d'odder end o'dat wheat fe'el by –
pass me dat las' loaf o'bread, ef'n y'please –
over by 'Fearson's. Just a 'lil coilin' o'smoke,
bu' she know'd Mistuh Clay was startin' t'cut down dat fe'el.
O Sarh. All dis heat an' its ben so dry,
an' smoke comin' up frum dat fe'el."

"Oh no! A fire?"

"Yeah! So she jumped intuh her Buick an' flew over dere,
an' dere was Mistuh Clay stompin' down de wheat
'round dat ol' green combine."

"The old one? Not the yellow one?"

"I know,
bu' dat yelluh un is waitin' fu' dat part
frum dat Sears Store in Jackson, so he t'ought he'd run dat old un,
an' Sarh, it was spittin' out sparks evy which a'way,
an' all dem workers was dere too, jus' stompin' down dat wheat,
an' it's ben so dry an' hot dis –"

"That field runs from there to here!"

"I know! Dat whole fe'el kud'a gone right up in flames!
So Miss Bessie come'd back shere
an' said dey's needin' 'bout twenty sam'iches fu' supper,
an' nobody 'ud be comin' home fu' a long time. So deez is fo' –
Brush off dem flies frum dem madders dere.
So we ain't havin' no supper tuhday. Miss Bess al'ys gits mad whin
Mistuh Clay wants t'eat in dem fe'els, bu' tuhday, she warn't.
She knows he's right. We's had quite 'nough fire 'round here, Sarh,
an' at dis time o'day too, an' at dis time o' –"

"What? Fire? What –"

"Ain't y'never hear'd 'bout dat?"

"No! What?"

"Y'know dat –
Start pullin' 'part dat roast beef an' puttin' dem pieces on dis here bread.
Y'know dat ol' stone chimney in dat back pasture
dat's jus' standin' dere like it doan b'long dere?"

"Yeah?"

"Long 'go, chil', long b'fo' you was born, b'fo' y'come'd t'us,
dere was a log cabin standin' dere frum long, long time 'go."

"From pioneer days?"

"O yeah, long, long time 'go. Dis farm was built 'roun' dat cabin.
Warn't hurtin' nobody, so dey jus' left it standin' dere.
It was 'bout dis time o'year, b'fo' you was born,
so hot we was havin' awful heat lightnin',
an' whin we was eatin', we hear'd dis **CLAP!** an' dat -"

"Oh no! Did lightning strike that –"

"O yeah, dat lightnin' done hit dat cabin somet'ing fierce.
An' den we smelled smoke an' went a'runnin' down b'hind dat barn,
an' dat cabin was a'roarin'! O Sarh, it was just a'roarin' 'cause dem –
SARH! Keep pullin' dat meat 'part fu' deez – *"Oh!"*
Miss Bess was screamin' an' all dem men was rushin' t'put it out,
bu' Mistuh Clay yelled at 'em dat it warn't nut'ing but a huge stack
o'kindlin', an' nobody kud put dat out nohow. So dey stomped down
all de grass all 'round dat cabin, wid Miss Bess screamin'
fu' evybody t'all git back, but y'know whut Mistuh Clay done?"

"What?"

"O glory, Sarh. I's never gonna fugit whut he done."

"What?"

"He stood by his barn, 'tween dat fire an' dat barn, an' he folded his
arms 'crost his chest, an' he din' say nut'ing, jus' stared at dem flames,
bu' we all know'd he was t'inking, 'You ain't comin' nowhar near
my barn! **You hear me, you flames? Is you a'hearin' me?**
Ain't none o'you comin' nowhar near my barn. Nowhar near!'

O Sarh, I's never gonna fugit him standin' dere, ef I lives t'be hundred
year old. An' dem sparks a'flyin' an' smoke evywhar, an' evybody
chockin' an' all dat roarin' - all dem men stompin', an' Bessie standin' in
dat lane screamin' at Mistuh Clay –
'Clayton! *Clayton!*
You's bein' crazy! Git 'way frum dere!
Clayton, you fool, git 'way frum –'
Bu' Mistuh Clay, he jus' kept standin' dere, ain't movin' no muscle,
jus' starin' down dem flames."

"Oh Mary, did it go –"

"O yeah, it went out all right, but it burned all dat evenin'.
Whin Leonard come'd, he seen all dat smokin', an' he an' all dem men
car'ied bucket aftuh bucket o'watuh frum dat cow trough an' wet down
all dat grass 'tween de cabin an' dat barn. Dem flames was still roarin',
but we kud tell dat fire was a'tamin' down. Miss Bess stopped her
screamin', bu' she still stood dere mumblin' an' cryin', an' Mistuh Clay
jus' standin' dere wid his arms folded 'crost his chest,
jus' starin' dat fire down."

"Oh Mary!"

"Y'know, I kin still see him jus' standin' dere, like he's still standin'
dere now, 'cept tuhday I 'spect he's starin' at his ol' combine, t'inking,
'Y'ain't burnin' my wheat fe'el down.'"

"Oh Mary, that was – Oh my!
Sister Martha always wants to hear stories from this farm,
so I can –"

"You sho' kin tell her, Sarh, how Mistuh Clay's still standin' dere starin'
down dem flames. Well, we got's all deez sam'iches done
fo' whin Miss Bessie comes back. Jus' got's t'pack 'em up.

She wants me t'has 'em redy, an' two pitchers o'iced tea,
an' I got's t'pack up dat cake frum d'odder day too."

"I was just down near that barn, Mary, talking to the echo-bird."

"D'whut?"

"The echo-bird. It's a little bird who lives all by himself in that
leaning red barn. Marvin says that bird is lonely, so I go down to
talk to him. And you know what, Mary? That little bird is so smart.
Mother Agnes would say he's a fast learner. He could be in our
Red Bird Reader's Group! Because when I call out, 'Sarah,'
guess what he says?"

Mary chuckled –
"I cain't 'magine, Sarh, jus' cain't."

"He calls back to me, 'SARAH, Sarah, sarah.'
The first time is real loud, but the other two times are quiet.
And guess what else? When I call 'Mary,' guess what happens?"

"I cain't 'magine dat un nedder."

"He says, 'MARY, Mary, mary,' just like 'Sarah!'"

"Ain't dat somet'ing! Who wud a'guessed."

"He's smart, but he has trouble learning longer words.
So I won't embarrass him anymore like I did last night."

"You 'barrassed him?"

"Yeah. I called out 'John Deere tractor.'"

Mary clapped her hand over her mouth, closed her eyes tight,
and quietly shook for a while. Then she said,
"Dat…dat 'ud sho' be a long wurd fo' dat 'lil bitty bird t'learn."

"Do you want to run down to that barn and talk to him?
Do you, Mary? He's so lonely living there all by himself.
He would like you, Mary. I've told him all about you,
and he already knows your name. Want to? We finished these –"

"I doan know how kindly Miss Bess 'il take t'me
standin' a'de end o'dat lane talkin' t'no bird."

"But we could hurry right back and pack up these –
and get that box – and then –"

"We's gonna has t'hur'y den, Sarh.
I 'spect Miss Bess 'il be climbin' intuh her Buick righ' quick."

"And after then you could talk to him everyday!
Sister Elizabeth calls that 'a formal introduction.'"

"I guess we kud – ef – ef –
Alright. Cover up dem sam'iches wid dat tablecloth,
an' whin we git back, we's gonna has t'move righ' quick!"

Squeeeek

SLAM!

"This door is almost falling off, Mary,
and still has that hole in that screen.
If Mr. Clay doesn't start taking care of this house,
it's going to fall in all around us someday.
That's what everybody says.

These pink roses are so pretty,
but all the spirea flowers are gone
I shook them all off. And you know what else, Mary?
Do you know why I talk to the echo-bird every evening?
I sure wish that breeze would change direction.
I don't like the smell of that compost heap.
I saw the birds pecking the watermelon rinds this morning.
Mr. Clay says Adelina grows watermelons in Havanna,
and they're really big!
You know why I talk to the echo-bird every evening?
Because Bessie's tabby cat from down in the barn
drags up a half-eaten mouse every day,
and puts it on the porch by Bessie's shoes.
That's so nasty!
That makes me sick! Makes me feel like I'm gonna be sick.
So I run down to the red barn and –
I sure don't like the smell of this gas pump.
And I don't like the smell of that compost heap either.
That makes me feel sick too when –"

Suddenly Mary took a hard hold on my shoulder -

"Sarh? Sarh, you's jabberin' wurst den dat bird.
You's 'bout t'talk my leg off!
Stop a minit. Yeah, jus' stop righ' shere. Jus' stop an' look a'me.
Yeah – jus' tur' 'round. Chil', you's talkin' like you's scared ag'in,
an' now you's bitin' yo' po' 'lil lip. Is you scared 'bout dat fire?
Is you wonderin' 'bout dat –"

"Oh Mary, that fire!
And that cabin! And – and that lightning, and those sparks,
and this heat, and no rain, and that field, Mary!
That field runs right over to our shed!"

"I know, yung'in. I know, bu' turn 'round ag'in.
Lemme show y'somet'ing."

Mary knelt down in the gravel sea, mumbled about her knee pad,
placed her hand on my back, and pointed beyond the shed
toward the horizon.

"Chil', look whar I's a'pointin'. See far ways over dere?
See over dere by dat road t'Jamestown? Whut's you see?"

"I see – I see yellow wheat."

"Yeah, an' whut else?"

"Yellow wheat and – and blue sky."

"Yeah, an' whut else?"

"Yellow wheat and blue sky, and – and tiny trees."

"Dat's 'xactly right, 'xactly right.
Ain't nut'ing dere but yelluh wheat an' sky an' trees.
Sarh, dat's whar de smoke used t'be."

"There?"

"Yeah, righ' dere."

"Oh!"

"See how dere ain't no mo' smoke? Y'see dat?"

"Yeah!"

"Ef'n dere ain't no mo' smoke coilin' up, dere ain't no mo' fire needer.
Dat fire's all put out, yung'in."

"Stomping?"

"Yeah, all dem men stompin' an' stompin' put dat fire clean out."

"Like that cabin?"

"Yeah, jus' like dey stomped by dat cabin."

"Our field is –"

" – safe, Sarh. Our fe'el is safe,
'cause dem men stomped dat fire clean out.
Now you jus' grab ontuh my dress an' be nice t'yo' 'lil face.
Come on now, an' doan be wor'yin' no mo'."

"Oh Mary, that fire could have –"

"Bu' dere ain't no mo' fire, Sarh. No need t'be scared no mo'."

"No need t'be scared no mo'."

"Dat fire is clean out, Sarh.
Just hol' ontuh my dress, an' doan wor'y dat head o'yo's no mo'."

"No need t'be scared no mo'."

"Gracious, chil',
look at deez roses climbin' right up t'de roof o'dis here barn.
Ain't dey purdy."

*"They smell better than that compost heap,
and better than that awful gas pump."*

I tugged at Mary's skirt so she would stop at the weeping willow which showered its graceful trendils over the side of the shed.

"This is where I call to him, Mary.
I've tried standing closer to that barn and hollering at him through those spaces between the boards, but he doesn't answer me then.
I think he's just shy. He must be like Katy. He's shy."

"Hol' still, girl. Dere's a 'lil bug in yo' hair. Just hol' –
O glory, dere's her Buick!"

"Where?"

"By de hog farm!
O gracious, Sarh, we got's t'run back!
Hang ontuh my dress, an' run!
O glory! All dem sam'iches jus' sittin' dere, an' dat box is –
I got's t'pack up dat iced tea, an' – an' git dat cake,
an' all dem sam'iches jus' piled up dere – dere – an' ain't nut'ing –
nut'ing in dat basket - **No, no, not dat way!**
She'l see us dat a'way.   Duck 'hind de gas pump.
If she know'd I was playin' b'fo' – b'fo' my work was done –
Gracious, I's gittin' ol'.
O Lordee, dere's her Buick turnin' up de lane!
Sarh? Run on 'head an' – an' git dat box –"

"FROM BEHIND THE WASHIN' 'SHEEN?"

"YEAH – YEAH, AN' – AN' PUT IT ON DE TABLE.
DAT'S RIGHT – STAY 'HIND DAT SPIREA BUSH
AN' RUN BY YO' TIRE SWING,
AN' TAKE DE TABLECLOTH OFF –"

"THE SANDWICHES?"

"YEAH – YEAH -
AN' START PUTTIN' 'EM IN DE –
BU' DOAN TOUCH DEM ICE TEAS,
AN' DOAN LIFT DAT CAKE, Y'HEAR?"

"YEAH!"

I ran behind the spirea and behind my tire swing, then ran around that colossal elm, then bounded up the three concrete steps into the pantry -

SLAM!

As I retrieved the box behind the washing machine,
placed it on the table, and took the tablecloth off the pile, I heard
Mary run panting up the three concrete steps, throw open the screen,
then quietly close the door.

"Did she see you, Mary? Did she?"

"I's so outta - outta breath!
I – I doan t'ink she seen edder o'us. Gracious, I got's t'breathe!
I - I's sho' she din' see us, Sarh, an' now - now we's busy ag'in enyhow.
You pack up deez sam'iches righ' quick
while – while I – I git dem iced teas."

My ol' Misses promise me
B'fo' she died, she'd set me free;
She lived so long dat her head got bald,
Den she give'd out de notion o'dyin' at all.

Several times each summer, Miss Bess, Frank, and Elaine left after lunch for Scranton, leaving Mary and me alone in that huge house all afternoon. I loved those afternoons, my absolute favorites. All morning she and I exchanged knowing glances about what we were going to do in Bessie's bedroom after they left. We looked at each other in the kitchen in the nightmare of the meal madness preceding lunch, but we couldn't smile, because then someone would know something suspicious was *goin' on,* and I would have to go too and listen to all the gossiping the grown-ups did about the DuPont's and their fortune, and who inherited what and who didn't. On one of those days, after the farm workers stormed into the kitchen, jostled at the sink, complained about the heat, then finally sat down, Miss Bess burst upon the scene, back from Greyson's backyard beauty shop.

SLAM!

The room fell silent, all eyes staring at her.

"Clayton, do you remember that –"

Mr. Clay frowned…squinted his eyes…and tilted his head - "Bessie?"

"Clayton, do you remember that –"

"Bessie?"

"Clayton, hush up! I'm trying to –"

"Was - was that blue rinse a little too *strong* today?"

"Oh, that'll tone down in a day or two."

Then everyone began to eat.

"Colored Mary, take this.
It's a nice bowl of Waldorf Hysterical Salad from Anna Zellner.
Doesn't she make the best Hysterical Salad.
Clayton, do you remember that young man last summer?
You said he was such a good worker?"

"Oh yeah. I remember. Good worker."

"That's what I just said.
Do you remember how his family was coming apart at the seams,
seemed like the plagues of Egypt, remember? Well it turned out –
Colored Mary, there are three quarts of strawberries
still in the car too from – Oh Colored Mary, you should see
Anna'a phlox. They have the mildew somethin' terrible!
I told her about that powder she could buy down at –"

"Bessie, could you just say it and be done with –"

"Say what? What was I talking about?"

"Henry!"

"Oh, that's right. Well, it turned out his father didn't die, and his mother doesn't have TB, and his sister didn't have to have both legs cut off, and his brother kept his job and – and – he's back!"

The young farm worker's fork froze again in mid-air.

"Back here?"

"No Clayton, not at Bluebonnet. At Porter's! You know when their son got back from that new hospital, well it's not new now, but it –"

"Bessie!"

"When their boy came home, then he got married and moved away, so Ike Porter was looking for someone to help farm for their stand. So when Henry came back into town, Ike offered him those back five acres to farm himself if he would help. Real nice piece of land, those back –"

"Bessie!"

"And if this doesn't beat all, Henry is sweet on Florencie. Oh yeah, can you believe it? I didn't think anybody would want her after all that. I try not to look surprised when I'm wrong,

but I sure was surprised today.
And that little baby girl is a fiery little red-head just like her mama,
being passed all around the beauty shop from dryer to dryer,
and back again from dryer to dryer, drinking her bottle then spitting
it up, then drinking her bottle then –"

"Bessie! Will you finish!"

"Looks like we'll be having a wedding
at the little Methodist Church. Isn't that something.
Who would have guessed? And you know what else?"

"Please, Bessie, do tell us so we can get back to –"

"Ike Porter said he didn't mind if Florencie's parents bought that new
family a tiny trailer and put it on that nice piece of land,
so Florencie could open her own beauty shop.
You know she learned all about that hair stuff from her mama.
And you know what else?"

"What Bess? We're all waiting!"

"Everybody is talking about this – just can't believe this.
That little girl is named Henrietta! Can you believe it?
When Anna told me that, I thought,
'What the devil? Is that the truth?'
Henrietta and her new daddy is named Henry.

Isn't that something. Who would have believed it.
You just never know how things will work out."

The young farm worker began to eat again.

"Oh the *disgrace* she put her poor mother through!
Oh the *shame* she –"

"OH BESSIE, SHUT UP AND *SIT DOWN*!
Somebody pass the chicken before it gets cold."

Bessie sat down and continued to mumble to herself.
When Mary set the second pitcher of iced tea on the table,
she was smiling.

After dinner, when the men returned to the fields,
Elaine said –
"Sarah, hurry up and get ready. Bessie, are you all right?
Frank's gone to gas up the car."

"I don't wanna go, Elaine. I just –"

"You don't want to go? You didn't want to go last time either.
What are you going to do here all afternoon?"

"Cut roses."

"Bessie! Pardon you! Roses, roses.
Every room in this house has jars lined up like soldiers
holding roses in every conceivable stage of decomposition.

This place is beginning to look like a funeral parlor."

"Miss Bess won't let me pick the buds,
and when I carry the flat roses back to the house,
the petals are already falling off. Today can I pick the buds?"

"No, Sarah, not if she said -
Bessie! What would Lady Manners say?"

"But Winston got to cut the buds when Annie was born."

"That was a special occasion, that was special.
You just cut the open or – or what do you call them?"

"Flat roses."

"Bessie! What's wrong with you?"

"Oh Laine, I'm dying over here.
Those cucumbers keep repeating on me."

"Those seeds were awfully big.
What else are you going to do all afternoon?"

"Try to read Moby Dick."

"Oh child, such foolishness. That book's bigger than you are.
How'd it get on this farm anyway? I don't see how it doesn't break
your arm carrying it everywhere like you do.

Who wants to read about dead whales anyway?"

"I don't have any other books.
Could someone take me to the library in Maysv-"

"No one is paying fifty dollars to get you a temporary card
for only three months. They said we'd get that money back,
but that's still highway robbery."

"Land sakes, Laine! There's another one!"

"Sarah, you and Colored Mary certainly look glum,
like neither of you wants to stay here.
Frank's back now. Do you want to go or not?"

"Oh, pardon me again, Laine.
Colored Mary, make sure you take those seeds out next time.
I keep belchin'."

"No, I'll talk to the echo-bird and cut -"

"I know, flat roses and —"

" -try to read Moby Dick and Farm Journals."

"Oh no, Laine. Excuse me again. I'm 'bout to burst."

As they were leaving the house, Mary and I stood absolutely straight-faced, having perfected this deception very well. When they finally got into the car, it was my job to carefully climb up to that first tiny bedroom over the kitchen, which had one of the only two north facing windows, and watch as their car disappeared down Rural Route 2.

Mary called up the stairway from the kitchen -
"Is you at dat winduh, Sarh?
Kin you see 'em, chil'? Whar is dey?"

"They're at the branch of the elm tree."

Mary chuckled.
"No, chil', not whar *you* kin see 'em. Whar is dey on de road?"

"Oh! By the cows."

"You keep a'watchin', 'cause dey might a'fugot somet'ing
an' den dey'l turn back in dat lane by dat beauty shop.
Dey by de corn fe'el yit?"

"No, they're still by the cows. They're just by the...Yeah!"

"Dat corn fe'el ain't es big es dat cow fe'el.
Is dey by de wheat fe'el yet?"

"No, they're still by the - Yeah! They're by the wheat. "

"Is dey slowin' down by dat lane?"

"No, fast, they're going real fast, Mary.
They're not slowing down at all, and now they're past the lane!
Can I come down? Please, can I come -"

"No, you watch a few mo' minites, just t'be sho',
while I git deez plates in some dishwatuh."

"They're not turning back, Mary.
I can't even see them any more. Can I come down?"

"Chil', whut's my gonna' do wid shuu?
I gots t'git deez plates in dis dishwatuh.
You jus' wait fo' a few mo' minits."

After Mary had deposited all the dishes in the sink, sure the car would not return until suppertime, Mary and I proceeded up the other narrow stairwell off the narrow hall between the kitchen and the dining room.

"Walk up here like I done taught ya, yung'in.
Dere ain't no banister here nedder, an' deez steps is so steep,
so hol' ontuh de step in front like –Yeah, dat's right.
Yo' sandle shoes on one step an' yo' hands on de next.
Yeah, dat's right."

At the top of those stairs was a rather long hallway which stretched from the back of the house to the front, its walls studded with pegs on which hung all Mr. Clay's clothes, overalls and work shirts, leather belts with huge buckles, lined jackets he wore in the winter in the large shed and barn, and his ties, what seemed to be a thousand ties, his hideously garish ties printed with a matador or a national monument, an Arizona sunset or a naked woman. When we came to the closed door of Bessie and Clayton's bedroom, Mary looked down at me as I looked up at her.

"Chil', y'know whut we's 'bout ta –"

"Yeah!"

" - we's 'bout ta –"

"Yeah!"

"Sarh, I's talkin' t'you. Y'got's t'listen.
Stop clappin' yo' 'lil hands an' jus' –"

"Yeah!"

"Sarh, I knows I says dis evy time, but it's 'potant!
We cain't never tell whut we does in dat room,
er Mistuh Clay, he'l tear intuh me like – like –
O Sarh, it'd be somet'ing terr'ble!
An' den, Sarh, deys ud send me far, far 'way,
an' you'd never see me ag'in, y'hear?
You'd never see me ag'in."

"I know. They would be mean and –"

"You an' me, chil', you an' me – we got's t'promise dat –"

"I promise, Mary, I promise. I always do."

"I know y'does, chil'. I knows it.
Fu' such a scared 'lil t'ing you is, ain't shuu somet'ing.
Fu' such a 'lil chil', you's somet'ing."

We tiptoed into that enchanted place and quietly closed the door. I was almost afraid to enter, because it seemed so delicate a place, with its subtle wallpaper of flowers and stripes, its small fireplace with carved mantle and dainty figurines, its high four-poster bed with crocheted bedspread and lavender dust ruffle, a large free-standing cedar closet with a huge drawer at the bottom and Mr. Clay's weekend hat carefully wrapped in cellophane on top, and a dresser on either side of the fireplace, one with a large rectangular mirror and one with a small oval. On top of the dressers were long lace doilies, silver trays filled with pretty little bottles of lavender perfume and lavender spray, and Bessie's silver brush, comb, and mirror set, which was too heavy for me to lift. The entire room seemed to be swathed in a fine drapery of lace composed of the dust which softly billowed in from the window overlooking the lane and from the front shaded window looking into the fir tree, the same view I shared from my attic bedroom.

I was nearly breathless, hardly able to contain myself, as I watched Mary find the gold key in the dust on the silver tray, and with great hesitation, like the unrolling of a sacred scroll, she unlocked the cedar closet. Out blasted that scent which made me feel instantly sick, but what treasures were inside.

"Your fur coat, Mary!"

"Ain't mine, yung'in. Wisht it was. O I wisht it was."

"Try it on again! Try it – Mary? Why are you –"

"Ain't you 'memberin, Sarh?
We got's t''member dat it's hangin' facin' de winduh,
an' dis hanger is turned dis a'way. Is you 'memberin' dat?"

"Yeah. It's hanging that way, and the hanger is this way."

"Dat's good. We hast t'keep dat in our minds.
Now I kin try it on."

Mary carefully took out Miss Bessie's coat, gently laid it out on the bed,
then opened it to reveal the lining.

"O chil', dat dere is satin. Ain't dat somet'ing.
Silver satin jus' sparklin' in dis light.
An' look Sarh, see 'em?
Dey's 'lil lilies o'de valley all over dat linin'.
Y'know whut dat flow'r means, Sarh?
Some fo'ks say dem 'lil flowr's is Mary's tears at de crucifixion,
an' some say dey's Eve's tears whin she had t'leave dere garden.

So dat's why some say dat gardens dat has lily o'de valley
bloomin' in 'em doan has no evil spirits,
like dat durn snake in Eden.
Guess dat's why dere ain't none o'dem flowr's on dis here farm.
Dere ain't none dat blooms nowhar on dis here farm.
Dat's so purdy. Gracious! Sarh, ain't dat somet'ing.
Evy time I see dat linin', I jus' cain't b'lieve it."

*"Oh Mary, wear it inside out.
Those little flowers are so pretty."*

"Chil', fur coats keeps dere linin' on de inside."

Mary carefully removed the coat from its padded hanger,
held it with both hands to ensure it would not touch the floor,
then tried it on over her faded housedress of safety pins.

"What are those?"

"Dem's de 'lil hooks dat keep out dem winter winds."

"No, don't fasten them, Mary. You'll burn up!"

"O I's a'fastenin' dem, chil'. I's a'fastenin dem, alright.
Dere. Doan I look purdy. Real purdy."

Mary lovingly stroked the fur on both sleeves –
"Ain't I real purdy."

"I can't see your dress anymore or your safety pins either!"

"Nedder kin I, chil'. Needer kin I. Now I's gonna pull out
dis bottom drawer, an' you 'member how yo' fox head is facin'.
Is you lookin' real careful?"

"Yeah."

"Whut's you seein'?"

"The eyes – the eyes are looking at the window,
and – and the tail is facing this way."

"Dat's good. 'Member dat. Now you kin try it on."

"Can the preacher's wife wear fox heads?"

"O sho'."

"It always feels like it will bite me in the neck."

"'T'ain't livin' no mo', Sarh. Dat fox is long gone.
Looks real nice over yo' yelluh shirt.
I kin see now why you wear dat fox head, Sarh. I know why now.
'Cause – well – way over in Afrika where my people comes frum,
fo'ks said foxes was tricksters, tryin' t'make bad t'ings happen.
Dey said fo'ks kud be like foxes, tryin' t'make good fo'ks do bad t'ings.
Bu' my mama, she said fo'ks dat b'lieve'd dat t'ought dey
was tryin' t'do bad t'ings in a good world,
tryin' t'make good fo'ks do bad t'ings in a world dat was good.
Bu' Sarh, you an' me knows dis world ain't good.
Dis world just ain't fittin' a't'all.
So foxes in a bad world tries t'make fo'ks do good t'ings.
In a bad world, fo'ks who's like foxes tries t'git people t'do good t'ings.
Dey's still tricksters like de bad foxes, bu' dey's good tricksters,
'cause dey's tryin' t'git fo'ks' t'do good.
I kin tell alredy dat you's a 'lil fox, a good fox in a bad world,
jus' like yo' fox head."

"That's not nice, Mary, calling me a fox. I'm not a fox!
Jesus called that Herod man a fox, because he was so nasty,

Killing all those children like that fox in the hen house last week.
That wasn't nice calling me that, Mary."

"Bu' Sarh, Sarh, now listen.
Dat Herod man t'ought it was a good world,
'cause it sho' was a good world fu' him.
So he was tryin' t'do bad t'ings in his good world.
Bu' Sarh, I's sure Mistuh Herod t'ought Jesus was a fox too,
'cause Jesus know'd dis world ain't good, ain't good a't'all.
So I's sho' Herod t'ought Jesus was a fox tryin' t'git fo'ks t'do good
t'ings in a bad world. Dey both t'ought d'odder was a fox,
bu' a fox in a diffunt world.
Dat's whut I see you tryin' t'do, Sarh.
You's de fox in a bad world who's tryin' t'make fo'ks do good t'ings.
O Sarh, why's y'got's tears in yo' eyes?
Why's you cryin'? O chil', whut'd I say t'make –
O chil'! Why's you cryin' so hard?
O gracious! Here, lemme wipe yo' eyes on my apron.
We doan want no tears on Miss Bessie's furs."

"Oh Mary, I can't figure out anything – anything on this farm,
not anything! And now I'm a fox! The Sisters say I'm nice
at the orphanage, but here I'm a nasty old fox. Everything here
is upside down. The Rules of Christian Conduct aren't even here.
They're everywhere at the orphanage. There's no rules here except
Preacher's Wife and Bessie's perfume and – and – how to pick
blackberries. I never know why Bessie and Frank and Elaine and Mr.
Clay get mad at me for trying to be nice. I was nice to that migrant,
but why didn't they want him to have green beans? And I don't know
why they don't like it when I'm sitting next to you when we're looking
through the Monkey Ward, and why I have to move away when they
come into the kitchen, and why can't Mr. Clay pay you more so you
can buy pretty dresses and be the preacher's wife? I know the
asksident was an asksident, but this farm is just mean!"

"O gracious, chil', sit down righ' shere on dis here bed. You's so upset!"

"But I'm scared to sit on that bed!
Please, please don't make me! I'm always in trouble now!
Bessie will get so mad at me again if we sit on her bed!"

"Now, now chil', si' down righ' shere. Jus' si' down an' listen.
I got's a 'lil penny in my pocket. Doan know why, I jus' keep it dere.
An' whin we's leavin' tuhday, we kin stretch dis here bedspread so durn
tight, my penny's gonna bounce clean off o'dat spread an' right out
dat fir tree winduh. Now si' down righ' shere."

"And why can't I hold your hand? I hold onto Elaine's hand, but why
can I only hold onto your dress? I don't have to hold onto
the Sisters' dresses. I can hold their hands. And why did everyone
sound like snakes when I invited Jesus for dinner, and why were
there snakes at the door? And why didn't they like that little girl with
my yellow dress? And why can't I set the table anymore, and why
can't you sit by me? At the orphanage, I have fun, but here I just stare.
And at home, they say I'm smart, but here, I'm dumb. Clifford even
called me a 'simpleton.' That must mean something bad. And
Elaine's always mad at me, and says, 'I can't find any evidence of
that.' At the orphanage I have night merzs, but I have day merzs here.
Everything is wrong, Mary, and I can't figure it out,
and now I'm a fox!"

Mary wrapped her arms tightly around my shirt
and slowly swayed me back and forth.

"Dere, dere chil', you's safe wid me. Jus' stay righ' shere, an' you's
gonna be safe. Stop talkin' fo' a minit an' jus' breathe fo' a while.
I know how y'git. Here, let's wipe yo' tears on my apron ag'in,
an' you's gonna be fine. Now take a few mo' deep breaths,
an' settle yo' 'lil heart down.

"Sarh, chil', de truth is dere just ain't no answers t'dem questions. Nobody knows dem answers, not ev'n dem Sisters at yo' orphage. Not ev'n dat 'brarian who's readin' dat whale book. Nobody knows. Dere's jus' nobody who knows. All we kin do, Sarh, is keep doin' de righ' t'ings, 'cause we knows dey's de righ' t'ings, an' not 'plain none whin dem righ' t'ings git us whut dey git. Al'ys doin' dat clean dirt – dat's all we kin do. Chil', look at me. I wanna see dem big brown eyes. Sarh, you was right invitin' dat man intuh dis house, but y'cain't do dat no mo', an' you was right settin' dat plate fu' me, but y'cain't do dat no mo' needer. An' ef we cain't sit close whin Miss Laine er Miss Bess comes intuh de room, we kin' sit righ' shere now. Dat's all I know, Sarh. Dat's all I know. I's so sor'y. I's real sor'y, bu' nobody knows dem answers t'yo' questions, not ev'n yo' school teachers."

"I keep trying to figure out all the rules on this farm, but they're not the same as Jesus said."

"I know, chil'. I know dat, an' you bite dat po' 'lil lip o'yo's 'til it's a'bleedin' tryin' t'figure all dis out. An' dat makes me sad 'bout you, 'cause dere ain't no way t'figure dis out. De truth, Sarh, is dat evyt'ing you's learnin' at dat orphage doan wurk here. Dat's de raw truth. Dat's de Gospel truth. Maybe it's 'cause dere ain't no lily o'd'valley in Miss Bessie's garden. Might be es simple es dat. Maybe dere ain't none o'dem flowr's t'purtect dis garden frum dem evil spirits. Bu' nobody knows, Sarh, why dis world ain't fittin'. It just is. An' nobody knows why t'ings is all upside down on dis here farm. But you's figurin' out how t'be a fox like Jesus, chil', a good fox in a bad world. An' chil', dat's a good, good t'ing. Dat sho' is a real good t'ing. Now, you look like you's feelin' better ag'in."

*"yeah.
If I'm a fox in my fox head, Mary, are you a bear?
That's funny. Mary is a bear."*

"Why yeah, Sarh, I reckon so. I's just a big ol' bear puttin' one foot in front o'd'odder. Ain't dat somet'ing. Mary's jus' lumberin' 'long."

Mary and I both laughed as Mary wiped my face again
with her safety-pin apron.

"Now, chil', we ain't gonna spend de rest o'dis aftuhnoon talkin' 'bout no critters. We's gonna dress up like great ladies 'til it's time t'git dat supper on dat supper table. Dat's right. Let's git up frum dis ol' bed an' purtend we's great ladies."

Back and forth and round and round, we paraded before the oval mirror. Mary's forehead beaded with perspiration as she bore the burden of a full length fur coat in ninety degree heat, and I glanced periodically to discern if the jaws of my foxhead were safely closed. Then Mary opened the top drawer of that bureau where Miss Bess kept all her jewelry.

"No, no, Sarh! Doan touch 'em yit. Jus' look at de –"

"Oh! I forgot. The ropes are here, and the sparkles are there,
and – and the bracelets are there.
What are these? I forget."

"Dem's her hat pins, bu' we woan be needin' none o'dem."

We coiled around our necks and wrists ropes of jewelry,
and Mary pinned as many 'sparkles' as my shirt would hold.

"Chil', you's lookin' real nice. Sho' do. Real nice."

Heavily burdened with all our regalia, Mary quietly pulled open
the bottom drawer where Miss Bess stored her nightgowns.
Puzzled for a moment, Mary and I both paused…

"W – Where's all the pink ones?"

"Whar'd dey go? Dey was righ' shere las' –
I bet I know. Las' week, Miss Bess done got a package
frum dat Monkey Store in Jamestown. Deez must'a ben in dat box.
Wunder whut she done wid dem ol' uns?
Dey sho' was purdy."

"What's that color, Mary? It isn't blue but –"

" – t'ain't green nedder. I doan righ'ly know.
Looks like watuh. An' look, Sarh, it has dem sparkle buttons,
an' dat 'lil bow is real – No! No, Sarh. Doan pick dat up.
Gracious, chil', we kin jus' peek at deez."

"But we picked up the coat?"

"Dis coat's gonna be a lot easier t'hang back up den put deez gowns
away. We got's t'leave deez in de drawer, bu' we kin touch 'em."

"Just peekin'."

"Dat next un is yelluh. O, look at dat dere lace. Ain't dat somet'ing."

"So soft, and like sunshine, Mary.
Can Miss Bess wear that when she's the preacher's wife?"

"Sho' can. An' dat un down dere is purple, real nice.
An' look Sarh, see dat?
Looks like dere's ruffles 'round dat hem."

"Mary?"

"Uuu huu."

*"Why doesn't Miss Bess slide out of bed
and hit the floor with a whallop?"*

Mary chuckled.
"I doan righ'ly know, chil'. Seems like she otta.
All dat slinkly. Wunder whar dem pink uns is gone?
All dem purdy uns? I wonder – I guess – I guess she must'a –
I reckon she must'a give'd 'em all 'way."

Mary's face suddenly assumed a faraway look as her eyes drifted
toward the window overlooking the lane where slants of light filtered
through the lace curtains which billowed gently in the afternoon breeze.

After a moment, Mary spoke –
"Chil', we has one mo' t'ing ta –"

"Perfume!"

"Dat's right.
All us great ladies got's t'wear dat purdy perfume.
Is you 'memberin' de rules 'bout –"

"Only one spray for you and me, because – because?"

"One spray so deres none o'dat smell –"

"Oh! - hanging in the air when they come home for supper."

We proceeded to the smaller dresser with its oval mirror and its
silver tray with little glass bottles of lavender perfume and cologne
standing on a long lace dresser scarf upon the marble top. Mary gave
herself one spray, then asked if I wanted mine on my neck or my wrist.
Wearing our furs, ropes of jewelry, sparkles, and now enveloped in the
scent of lavender, we admired ourselves once again in that oval mirror,
standing transfixed because this little ritual was drawing to its close,

wanting this moment to be frozen in time, a white child's imagining and a black woman's fantasy of being one day great ladies.

And then it was over.

"Now we got's t'be very careful like, Sarh,
'cause we got's t'put evyt'ing back 'xactly de way –"

" – it was. I know. Because if Miss Bess found out –"

" – dat ud be somet'ing – "

" – terrible!"

With great reluctance, we replaced the perfume bottles exactly the same way on the tray, straightened the lace dresser scarf, coiled the ropes of jewelry exactly right in the drawer, replaced the 'sparkles over there,' lightly smoothed out any wrinkles in Bessie's new nightgowns, carefully closed the drawers, rehung the fur coat "That way, Mary. It was facing the – Yeah, and the hanger was – Yeah – this way," replaced my fox head - "The eyes need to look at the window, and the tail should – Yeah – this way" exactly as it had originally been, closed those magical doors, replaced the gold key in the same absence of dust on the silver tray exactly where Mary had found it, and firmly smoothed Bessie's bedspread of elaborate crochet.

"Why's you laughin', chil'?"

"Oh! I was thinking about your penny flying out the window. That's funny."

"I doan t'ink we got's t'do dat tuhday.
Dis here bedspread is es tight es a board!"

We stood for a while in the doorway, checking and rechecking that nothing was out of place. Mary undoubtedly felt the enormity of the danger, and I felt that my little heart would burst for joy. I don't know the length of time devoted to this wondrous ritual, but for me, time stood still, because Mary, whom Elaine said was *"black as the ace of spades,"* and me the scrawny white girl with broomstick legs and knobby knees, had stolen a magical moment worthy of a fairy tale, dressed in the finery of queens.

"Til' next time, Sarh?"

"Till next time, Mary. Sarah and Mary,
the fox and the bear and the penny flying out the window.
That's funny."

O Give me yo' hand, Give me yo' hand,
You must be lovin' at God's command.
You say de Lord has set you free,
You must be lovin' at God's command.
Why doan you let yo' neighbor be?
You must be lovin' at God's command.
O Give me yo' hand, Give me yo' hand,
You must be lovin' at God's command.

Mary possessed three three talents which absolutely amazed me. Her palms were so tough from years of hard work that when fires sprang up on the stove top, as they often did in those frantic hours of meal preparation, she simply patted them out with her hands, while I either stood speechless nearby, absolutely aghast, so sure that her tiny frame would ignite and disappear into a puff of smoke, or shrieked her name at the top of my lungs!

Her astounding ability to peel a potato in one long elegant spiral is an artistic achievement I have never attained, though as a child I made courageous but futile attempts to acquire that skill each day. Every morning, in another of the little rituals I originated to punctuate my little life, I was determined that this was the day when I would not only peel a potato in one piece, but I would actually do it faster than she. Since all my efforts on that farm, from the sublime to the ridiculous, were doomed to failure, I never succeeded. After we had dug up the potatoes from the hedge row, Mary would sit on her stool by the old wood stove with me on a chair beside her. In a large metal bowl floated the potatoes in water. Mary would take each one, and using her sharp paring knife, proceed to quickly peel the skin away in one long elegant spiral, while I with my butter knife proceeded to maul each one. After three or at most four humiliating attempts, I left my chair, experiencing yet another of my daily defeats, but feeling the sense of accomplishment that I had bravely tried, plus the firm resolve that tomorrow I would succeed.

She could beat egg whites into lofty peaks of meringue using a fork alone, never seeming to tire, and I'd watch her beat egg yolks with a fork which moved back and forth so quickly, it effectively disappeared into the rising foam. I was always puzzled why she could perform such a simple task with all the efficiency of an industrial machine.

One afternoon, as Mary sat on her stool at the kitchen table and I sat on a chair beside her, she produced lofty peaks of meringue in a blue-willow bowl while delicately sprinkling sugar into the bowl with her left hand.

"The ladies at the orphanage cooking in the kitchen
all wear pretty white dresses, Mary, and white shoes too.
They could be the preacher's wife.
And they always wear little net things on their heads
just like brides with veils."

Mary quietly chuckled again and shook her head from side to side as though she were saying 'No.'

"Oh! They 'probly bought those dresses in the Monkey Ward Catalog."

"I bet dey did, Sarh. I bet dey did."

*"All year long, we have soup. Soup for lunch every day.
But at supper on Friday, we have fish and brussel sprouts."*

"Gracious, chil', I kin tell by dat face y'doan much like dem sprouts."

*"I hate them. The Nuns grow them in the garden
behind St. Francis Hall, but I sure don't like them.
Every year I hope for one of Mr. Clay's 'crop failure.'
Mary, I can't even see your fork. It's disappeared in the foam again.
How can you –"*

"O chil', I ain't had no truble wid egg w'ites since de asksident."

"You had an asksident?"

Mary gave the bowl before her a stern focus of attention, determining if the critical mass of meringue was sufficient for the three lemon pies waiting nearby.

"I do b'lieve we ain't gonna has 'nough, Sarh. Wish we had a few mo' eggs. Dem hens sho' ain't layin' like dey's 'posed t'be layin'. You ain't ben scarin' dem chickins half t'death in dat coop ag'in, has you? Has you ben runnin' in dere ag'in yellin' wid y'arms all wavin' like some wil' woman, hens screechin' an' feathers flyin'? Such commotion in dat 'lil house! Y'ain't ben doin' dat, has you? Sarh, y'ain't, has you?"

I said nothing.

"An' I know whut else you's t'inking.
Sarh, I know whut you's wantin' t'do.
You's t'inking 'O glory, I cain't wait til' Mary ain't lookin'!
I jus' cain't wait!' You's wantin' t'grab deez lemon peels,
den sneek out intuh dat pantry, an' hide 'hind dat washin''sheen,
t'inking, 'Mary doan know whar I's at! She sho' doan!'
Den you's gonna spend de whole aftuhnoon dippin' deez lemon skins
intuh dat sugar tin on dat floor, jus' gnawin', an' gnawin', an' gnawin' –
Girl, ef you doan stop dat sneakin',
y'ain't gonna has no teeth by de time you's seven year ol'.
Gracious! We'l be droppin' yo's in a glass an' linin' it up on dat sink
like we line up Bessie's an' Clayton's!"

I said nothing.

Mary continued to beat with her invisible fork as I brushed two
flies from the lemon filling.

"You ain't never ben in dat shed,
bu' near dat door on de side by dat weepin' willuh tree,
dere's a shelf on dat wall whar Mistuh Clay keeps some o'his tools.
Long 'go, b'fo' you was born, b'fo' you come'd t'us, I was goin'
intuh dat shed t'git some tatters, an' dat durn shelf fall'd off an' broke
my arm. You's sho' right, it was awful! I jus' sat dere in dat dirt,
not knowin' whut t'do, my arm just a'hangin'.
Miss Bess took me t'dat horsepital in Jamestown,
it was new den, an' dat doct'r say he has t'operate.
Sho' 'nough, dat bone was broke somet'ing fierce in t'ree places
an' good fo' nut'ing, so dey took it clean out an' put in dis metal rod
whar dat light brown line is dere. See dat? An' since dat dere day,
I kin make deez egg w'ites jus' –"

"You didn't get tired?"

Mary gasped!

Her fork suddenly stopped!

Mary and I were silent.

She then quietly tapped the fork on the side of the bowl, placed it slowly on the table, then turned solemnly toward me. After a pause, Mary said -

"O chil'. I - I's so sor'y. I din' mean ta –
I was t'inkin' mo' 'bout deez egg w'ites den 'bout you. I din' -"

"You didn't get tired?"

"No, no chil', I din' git tired,
an' I ain't gittin' tired es long es you's needin' me.
Dat's my promise, Sarh. Dat's my promise.
You doan need t'be wor'yin' none 'bout – 'bout -
I's gonna be righ' shere es long es you's needin' me, 'cause –"

A horn abruptly sounded in the distance…then sounded again.

"Was dat a –"

"Oh Mary, it's Tuesday!"

"O chil, we plum fugot. Dat's de –"

" - Rag and Ware Man! Mr. –"

" - Carlson! Ain't he just in time. Maybe he has some eggs fu' deez
pies, 'cause it sho' doan look t'me dat we has 'nough."

As the honking continued accompanied by an occasional backfire, Mary hurriedly covered her blue-willow bowl with a blue-willow plate as I covered the pies with the tablecloth. Then we both hurried out the squeeeeky door –

SLAM!

and stood on the porch near the two concrete steps.

A sorely dilapidated blue truck which read *Carlson's Fish or Cut Bait* meandered slowly up the lane past the lavender Rose of Sharon…

past the rose-petunia patch…

and shuddered to a backfiring stop
near the tub of pink portulaca by the old blue pump.

"Mistuh Carlson? Sarh an' I jus' plum fugot you was a'comin'."

The door opened on the other side of the truck,
and an invisible voice called out –

"Oh yeah, Miss Mary, it's the second Tuesday,
and I'll be back on the fourth one too, just like always."

"Sarh an' I was so busy talkin', we's jus' plum fugot."

"Well, you'll both be quite happy I came,
because I've got a big box of gifts for you two."

He suddenly appeared near the back of his truck wearing his customary patched overalls and a battered fishing hat. He held a large cardboard box which he deposited near Mary's safety-pin sneakers as the fishing tackle hanging from his brim glinted in the afternoon sun.

"I see you have your little companion again today,
hanging onto your dress again."

"Sho' is. Al'ys a'clingin', just al'ys a'clingin'.
Good gracious, Mistuh Carlson,
I ain't never seen such a huge madder!"

"Me neither. That sure is a duzzy, Miss Mary.
Big enough for the State Fair. Ida May Anderson said there was no way
she and Abel could eat all that, so she thought your farm hands might
like it. She had it hanging on a vine with a silk stocking when I came,
so it wouldn't fall clean off into the mud. And here's a pint of Caitlin's
pickled zucchini, and look at these cukes from Dorothy Baxter. Huge!
And here's a jar of her dill pickles. She said they're coming on
so hard now, she just can't make pickles fast enough.
And - and here's a pint of preserves from the last of the strawberries.
Anna Zellner sends her regards. Oh, this is a bag of Avon from Detsie
Sanford. Thought that would save Miss Bess a trip,
and – here's a few green onions from Massie Malcom,
dead cows, and here's some powder that Maybelle Porter is using
on her roses. Said she's having good luck with it."

"O dem beetles is terr'ble dis year."

"I know. I saw Miss Bess just now fussing in her pink roses
down the lane."

"We do t'ank you, an' Miss Bess 'il too. Dey's all be most 'preciated."

"And now look way down in there, Miss Mary.
Down in the bottom."

"Ah - is - is dat a green watuhmelon? – er a –"

"*That*, Miss Mary, is a zucchini!"

"Gracious! Lord have mercy.
Look Sarh, it's 'most es big es Mistuh Clay's watuhmelon spuds."

"It was hiding under the leaves through three rains, and now look
at that whopper. Comes from MacPhearson's."

"I ain't never seen one dat big in all my born days.
I's gonna need 'nudder six fryin' pans!"

Mr. Carlson was a refreshing anomaly in my early little life
which I could not have hoped to understand standing there by those
concrete steps, clasping Mary's skirt. He and his wife had always lived
simply, piecing together a modest living from his fishing expertise and
his peddling door to door. That spring though when both his sons were
killed in a tragic boating accident, Mr. Carlson's dilapidated truck
disappeared from view for one full year. During those twelve months of
immense grief and enforced introspection, his virtues were forged in a
dark crucible of suffering too painful to be imagined. When he emerged
the following spring, he radiated a peaceful trust in the benevolence of
God, an unwavering endorsement of human dignity which simply did not
recognize the color of anyone's skin, and a generosity which nearly
always elicited a generous response from others. In the racially charged
atmosphere of my childhood, Mr. Carlson was a welcomed relief for me,
as I am sure he was for Mary. For a short time twice a month, Mary was
simply a woman enjoying the company of someone who regarded her as
his equal. For those moments, she could simply be herself.

"And what will you be needing today, Miss Mary?"

"Ah, like we was just a'sayin'
dat we wisht we had 'nudder egg er two fo' –"

"Sure, I've got another two dozen."

I yanked on Mary's dress -
"Knee pad."

"An' wud y'happen t'has 'nudder box o'dem safety pins
an' one box o'cornstarch? Dis yung'in loves dat puddin' recipe."

"Sure do."

I tugged even harder at Mary's dress -
"Knee pad!"

"Will you be needing one dozen eggs or two?"

"Just one doz - Sarh, why y'keep yankin' at my durn dress?"

*"KNEE PAD! YOUR KNEES IS 'PLAININ'
JUST A BIT!"*

"O Sarh, I plum fugot ag'in.
Dis heat is makin' me lose my mind! I's a'needin 'nudder knee pad
'cause –"

" - her knees is 'plainin' just a bit!"

Mary chuckled again
and shook her head from side to side
as though she were saying 'No.'

"Well Miss Mary, I started out this morning with seven knee pads,
and I only have one left. Miss Caddie's and Miss Dilsey's,
and that new woman who helps with all the little Blackwells –
everybody's knee pads wore out all at the same time.
But I do have one left."

Mr. Carlson disappeared into the back of his truck as Mary and I marveled at the size of that zuchinni and tomato. Then he reappeared with a smaller box which was topped with a napkin bundle spotted with blue.

"Here is what you were needing, Miss Mary,
and this on top is from Betsie Blackwell.
She was making dozens of these today for her brood
and thought you and Miss Sarah might like two for yourselves."

"O Sarh, ain't dat nice.
Dey's blueber'y muffins, an' feel, dey's still warm."

"And for you, Little Miss Clinging Always Clinging,
Mrs. Blackwell sends this coloring book for you,
and this little box of crayons. It's *Cinderella*.
She thought you might like coloring all those pretty -"

"I can wear colored when I'm the preacher's wife, because -"

"Ain't we ben havin' nice weather!" Mary shouted.
"Sho' has ben nice weather, sho' has!
I's never seen such nice weather!
Mistuh Carlson, we sho' do t'ank you fu' all o'dis.
How much do we owe ya?"

"Oh Miss Mary, since you're my last stop,
and now I can go home to my Mrs.,
how about we charge it to the dust and let the rain settle it."

"We sho' do -"

"That little lady with those big dark eyes -
she's gonna break many a'heart when she grows up."

As Mr. Carlson closed the back door of his truck
then climbed into the driver's seat, Mary called out –
"Eny mo' gran'babies on de way?"

"Oh yeah, Miss Mary. Two next winter,
and Emma's three boys are growing up to be fine young men."

"I's real glad t'hear dat, real glad. Caught eny fish lately?"

"Oh yeah, Miss Mary, a real nice bass the other day."

"But de big un got 'way ag'in?"

Mr. Carlson chuckled as Mary herself chuckled -
"Always does, Miss Mary, always does."

The door closed, the engine started,
and the truck turned around in the wide gravel sea.
Then that dilapidated *Carlson's Fish or Cut Bait* meandered
down the lane, honking and backfiring all the way.

Mary stood silently on that porch gazing out over the potato field,
with me clinging as usual to her dress.

A heavy peace had fallen
upon those one thousand acres,

solemn

pervasive

a peace rarely felt on that farm.

After a moment, Mary spoke -

"O my, Sarh, we sho' do has wurk t'do
gittin' all dis intuh dis house.
An' den, we has even *bigger* wurk t'do."

"What?"

"We got's t'eat deez muffins,
an' while you color yuse'f a purdy dress
fo' whin you be de preacher's wife,
I's car'yin' dem lemon peels out t'dat compost heap.
Ain't no chil' o'mine droppin' her teeth intuh no glass
by de time she's seven year ol'!"

INTRODUCTION TO THE TRINITY

God has promised life fuever
At dat camp meetin' in de Promised Land
Doan git weary, doan git weary
'Til dat meetin' in de Promised Land

Jesus is a'comin', see Him, see Him
At dat camp meetin' in de Promised Land
Doan git weary, doan git weary
'Til dat camp meetin' in de Promised land

Cain't you feel de Spirit movin'
At dat camp meetin' in de Promised Land
Doan git weary, doan git weary
'Til dat camp meetin' in de Promised Land.

At the orphanage, the dogmas of Catholicism were presented in symbols which we children could easily understand. The font meant baptism. The manger represented the birth of Christ. The crucifix with a corpus meant the Passion, in contrast to the plain cross, lacking a corpus, which meant that God's plan for redemption was complete. The more abstract symbols, such as atonement represented by the pelican feeding her young with her own blood, were mercifully omitted as too difficult for orphans struggling with nightmares to comprehend. These symbols were presented in an orderly, unvarying sequence. Christmas was always followed by Lent, and Good Friday always preceded Easter. Symbols were always presented with their appropriate associations. Nails were never displayed near the baptismal font, neither were the Wise Men ever depicted during Lent.

In the many oil paintings and the many photographs of oil paintings which lined the walls of the orphanage, the Trinity was also presented as understandable to the consciousness of a child. God the Father was shown as an elderly man seated upon a throne. His clothing, though voluminous, was of humble rather than opulent appearance. He was sometimes presented near or upon clouds, and I noticed that He rarely looked at me. Mother Agnes always taught that because no one could see the face of God, artists presented His face in a dimness that resembled dusk.

` Portrayals of the Son of God included His gentleness, and the power of Christ as a miracle worker. The more graphic portrayals included His Agony in the Garden as well as images of His Passion. The artistic renderings of Good Friday were balanced by portrayals of Christ's rising from His tomb as He triumphed over physical death. Paintings of the ascended and glorified Christ included stars, since Father Anthony taught that the Christ of Revelation holds seven stars in His hand. Mother Agnes said that was important to remember, because Jesus was prophecied to be the star rising out of Jacob.

The Holy Spirit was simply a dove or a flame of fire, both images of movement. We were taught that the Spirit of God alters history according to the designs of God, and that the major thrust of the Spirit is movement toward the good.

Fortunately, these elemental images were instilled into me so deeply that I was able to transcribe their essence from metaphor to direct life experience. The Trinitarian God who is paradoxically Three Divine Persons in One - an elderly man seated on a chair, the beauty of the Son knotting into unimaginable horror before rising in triumph over death, and the movement of the Spirit which is sometimes gentle, sometimes violent, yet always irresistible - were presented to me as a six year old in three events which appropriately occurred on the same road.

When we drove out the lane of Bluebonnet and turned left onto Rural Route 2, we drove about half a mile to Baxter's hog farm. Across from their farm, another one-lane road branched to the left at a right angle to Rural Route 2. That little country road meandered past a dirty-white two-story wooden shack which leaned alarmingly to the left, beside which one solitary armless kitchen chair, with ripped and tattered vinyl, stood facing our alfalfa field in majestic isolation. The house was in as conspicuous disrepair as its neighboring chair, in serious need of paint, and was in desperate need of weather-proofing, because the wooden planks had aged to the point that wide gaps appeared in the walls. Gale-force winter winds, blasting across those fields, must have tormented the inhabitant of that humble home.

That road continued for miles past farms and tiny hamlets of no more than five houses, until it widened into a four-lane highway near Sterling Downs, the nearest racetrack where Donald MacPhearson raced his sulky horses and won a considerable fortune. That highway then continued to Jackson where Clayton owned his bar, and where Miss Bess frequented the Sears and Roebuck Store. After Jackson though, that highway suddenly remembered its humble origin near Baxter's hog farm, and gracefully returned to a one-lane country road which then terminated in Jamestown. Though that once tiny hamlet had grown significantly to now include a modern hospital which was the pride of the region, that road itself lead not into the newer section of the town, but rather into the old sector with its infamous trailer park and where the little one-room schoolhouse from long ago still stood.

On this road I was introduced to the Trinity. Each experience included a depth of fear which imprinted each indelibly upon my mind, heart, and soul. Each brought the consciousness of this skinny little orphan with broom-stick legs and knobby knees to the end of her mind's comprehension, but paradoxically to the brink of spiritual understanding.

God has promised life fuever
At dat camp meetin' in de Promised Land...

CLANG! CLANG! CLANG!
"DINNER'S REDY! TIME T'GIT WASHIN' UP!
CLIFFORD? YEAH! TIME T'GIT WASHIN' UP!"
CLANG! CLANG! CLANG!

Mary rang the dinner bell,
shouting in her loudest voice toward the open door of the shed,
and the echo-bird became embarrassed again.

SLAM!

"Dey hear'd me. Clifford was a'wavin'. Dey hear'd.
Durn bugs, all summer long deez durn bugs.
Shew! Why God made bugs, I never know'd."

"Clayton still hasn't fixed the hole in that screen, Laine,"
Bessie grumbled.
"How many summers has it been?
He spends all winter fixing machines down in that cold shed,
but he can't spend a few minutes on a warm day and fix that screen."

"It's about to fall off, Bessie, from all that slamming.
Frank, do you think you could – could –
At least the hole in the screen – could you –"

"A new door," was all Frank said.

"I know, Frank, in a perfect world,
but I don't know that Clayton would like us to buy a new one.
On the other hand, I doubt he would even notice.
In the meantime though, could you just fix the screen?"

Frank began mumbling to Elaine more words
than he ever spoke aloud, accompanied by grand gestures,
to which Elaine responded mumbling tensely with obvious annoyance -

"I know, Frank, I know. The problem is not just the door...
The swirling corn in the - Yes, I know, it's disgusting...
Even after it's flushed, yes. If this were our house,

we would have called the plumber eight years before yesterday. . .
I understand, but we don't live here...
I remember the. . .yes, Frank. . .the cholera epidemic. Yes, I know.
A century ago in Maysville. . .Yes, half the town. . .
I know, Frank, I know, but we don't live here! In the meantime –
Bessie do they sell screens at Carpenter's Hardware Store,
or at least patches?"

"I would guess they do, Laine. Clyde sells about everything else."

"Then Frank, let's drive into Maysville today after -"

"Colored Mary?" shouted Bessie.
"Did you bring up that banana ice cream from the cellar?"

"O Miss Bess, I plum fugot! Will go git dat righ' now!"

As Bessie began her customary remarks about
"the laziness of house niggers,"
Mary rushed around the stove, rushed down the short hallway,
hurried up the two steps, and quickly crossed the dining room
toward the cellar door.

"Sarah? Where do you think you're going?"

"I have to go with Mary."

"No. you don't. Stay right here and put this bread on the table."

"No, I have to go with Mary!"

"Young lady, you are too assertive for your own good.
A little too high and mighty.
She's always been cocky, Bessie.
Thinks she rules the world. We'll take her back to that orphanage,
and those old Nuns will whip her back into shape.
You know what that Catholic Church is like."

"I hardly think that's likely, Laine.
She comes here more determined every summer.
Remember last year with that plate? Where's common decency?
I wouldn't be a Catholic if you tied me to a tree
and flogged me half to death. Damn cross-backs.
I don't know how Donald and Caitlin MacPhearson
escaped being so high and mighty.
Oh I know all right what that Catholic Church is all about.
I've heard stories that would curdle your blood.
That's where she gets it you know, all that high and mighty."

But I rushed out of the room.

Almost everyday, Mary descended the steps from the dining room into the cellar where the meat and ice cream freezer was kept and where the rats lived. Every day I was terrified that, as she was getting our food, she herself would be theirs! She never took my fear seriously, which worried me all the more, because in my childhood mind, she just didn't seem to realize the enormity of the danger.

"Sarh, jus' sit righ' shere on dis here top step an' wait fo' me.
Yeah, right on dis here step like y'al'ys does.
I got's t'go down an' git dat ice cream Laine made,
'cause Miss Bess, she be mad at me ag'in.
O chil', you's lookin' like you's frettin'.
O chil', doan wor'y none, Sarh. No need t'fret.
I be righ' back. I promise I's gonna be righ' –"

"But there's rats down there, Mary!
Those – those awful rats! They could –"

"O chil', you's al'ys frettin' 'bout somet'ing.
Sarh, you doan has t'al'ys fret.
I's bigger an' scarier den dem rats is enyhow."

Her words did nothing to alleviate my fears. Each time I'd sit on that top step and watch anxiously as she descended into the cellar. When she reached the dirt floor beneath that suspended naked light bulb and disappeared, I began calling to her, a continuous dialogue, always the same -

"Mary, are you all right?"

That reassuring voice from far below –
"Uuu huu."

"Mary, are you still there?"

Chuckling to herself –
"Uuu huu."

"Mary, do you see any rats down there?
I don't want them to –"

"Sarh, doan shuu wor'y, yung'in. I's comin'. I's a'comin'."

"Mary? I can't see you. Are you still —"

"I's comin', chil'. I's comin'. Dis freezer door's done stuck ag'in.
Durn ice cream's gonna be hard es a brick ag'in.
Dis ol' house comin' 'part at de seams, an' nobody seems t'care.
Cain't git no ice cream ef'n dis door cain't open."

"Mary?"

"Uuu huu."

"Are you coming back now?"

The whole time she was in the cellar, I was worried sick. But
then I'd hear the freezer door open...then close...and then I'd hear Mary
moving...and then I'd see Mary herself coming back into view...and
back up the cellar steps. Each time she chuckled to herself and shook her
head —

"Whut's I gonna do wid shuu, yung'in?
I goes down dere 'most evy day, an' no rat's done got me yit."

Only then would my heart stop racing, and only then would my
fear evaporate away. Everyday she attempted to reassure me with her
familiar chuckle -

"Yung'in, Sarh, I's bigger an' scarier den dem rats is.
I know I's bigger. Dey's scared o'me! Dey is!"

But I didn't believe her, since I had never actually seen one.

By the time Mary and I reentered the kitchen, everyone was
seated around the table as Mr. Clay held up an ear of corn, pronouncing
the same agricultural lesson he provided at least once each summer -

"Look at this. Everybody see this?
See how these rows are even here, nice and parallel,
but down here they waver a bit?
Remember that dry spell we had about three weeks ago?
That wavering here, just a bit right here,
means the corn was stressed, just for a bit,
because here the rows are even again.
Can always tell what the weather patterns have been
by observing an ear of corn."

"Frank and I picked these three dozen ears this morning, Clayton.
They're coming on hard now with all this rain and heat and humidity.
We definitely didn't take Sarah this time though.
Last time, she just wandered off – just disappeared in the field.
Couldn't find her for the longest time.
She had wandered off from where we were, so –"

"I was trying to find the stream."

"The what, Laine?" Bessie asked. "What'd she -
You can tell these green beans came from Porter's.
He always has the best green beans."

"She said she was trying to find that stream, Bessie,
you know, that runs beneath that stone bridge
beyond MacPhearson's, near Clifford's."

"Oh yeah, by that oak tree. That huge old thing's
been hangin' over that stream forever, even when I was a kid."

"I couldn't breathe, and it was so hot,
so I was trying to find that stream."

"She was trying to find that stream, Bessie,
and then she fainted dead away.
She passed out, and I mean out cold, in that field
last Sunday when Frank and I drove down there
in the pickup to get corn. Oh yeah, she was face down
in that corn field when we finally found her, white as a ghost.
Frank carried her to the truck and fanned her down good,
but even then she was grey and green.
We're not taking you there any more, Missy,
even if you want to go.
Goodness. You provide a new ordeal every day."

"She'll be white as a ghost when she sees the Boogie Man!"

"Oh Clayton, don't start that!
You terrorized all our own children with that nonsense."

"The what?"

"Oh Sarah, the Boogie Man, that awful Boogie Man.
Lives on that road 'cross from Baxter's. Lived there a long time.
Bessie, I do believe these chompers will last me another year.
I'm eatin' this corn like these teeth are my own!"

"I've never heard of a Boogie Man."

"Oh Sarah, you don't want to know.
He's that monster that lives across our field.
Lives all by himself in that little shack,
but he sure does love to eat little girls."

"Clayton? Just stop before –"

"He – he eats little girls? He'd eat – he'd eat –"

"Oh yeah! He 'specially loves little girls
with brown hair and big brown eyes.
And you know what?"

"Wh– What?"

"He's so big, Sarah, so big, he's as big as the whole sky,
but he lives all by himself in that little house,
and every night for supper he eats a little –"

*"Oh Frank, she's looking green and grey again,
like she's about to pass out again."*

"Tonight Sarah, you can see him, and he will see you.
I'm going to drive around all the hedgerows,
and you can go with me, so that Boogie Man
will have a chance to see your brown hair and big brown –"

*"Clayton, that's enough! Please!
She'll go stiff in a minute, if you don't stop,
and you know what an ordeal that is."*

That evening after Mary left, Clayton drove out the lane with Bessie in the front seat and me in the back, then turned left onto Rural Route 2. When we came to Baxter's hog farm, Mr. Clay turned left onto the Boogie Man Road.

*"Oh Clayton, look how you've terrorized that child.
She's shrinking over in the corner of that back seat
like she's trying to fall out outta the car."*

"Sarah, have a look. His house is on Bessie's side.
I'll drive real slow now, so he'll get a good look at –"

*"Clayton, stop that teasing! Sarah's shoulders are up past her ears,
and her eyes are squeezed shut so hard,
like somebody's gonna punch her!"*

"I can see his house now, Sarah.
Let's see if he's waiting for you on his chair."

"Clayton, stop that nonsense! She's not breathing!"

"Well, well, well. What a shame. I don't see him sitting in his yard.
He's probably still inside having a little girl for supper."

"That's enough of this foolishness! Just stop right –"

"Let's drive around to those eastern fields by Anderson's,
then drive back, so that monster will know what you look like
for his supper tomorrow night."

"If you don't stop, Clayton, we'll have a fainting kid on our hands!"

I don't remember where we drove, because I had tightly covered my face with my hands. Mr. Clay's observations of weeds, the familiar quiet of the country evening, and all the familiar rural scents failed to register to my senses, so sunk was I in the sheer terror of knowing that soon the Boogie Man would see me. But eventually, as our car turned right and Bessie simultaneously called out the window to Clyde Carpenter, marveling that the brown-eyed susies by his mailbox were spreading like wildfire, I knew with a sickening dread that we once again were on the Boogie Man Road.

"Oh good, Sarah. Just as I hoped. I see him now,
there on our side of the car. There –"

"Don't start, Clayton, please! She's grey and green again!"

Despite my profound apprehension, I dared to peek through the rigid slats of my fingers as our car slowed to a creep before that little leaning house. Suddenly my senses resurrected.

An elderly white-haired black man, so thin and so frail, was seated so simply on that armless kitchen chair, his gnarled hands meekly folded in his lap. His ancient bib-overalls were faded, torn, and tattered, each suspender fastened not with brass, but with common safety pins. Each pant leg was rolled up to clearly reveal his own dirty, safety-pinned sneakers. He wore a yellow-ish white shirt which had obviously been worn for decades, so patched and repaired that it closely resembled the condition of Mary's own dress. He paid no attention to us, or to me, or to our slowly moving car, his quiet gaze fastened solely upon the clouds of glittering firefires hovering over our alfalfa field under the shimmer of a cresent moon. In the fading light of the setting sun, his diminutive nature was magnified to powerful presence as burnished rays lengthened his shadow and the shadow of his chair across the entire lawn. So transfixed was I at that magnificent, lowly image, that I was startled when Mr. Clay laughed his wicked laugh and said –

"That's the Boogie Man."

With those words, my mind came to its end. All thought stopped with a shock. I was too young to reconcile the terror and the meekness of this immortal figure. I simply felt like my mind was standing on a cliff, and beyond that I could not step.

Jesus is a' comin', see Him, see Him
At dat meetin' in de Promised Land...

"Hi Mary,"
I said as I skipped into the kitchen.

"Dere you is! I's ben a' callin' you. Whar's you ben, yung'in?"

"Oh, I was resting up on Frank and Elaine's bed
trying not to catch The Polio from Jeffery.
Wha' cha doin'?"

"Makin' brownies.
Why Mistuh Winston wants brownies in dis here heat,
I never know'd. Gracious! No need t'melt de chocolit.
Jus' sit it on de table an' it melts its own durn se'f. O my, lookee you!
Ain't dat purdy. 'Nudder dandelion necklace."

"Yeah. And see in the back, Mary? Can you see back here?
I fastened it with a safety pin."

"O I see dat. Jus' like Miss Bessie's fancy necklaces.
Real nice. Whut's you talkin' 'bout Jeffry?"

"Oh, he caught The Polio on a hot day,
so Sister Angela says on hot days, we have to spend time

on our beds in the afternoon, so we don't catch it.
That's when Katie and Mimi and I put our faces on the metal."

"I see."

"Jeffery has hard bars on his legs, so he's the scorekeeper,
but David can still play ball. He has The Terrible Palsey,
so he has to sit in a chair with wheels all day long.
When he hits the ball, Sister Margaret runs for him,
and he pushes his wheels behind her."

"I'd like t'see dat!"

"Yeah! The boys put their hands over their mouths and laugh,
because she lifts her skirts so high."

"I'd like t'see dat too! I hate t'turn on dis stove ag'in."

"We can't have brownies at the orphanage. The Nuns say they are
'excessive.' But we have a birthday party the last Sunday afternoon
every month. We have a party then with a flat cake for all the
children who had birthdays that month. But you know what, Mary?
In November we have to have two flat cakes, because so many children
have birthdays in November."

"Valentine's Day," chuckled Mary.

"That's silly, Mary. Valentines Day isn't in November!"

Mary chuckled again.
"O dat's right. I plum fugot.
I hear you's goin' t'de race track tuhnight?"

"Oh yeah, to see Mr. MacPhearson drive his big horse!"

"Ain't dat somet'ing. I shu'ly hope he wins.
Maybe I kud jus' leave dis pan on de table righ' shere.
By suppertime, dis batter ud bake its own durn se'f."

Donald and Caitlin MacPhearson were third generation Irish immigrants who charmingly fulfilled every stereotype of their native land, though because of their amiable personalities, their staunch Catholic faith was politely overlooked in this staunchly Protestant region of the world. Donald always wore a green hat, smoked an Irish pipe, and spoke in faint whispers of the Irish brogue of his parents' ancestral home. They bartered their voluminous cabbages for Mr. Clays bountiful potatoes, and Caitlin was famous the region round for her quintessential Irish kraut. Their conversation was laced with the Irish idioms which have become an indelible addition to American speech. It was Donald's sense of humor as well as his abrupt recovery which forever changed the name of Mr. Clay's bar.

When they were newly married, their six children arriving in rapid succession, Donald had struggled with a drinking problem and a fondness for green ale, an addiction from which as an older and wiser man, he had fully recovered. The impetus for that dramatic reversal was that his drinking had brought that family from rags to unexpected wealth.

Every Saturday evening, Donald fulfilled the ritual which was so famously enacted each week in the life of Clayton Clay, when Donald spent his evening out talking to the other farmers leaning back on those straight back chairs beneath Maysville's revolving barber pole, bragging about his crops and the enormity of his cabbages, or lamenting about the weather. One Saturday though long ago, when Clayton bragged to that group about the new bar he had just purchased, all those farmers left those chairs and drove in their pickups down to Jackson to Clayton's bar, *Suds and Spuds.*

Caitlin, like Bessie, never bothered to wait up for her husband on Saturday night. She cleaned up after supper as the children played among the fireflies, gave them their baths, sang to them Irish songs, told them Irish folktales, then put them to bed.

In the wee hours of that famous morning, Caitlin heard a man singing at the top of his lungs on that one-lane road to Jamestown –

In Heaven there ain't no beer... my dear
That's why me drinks mine here... right here.

Since their farmhouse stood at the very side of the road, she called urgently out the bedroom window in a hoarse whisper –

"There's children asleep here!"

The singing continued. Then after a pause, a voice called up from the darkness, "Ma'me?"

"May the devil tear into your worthless hide!
I said there are children asleep here!"

"Oh - oh Ma'me," that drunken voice sing-songed back. "I'm so – so very sorry. I have - I have – Do I have six? Yeah Ma'me, I do believe I have six home meself!"

"Donald? Donald MacPhearson - is that you?
Donald, it is you! You're drunk again?
Why you no-good blackguard bullocks bowsie! You stocious sot!
You fluthered mouldy drunk! You –"

"Caitlin – me love – now, now don't get so -"

"There's not a full shilling in your entire head! You – you rotten -
I'm gonna scraw your – Mother of God, what have you done?
Donald, what have you -"

"Oh - oh love. Oh – me love. Don't be mad, Caitlin.
You ain't so pretty, hun, when you's mad.
No need t'be mad this time nohow.
I won this – this fine horse! Can you see him here in the dark?
And – and where's my truck? Where'd my durn truck go?
Well, wherever my damn pickup is, me love, the back – well –
the back is full of zucchini!"

"What the devil? You no-good -"

"And the barmaid - Clayton's barmaid - that little sweetheart –
that pretty one in that tight sweater?
Well, hun, she – she sends her regards."

No one knows what happened in the MacPhearson bedroom that night, but everyone surmised there must have been a marital row of cosmic proportions. Everyone did know, however, that the next morning the countryside between that farm and Jackson was combed until that pickup was discovered wedged in a ditch. As promised, the back was piled high with zucchini. That night forever changed the history of that county.

Caitlin knew from those dire stories of the Irish potato famine told and retold down through the generations, that whatever zucchini her family could not eat or she could not give away, had to be used somehow. Out of sheer desperation at the enormous pile still dominating her kitchen, she invented her now-famous recipe for *Pickled Irish Zucchini*. Because her recipe was so well received by her friends, and was so welcomed when pint after pint was shared from Mr. Carlson's delapidated truck, she decided to enter a jar in the State Fair. Much to her surprise, her *great* surprise, she won the blue ribbon.

This meant that for the first time in sixteen consecutive years, Ida Mae Anderson did not win first prize for her *Spicy Pickle Relish*. Sixteen blue ribbons, in one long solemn row, lined the wall of her dining room, their color perfectly complementing the blue accents in her floral wallpaper. Not wanting those ribbons to fade, she carefully hung them on the southern wall away from the windows. Winning only second place was a serious blow to Ida Mae's self-esteem. Abel did his best to comfort his wife, and her children and grandchildren assured her that her relish was still their favorite. Her youngest granddaughter, who was by far the most outspoken, blurted out that the contest was flawed, the judges should be fired, and her entry should be tried again! Ida had several good cries about her defeat. Then with a paradoxical blend of reluctance tinged with haste, she hid away her failure in the bottom of her cedar closet, assuring herself that until the winter winds began to blow, she would not have to lay her unhappy eyes upon the color red.

By the time September had faded into October, and October progressed into November, when she knew she had to retrieve Abel's and her own winter coats, Ida Mae had finally adjusted to her defeat with a modest grace. As three generations of her family gathered round the table that year for Thanksgiving dinner, there at the end of the solemn row of blue ribbons was nailed to the wall a red ribbon still smelling of moth balls.

Though Ida Mae's fortune went from blue to red, Donald MacPhearson's history reversed from rags to riches. That huge black horse of which that family was so enormously proud, which Caitlin had had so much difficulty perceiving in the darkness of that now-famous night, was kept so brushed and polished that I could very nearly see myself reflected in its coat. Because that animal was so beautiful, so huge, and so brutely powerful, Donald affectionately named it *Clyde's Dale*. Donald quickly learned he had an inborn talent as a trainer and sulkey driver, and eventually he acquired other racehorses from the fortune Clyde's Dale earned.

As fond as he was of all his horses, it was Clyde's Dale which was responsible for the termination of Donald's addiction. Because of that reversal, for which Caitlin was eternally grateful, Clayton Clay changed the name of his bar from *Suds and Spuds* to *The Sobri-a-Tea*. That was the horse I was to see race at Sterling Downs that evening. Farther down the Boogie Man Road was the race track.

Early the next morning as the dew rose from Mr. Zellner's strawberry field, and the full moon faded from silver to hazy blue, I heard Leonard's car stop abruptly at the end of the lane. Their car door open and Mary called to me -
"Chil'?
Whut's you doin' sittin' in de grass ways down here so early?
Whut's you doin' sittin' by dem iris?"

I continued to stare motionless into the expanse of the field across the road, as Mary's voice became suddenly muffled as she leaned into the car –

"Yeah, Leonard, 'bout six. 'Bout six be fine.
Tell Mattie dat I's gonna be at de church by seven fu' sho'.
All's I need is 'bout an hour. I got's t'go an' see whut dis chil' is doin'.
'Bout six den. Yeah, 'bout six."

As Leonard's ancient car backed out the lane,
Mary rushed over to me sitting by the iris as still as a stone.

"Chil', whut's you doin' down here dis early?
Dere's a chill in de air dis mo'nin', an' you's shiverin'. Gracious!
Here, take my sweater. T'ain't got's no buttons,
but here - lemme wrap it round yo' shoulders. Real purdy color.
Dat church in Maysville brung me nudder bag las' night, shirts
fu' Leonard an' a real nice pot. Here, lemme take one o' my safety pins
an' pin it under yo' – Hold dat chin up a bit, yung'in, whiles I – I –
Jus' a second mo' - Dere. Dat looks real nice over yu' yelluh shirt.
Whut's you doin', yung'in?
Why's you starrin' like you's scared ag'in?"

So overwhelmed by the previous evening, I could barely whisper -
"Oh Mary - that – that horse!"

"O dat's right. Y'all went t'de races las' night. Whut –"

"Oh Mary – the horse – and – and the screaming!"

"O yeah. I know. Dem races gits so loud,
wid all dem fo'ks so 'cited 'bout –"

"The screaming and then – Oh Mary – then the ambulance came!"

"De *whut?* The amb'lance? Gracious, was dere an asksident? Sarh!
Was you hurt? Is you hurt? Was you –"

My voice was low and hesitant, uttering words too powerful
for a child's understanding -

"I – I was standing down at the starting line – you know –
by that metal - that chain fence."

"Yeah?"

"The loud speaker man was shouting about 'bits' – or 'bets' –
and everyone was talking about winning money.
People around me were talking about a 'double',
and everywhere smelled like popcorn."

"Yeah?"

"There were so many people, Mary - crushing all around me,
that I had to hold onto the fence so tight - like this –
real tight – like this - to save my place by the starting –"

"Whar was Frank an' –"

"I don't know. They were in the stands.
Somewhere – I don't know – up in the stands.
I don't know where they were, but they were in the stands."

"Chil', hur'y up an' tell me whut happened!
Here, lemme rub yo' back so you kin warm up.
Yo' fingers is so tight, chil', like you's still holdin' ontuh dat fence!
Gracious yung'in, tell me why dere was d'amb'lance!"

"The horses, Mary – the horses were warming up like they always do –
just trotting up and trotting down the track – and their sulkys were
going back and forth by me. I waved to Mr. MacPhearson once - when
he was going slow, but he didn't see me. There were so many people
taller than me, that he couldn't see me. Clyde's Dale was the only
horse with a tail, Mary. All the other tails had been cut off, but
Clyde's tail in that breeze was so pretty. I could see it shining under
the lights, like his tail had little sparkles like stars."

"Chil', you's lookin' like you's shiverin' now frum fright.
Unlock dem fingers, Sarh. Yo' knuckles is w'ite.
Chil', look at me! Look at me righ' now. Whut happened?"

I forced my gaze away from the fields…and looked at Mary.
Our eyes locked.

"Oh Mary, I was so scared. My heart was – was – Those horses are so
big, and they were so close by! That yellow car with the long poles on
each side drove out onto the track and parked on the far side, and then
all eight horses one by one lined up behind those poles. I couldn't see
where Clyde's Dale was that far away, but he wasn't at my end.
Then the car started moving very slow with the noses of the horses
nearly touching those poles. Then that car started going faster and
faster, and all those horses starting trotting faster and faster until
the car rounded the track on my side. All the horses were running so
fast – you know how fast they run - except one horse in the middle.
He was – he was almost running sideways. He seemed nervous,
Mary, like – like he wanted to go home, so he was trotting with his

head turned sideways - like this - like he was trying to get away from that pole. The car went faster until it got to where I was standing, and when that car raced away, that horse that was so scared, he – he stood up on his back legs and pawed the air!
Oh Mary!"

"O Sarh!"

"Oh Mary! And then the other horses reared back too and did the same thing! The drivers were shouting 'Whoo! Whoo!' and the women by me were screaming, 'Oh my God!' and I couldn't run because my hands seemed stuck to the fence! They were grabbing that fence so hard, I couldn't make them move.
All those horses were pawing the air just like this, and the sulkeys were going a little back and a little forth, and those horses were so loud, and those drivers kept shouting 'Whoo!' And then one sulkey upset. Oh Mary, a driver was on the ground! I could see him in the dirt with his arms covering his head, with all those horses rearing up all around him, and then I heard the ambulance siren and –"

"O chil!"

"Oh Mary! And then –"

"O Sarh, tell me whut – "

"Then – then – Clyde's Dale jumped into the air!"

"De *air*?!"

"Yeah! Mr. MacPhearson and the sulkey and the horse and his tail were all in the air! Everything was in the –"

"O my God!"

"He jumped, Mary! He jumped over everything!
He jumped over all those horses and over the man on the ground
and over all the sulkeys, and I – I was so close, Mary, I just couldn't
move! And then I saw him in the air – just hanging there, Mary –
like I see him still hanging there now."

"O Glory! O Lord, have mercy!"

"Just now – before you came – when I was looking out over the
strawberries, it's like I still see him hanging there now,
like he's still hanging there now.
And I still hear the loud sound of the ambulance siren,
and I still see him in the air – and – and I still hear all the people
shouting, "Oh my God! I still hear them shouting – still hear –"

"O my God!" Mary whispered, "O my God!"

Mary sat wide-eyed and still as the shadows on the grass grew
shorter. Little by little the sun was becoming more firmly established in
the sky. She and I were silently processing a series of images too holy to
be expressed, of a living being so beautiful, knotting into such horror,
then rising so utterly glorious.

Then Mary herself whispered hesitantly from a world far away –

"I's so, so grateful, chil'. I's so, so grateful t'God. O Sarh!
I's so grateful dat you warn't hurt. I's so glad you's safe.
Po' t'ing, you's still shiverin', an' looks t'me like dem 'lil fingers
is still stiff. I got's t'git you back intuh dat house, chil',
t'git somet'ing warm in you. I bet y'ain't had nut'ing t'eat."

"I've been down here a long, long time," I whispered.
"A long time."

"I's gonna built you a 'lil fire in de old wood stove
an' you kin sit on my stool an' warm up."

We rose simultaneously from the earth once again, as though by intuitive understanding. With Mary's hand on my back and me clasping Mary's skirt, we walked past the hollyhocks, yarrow, and the yellow roses on the old wagon wheel.

"Mary?"

I asked, my voice still trembling –

"Uuu huu."

*"W – will I always hear that ambulance siren, Mary?
Will it always be in my ears – like it is now?
Will I always hear it? I can hear it still so loud."*

"I 'spect not, yung'in. No need t'fret,"
said Mary as she brushed away the first of the daily flies.
"But I 'spect whut 'il happen t'you is whut 'il happen t'me. I woan hear
dat siren no mo' nedder, chil'. Dat sound fo' us both 'il die 'way.
But you an' me, Sarh, you an' me –
I 'spect we's gonna al'ys see dat horse in de air,
an' al'ys hear dem people shoutin',
'O my God!'"

❍━━❍

Can't you feel de Spirit movin'
At dat camp meetin' in de Promised Land...

The annual summer event toward which everyone in the county eagerly looked forward was the square dance held the second Saturday of August in the little one-room schoolhouse in Jamestown. The high-school square dance held in a similar schoolhouse in Jackson was that infamous gathering which Miss Bess adamantly insisted was -

"as good as a hayride.
No tramp can go there more than once,
because the next August, she's up to her eyeballs in diapers!"

But the dance in Jamestown was a reunion for adults, since nearly every farmer in the county and nearly all their wives had attended that tiny school at some time during their childhoods. Many of those boys and girls had formed friendship which later blossomed into marriages celebrated in the little Methodist Church in Brueston.

It amazes me now that that building was chosen at all to accommodate such a large number of people. Mercifully, throughout all the summers of my childhood, it never once rained on those particular Saturdays. The structure possessed only one door in the center of the front, only three windows on each side, and no air-conditioning or indoor plumbing. Though the grounds surrounding it were planted each May with zinnias, marigolds, and geraniums, the building itself could not be renovated, because The Historical Society had declared it a national landmark. Though the school truly did possess great historic value, the three outhouses standing out back generously swathed in sweet-pea vines were of even greater interest, because one was the county's famous *two-seater*. The schoolhouse had once stood proudly on the main street of Jamestown, but as the town grew, that tiny building seemed to have wandered off of its own humbled accord. It now stood on a back street next to the abandoned doctor's office, since Dr. Schumacher, known affectionately to some as Dr. Shoe and to apprehensive children as Dr. Shew, had moved his practice to the hospital back in the days when it was new.

As Frank parked our car on the already crowded grass, I saw once again a scene of Americana so perennially persistent, it could very well have served as the cover of a Norman Rockwell calendar. To the left of the front door stood a flagpole from which hung an Old Glory so huge and so heavy that I never once saw it wave over the Land of the Free. On the grass to the right of the front door stood the long table, borrowed from the local church hall, upon which desserts of every conceivable variety were proudly displayed among mason jars of zinnas and cold drinks stored in buckets of ice. On that table too was the box labeled *Door Prize for Best Recipe.* That wrapped and ribboned gift ensured that the Jamestown square dance was a highly caloric affair.

"Hello Elaine. Well if it isn't little Sarah again!"
exclaimed Anna Zellner as she placed a tray
of double-layer frosted cookies on the dessert table.

"Oh Anna, you must be so proud that your square dance skirt
still fits after all these years."

"Elaine, if the truth be told,
I had to take it out a bit here and -"

"Sarah, put your dress down."

"But Elaine, I just lifted it a little so Mrs. Zellner
could see my slip under my ruffle.
See, I wore my blue dress with this ruffle, and see my -"

Elaine made another quick downward motion with her hand -
"Sarah, put your dress down! That's not polite in public."

"And I also have lace on my socks."

"Oh, how beautiful!" exclaimed Anna. "How very, very pretty.
Don't tell anyone, Sarah, but I have lace on my slip too.
Now we're both dressed up for the dance!"

"I wanted to wear my dandelion necklace, but Elaine said –"

"Well, if it isn't Clyde Carpenter!"
shouted Clayton, as he and Bessie stepped up to the table.
"What the devil happened to your arm?"

"Oh Clayton, it's a long, long story.
Will go down in the family lore, I'm sure."

"How many more weeks for that cast?"

"Only two, Clayton.
Good thing, 'cause as you can see, the grandkids
have completely covered it with crayon."

"Doc Dobson just went in, Bessie," said Anna.
"Dorothy called him early this afternoon.
Apparently there was a minor crisis with one of those Baxter hogs."

"Sloane's truck is here, Elaine. Have the Carlson's arrived?"

"I think so. I saw them head inside a while ago.
Must be like an oven in there my now. Always is."

"Oh I know, Anna. Why last year, I nearly passed out."

"And on top of the heat - that Avon!" exclaimed Elaine.
"I just know Detsie will be –"

"We know!" Bessie and Anna agreed. "That box! Every year!"

The atmosphere resounded with music. Each year Ben Glacie, wearing his battered straw hat, played his banjo on the lawn as guests arrived, and each year, Abel Anderson and Ike Porter offered Appalachian folk tunes on their harmonicas as they strolled among the parking cars. Both Abel and Ike had learned to play when they were little boys, and during his army days, Abel had learned how to perfectly tune multiple harmonicas with a draw scraper and file.

"Blackwell's got here a while ago, Elaine,"
said Anna as she placed upon the table another glorious dessert.

"Yeah, I think I just now saw them wander off toward the back."

"When is she due again? Is it one per year now?"

"I don't know, Anna. After so many, I just lost track."

The dance committee had asked Betsie Blackwell to help serve those desserts from behind that long table. Though she politely declined, she privately fumed, *"There's no way I'm going to serve the entire county when I serve so many of my own children each and every day!"* So she and her husband, William, spent the evening mercifully away from their ever-expanding brood, admiring the daylilies, tiger lilies, and other glorious flowers which thrived in the fertile soil near the old outhouses, with Betsie wearing her favorite flowered maternity dress, and Bill providing her a constant supply of iced drinks.

Gracie Lynn was another bit of annual local color at that school-house, appearing each and every August with a new and often elaborate hairstyle fashioned by Grace Greyson in her backyard trailer beauty shop. Being an aging spinster who had spent her entire adult life managing the switchboard for the Maysville Phone Company, she viewed the selection of eligible widowers at the Jamestown square dance as *one last chance.*

Though the scene outside was charming, enchanting, and as all-American as mother and apple pie, the music thundering through every opened window and through that opened door promised to shake that tiny structure to its very foundation.

We entered that room to find it absolutely stuffed with people. Farmers and their wives sat all around the perimeter where benches had been pushed up against the walls which were decorated with individual quilted squares of the original quilt pattern called *The Schoolhouse,* Some blocks had one chimney, some had two, and a few had quilted shrubs near a rectangular door. Each block was discreetly fastened to the walls with tiny tacks to avoid the consternation of the Historical Society. The Sloane's, Malcom's, Wilson's, Donald and Caitlin, many farmers I didn't know, and Doc Dobson, the widower of over one year, who was sure to be cornered by Gracie Lynn later that evening, sat beneath those quilt blocks upon those benches drinking various drinks from paper cups and sampling various desserts on paper plates. In that stifling heat, all the ladies waved before their faces elegant fans which featured a glorious bouquet of peonies on one side and *Thompson's Funeral Parlor* on the other. While this was a purely social occasion for all, it was serious business for Detsie Sanford, who monopolized one entire corner selling Avon from a box, spraying the newest fragrance, *Persian Woods* with grand sweeping gestures both into the air and onto so many wrists that everyone in that vicinity was threatened with suffocation.

A crushing crowd extended from the door to beyond the pot-bellied stove positioned in the center of the room, and the fiddle music resounding from the back of that room was deafening. I pushed my way toward the origin of the music, and when I reached the edge of the crowd, I saw the original blackboard, now seriously chipped and battered, upon which were written words in a cursive script which rivaled Mother Agnes' own - *Welcome Back Ladies and Gents from Whenever Ago.* Before that blackboard, four couples swirled around in a circle which was simultaneously a square, the dancers sometimes dancing to the left and sometimes to the right. Two violin players and a man shouting strange words seemed to be competing for the maximum volume and the most reverberation, because the bodies of the fiddle players literally shook to the rhythm of the music, each man's knee nearly striking his chin before he slammed it into the floor.

> *Had a 'lil gal and her name was Clair*
> Stomp Stomp Stomp Stomp
> *Pea green eyes and flaxen hair*
> Stomp Stomp Stomp Stomp
> *Purdy 'lil smile and ways so fair*
> Stomp Stomp Stomp Stomp
> *There's her husband over there*
> Stomp Stomp Stomp Stomp
>
> *Gals that do and gents that know*
> *It's right by right by wrong you go*
> *You can't get to Heaven if you carry on so*
> *It's home little gal and do-si-do*
> Stomp Stomp Stomp Stomp
> Stomp Stomp Stomp Stomp

I understood when the loud man shouted *left* or *right,* but other words like *alla man* and *dough see dough* were nonsense to me. Apparently the dancers knew what to do when the loud man yelled at them. I watched the couples reeling and shuffling around, holding each other's hands in strange ways, when suddenly a man rounding the bend shouted "Sarah!" before he grabbed my two hands and lifted me off the floor! He swung me through the air as the other dancers made that chuckling sound Mary often made, and the caller rang out the words -

> *Oh my gosh and oh by Joe*
> *Sarah is a'twirlin' and do-si-do*
> *One to the left and one to the right*
> *Swing her high boys 'cause she's so light*

I was swinging this way and that as the loud man stomped, swinging sometimes forward and sometimes backward, sometimes with my feet on the floor and sometimes not. I remember shouting to a woman twirling toward me, *"I don't know how to - I can't -"* and she laughed and shouted back, *"It's the fun of the dance!"*

Follow your partner and spread your wings
Come on 'til Sarah and weave the ring
Round the world and let it whirl
Give that filly another twirl

After a minute or two of being absolutely bewildered, feeling that familiar childhood terror of being absolutely out of control, something in me broke. Then the dance became delight. I never knew which way I was going, whether or not my feet would touch the floor, but it quickly became apparent that the friendly hands of a smiling adult would always be extended to me, that I'd always be close to someone who cared, that though I never knew exactly what I was doing, the caller always did.

Have a little gal and her name is Clara?
No, by Joe, her name is Sarah
Round the world and round the bend
Dance in a square makes a circle of friends.

For however many minutes that dance continued, I felt absolutely safe in a vortex of happiness, all those pretty skirts and lace slips flowing around me, all the laughter and all the joy. Those minutes were extraordinary, unforgettable for someone so neglected as I, because in all the chaos, I knew total security and a deep, deep stability. The whirl had become the peace.

Doan git weary, doan git weary
'Til dat camp meetin' in de Promised Land

Dis world just ain't my home, I's just a'passin' thruu
My hopes an' all my treasures lay somewhars in de blue
De angels is a'beckonin' me frum Heav'n's open do's
An' I jus' cain't feel at home in dis world no mo'.

Further down Rural Route 2, about two miles past Baxter's farm and the Boogie Man Road, stood two farmhouses facing each other positioned very close to the road, one owned by the parents and the other by a son. Those houses were so close to each other, with only the road dividing them, that I always pretended that as our car passed, it was splitting one front porch in half. Another mile or two beyond those houses, the road dipped down into that wooded area near Clifford's and MacPhearson's farms. Those woods served as a windbreak for a wide vast area, because its two extensions, viewed from our side porch, stretched across the entire horizon.

Those woods were bisected by a narrow one-lane stone bridge which arched elegantly over a narrow burbling stream. To it's left, an ancient oak tree with a massive trunk, whose mighty boughs had witnessed the history of that region through hundreds of years, leaned protectively over the brook. The humidity shimmering up from that steam contributed to the mirage of heat I saw from our side porch, that mirage which looked to me as though it was always raining down at MacPhearson's. It was that stream, which quietly gurgled under that bridge as it bubbled over several flat grey weathered stones in the merciful shade of those woods, which I was attempting to find when I fainted in the corn field. As an adult, I remember that scene as reminiscent of a painting of Cezanne, but as a child, it was as filled with fantasy and fairy tales as Bambi's woods...until tragedy intensified its loveliness into horrific beauty.

One morning I ran into the kitchen expecting to round the bend by the stove and throw my arms around Mary at the sink, but the atmosphere in that room was so tense, it felt rigid. Since Miss Bess, Elaine, Frank, and Mary were there, I automatically assumed Mary was in trouble again. As I turned to run out the door, Elaine called -

"Sarah, stay right here."

"But I –"

"Just stay right here. Something's happened,
Yeah, just stay in the house."

The three white adults wandered aimlessly round and round that wooden table, stammering to each other words incomprehensible to me, as Mary stood a mute unblinking statue staring toward the screen.

"Bessie, you said the crash happened at –"

"Midnight, Laine, is what the sheriff said."

"Oh Bessie, how – how many, do you know?"

"Thirty-four is the number he gave us."

"Oh Bess, they must have all been standing up in that truck.
I hate to ask, but – but were there any children?"

"Sorry to say, Laine, but there was a baby."

"O God! Were they – well, drunk?"

"Oh yeah, I'm surprised you didn't guess that.
They had just gotten paid.
I didn't think they were as dumb as niggers,
but apparently –"

"Oh Frank, that huge old tree. It's so dark down there anyway,
and last night – with no moon – Bessie, where's Clayton?"

"He left as soon as he heard, Laine.
We got a party line call last night.
It rang, and rang, and rang, and rang apparently,
but we didn't hear it.
Then the sheriff pounded on the front door like to beat it in.
Said he pounded on the kitchen door too. Surprised you didn't hear.
Soon as Clayton heard, he left and hasn't been home since."

"What's he gonna do, Bessie?
The potatoes are only half harvested, and he's already called
the broker and scheduled two more trucks for today!"

"I would imagine Clayton's already cancelled them, Laine.
I'm sure he's called John.
But about the rest of the season, I just don't know.
We're the only farm 'round here that uses migrants
at this time of year, so I just don't know.
But there's one thing I do know now.
I never suspected those Chicanas, or those Chiconas –or you know –
those – whatever they're called – those pinto-bean people,
to be as dirt stupid as niggers, but apparently they are."

"Has anybody been down there, Bessie?"

226

"I suspect Clayton went down with the sheriff for the worst of it,
but I didn't go."

"Someone should go. Frank?
Do you think you and I should go?
Do you think we should – well, with Sarah - should –"

"Sarah?" was all Frank said.

Me? - Me? – Why me?

"There's no other Sarah here, is there?
Go out to the car and be quick about it.
After all, Frank – they were –
Sarah, we're not putting up with that stiff-knee thing today.
There's too much going on this morning to cope with your foolishness.
Just go out to the car and be quick about it.
Frank, let's go down and see what – what –
Oh God, Frank, there are moments – moments -
Disbelief, Frank – there are just some moments of disbelief."

As we drove down the lane, I saw Mary standing in the shadow of the screen door, staring with wide eyes across the fields toward the mirage.

As we passed the Boogie Man Road, I was terrified, imagining that I would see puddles of blood and dead bodies everywhere, so afraid there would be a dead baby on the road. Despite my fear, I heard Elaine talking to Frank in the front seat -

"There – there's something else, Frank,
something else that – well, that –"

"What?" was all Frank said.

"Bessie told me something this morning that –
Well, it just scared me and I – I -
Frank? Do you remember that oil painting
in the front parlor?
Used to hang over that second sofa near the marble top table?
That Wilson girl – can't remember her name –
remember when Clayton fixed their combine himself?
Then their daughter painted that picture of our potato fields?
Looked like the painting was a photograph
whenever we went into that room?
Well this - this scares me Frank, really does.
Last night, in the darkness,
Bessie heard something clunk in that room in the night.
Clayton had been busy all day, this harvest coming on so hard,
so she didn't wake him.
She tiptoed down the front stairway and turned on the light
in that room, and saw right away a vacant spot on that wall
where that picture used to be.
It had fallen, Frank - fallen down behind that table, fallen face down,
like it buried itself on the floor – that picture of this farm just buried!

She didn't touch it, just wanted to see what that clunking sound was, but when she got back upstairs, she noticed that the time was midnight.
Frank, that time was midnight!
Midnight was the time they – when those –
This scares me Frank!"

Frank continued to look straight ahead and said nothing.

Beyond the two houses facing each other, he parked our car on the side of the road. Then slowly...

silently...

we walked down toward the woods. I was scared out of my mind at what I was about to see. When we drew near the bridge and that monumental tree, we stopped and stared, almost unable to breathe. Elaine gasped then whimpered, "Oh God – Oh my God!" A moment later, overcome, she buried her head in her hands and began to cry. Frank held her in his arms and spoke so slowly...

so solemnly...

whispering to her an image I will never forget -

"On the trunk, Laine – on the trunk of that huge old tree –
scattered all over the trunk -
nailed to that bark with store-bought nails
are little torn scraps of lined notebook paper,
all over the trunk those bits of paper, just nailed there.
And – and it looks like – yes, it is –
they are written with messages and prayers
for all the dead."

Frank continuously ran his fingers through Elaine's hair,
and slowly stroked her back.

"Elaine, it will be all right, everything will be all right.
This is just death, Laine. This is just death.
It happens to everyone, no matter who we are,
and no matter how old we are,
and it's going to be all right, Laine, it's going to be all right.
Just cry all you want, as loud as you want.
There's nobody here but Sarah."

Birds chirped in the woods, and the stream bubbled over those stones,
as a breeze rustling through the leaves
brought the fragrance of the fields.

"And on the bark, Elaine, all over that bark
are little photos of some of the migrants –
those little snapshots we used to make in bus stations.
You remember those little snapshots when we were dating?
Their own little photos nailed into the bark with their own prayers.
It's all right Elaine, just cry."

"I can't bear this!"

"I know, I know.
Little pictures of the dead who only hours ago were living."

"My heart is – Oh God, I can't bear –"

"And there – there - nailed near that knot of bark –
is a framed picture of a beautiful woman wearing a beautiful dress –
Our Lady of Guadalupe.
I can't - just can't *imagine* the grief at this tree
when all these things were nailed here."

"Oh Frank, oh God, oh Frank.
I know they were only – well, just Mexicans,
but I can't bear the thought of them dying here."

"I know. And Elaine, around the base of the trunk,
just stuck into the ground,
all around the perimeter of this huge old trunk
are little crosses made of sticks tied together with twine.
Just two small sticks – tiny pieces we would use for kindling –
little sticks too small to do anything with – but make crosses -
just tied together with simple twine.
Must be over thirty of them, Elaine – probably thirty-four,
just stuck into the ground all around.
And there – there –
leaning up against the trunk is a large framed photograph of Eliseo."

"The leader of that group? My heart will break! I just can't bear –
That must have been – that must have been his baby!"

"Must have been. Father and son – father and son dying at this tree.
Eliseo? – Eliseo?
If I'm not mistaken, Eliseo means *God is salvation.*
Just cry, Elaine, it's all right. Just cry all you want. No one can hear.
Death can come to anyone, no matter how small.
It truly doesn't matter how old or how small.
My mother, she died, and I almost died too when I was a baby.
Just cry all you want, Laine. All you want."

"I don't know what I would have done if you had died then.
I – I just don't know if I could have -
could have lived a life w - without you."

"I know, Laine, I know. And there, Laine, above there -
above there in the lowest branches above,
just draped over those branches among the leaves are rosaries, Laine,
must be – must be at least fifty rosaries
just draped over those limbs, just sparkling there,
tiny stones just sparkling -
with their crosses drifting slightly in this breeze –
their colors sparkling in this morning light like a rainbow –
every conceivable color just glittering there in this tree.
Just glittering above, colors all above.
It will be all right, Elaine. Those are rainbows of hope in death.
Rainbows of hope – rainbows in death. It's going to be all right.
Everything, just everything will be all right."

As Elaine's sobs grew louder, I stood transfixed, spellbound, as though I were staring out over Zellner's fields, but instead I was staring at that mighty tree, that huge ancient tree draped with those necklacy-things with crosses on their ends, glittering so simply and shimmering so quietly in the breeze.   All those photos of the dead now at rest under their rainbow of hope, and all those little crosses patiently made with love only hours before.

I remember listening to the sound of the breeze, the muffled cries of Elaine, and Frank murmuring softly, "There now, there." I listened to the birds and watched as the broad slants of early morning light slowly saturated those fields. I observed the ever-shifting plays of sun and shadow among those trees and felt the cool mist from that narrow stream rising upward to materialize as a mirage. It seemed I was melting away into a benediction, a benediction with a beauty I simply could not bear.

It was as though all my life up to that moment had been but a preparation to see the colors of those beads flashing above me. I realized then that if I died that morning by that tree as all those people had died short hours ago, I would let go of my little life with joy instead of fear.

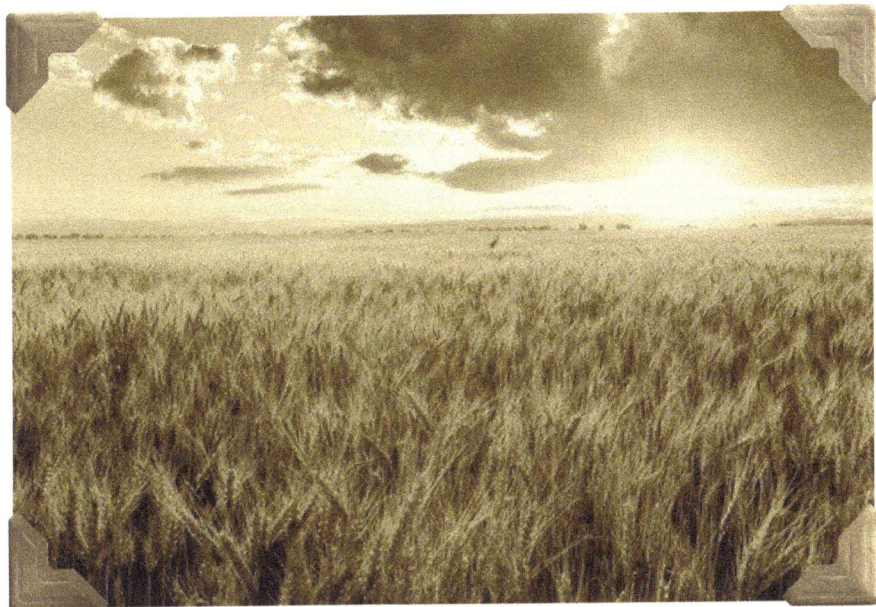

INTRODUCTION TO THE DEMONIC

De Devil hise'f cain't blow it out, I's gonna let it shine.
De Devil hise'f cain't blow it out, I's gonna let it shine.
De Devil hise'f cain't blow it out, I's gonna let it shine.
Let it shine, let it shine, let it shine.

That summer when Mary left beside my birthday cake a little bundle of seven pink candles wrapped in a rubber band, I was introduced to the insidious nature of the demonic.

When I was very young, my experiences each summer were largely confined to the parameters of Bluebonnet. I consequently assumed that the dramatic displays of racial hatred were unique and ugly characteristics solely of the Clay family. Though I observed horrible scenes of racial degradation at regular intervals in restaurants, I naively assumed that these extremes of feeling were localized in Bessie and Clayton. As I became increasingly conscious, however, I came to the shocking realization that racism was a systemic evil in our entire species, a demonic recessive gene which, reinforced over each sequential generation, had become tragically dominate.

That summer, I also learned that the demonic possesses the ability to change its form. Whenever I observed it lose power in one manifestation, it changed into an alternate phenomenon in an attempt to maintain its strength. I learned that evil was quixotic, ever-shifting, ever-sinister, alternating between constriction and expansion with a chaotic energy which often left me feeling faint. I learned that racism could be inverted, that I myself could be viewed as an enemy, a child who should be regarded with suspicion and contempt. In my innocence, I sometimes participated in this dimension, tormenting with generosity the very people who were not allowed to receive it, and torturing Mary with unanswerable racial questions which must have pierced to its core her innermost heart.

Like the snake in Eden which once stood upright before condemned to slither on the ground, or like the evil figure in *Sleeping Beauty* who abruptly mutates into a towering dragon, the little green snakes which I so profoundly feared when Mary and I dug potatoes when I was four years old had grown until that seventh summer, they figuratively struck at me with all the venomous impetuosity of a cobra.

The Rules of Christian Conduct displayed ubiquitously at the orphanage as well as the Sisters' vigilant care provided no context for learning to recognize this chameleon quality of the diabolical. Consequently, my daily experience on that farm was often so overwhelming that I of necessity was forced to discern the underlying adult motives beneath maddening, infuriating, contradictory, and radically offensive behaviors which were totally alien to me. Nearly every day I was forced to distill the teachings of Jesus to one abstract principle then apply that fundamental to a concrete situation. Though that challenging process was instructive and truly did add to my growth and maturation, that very process caused those summers to be profoundly disturbing and often exhausting. My little boat was navigating turbulent racial and immoral waters. Mercifully, Mary's behavior was the rudder of my ship; the teachings of Christ were my compass.

My introduction to the global dimension of racism began in Brueston.

At first glance, Brueston appeared to be an island of green in a vast sea of yellow wheat. The village wasn't visible from our farm during the day, but each evening as the hummingbirds darted by, I watched its lights on the horizon twinkle on one by one. The quaint essence of its early American atmosphere could be accurately captured in art only by the delicacy of watercolors or the finest brushes of oil paints. Even black and white photography of that era would have been too harsh for Brueston's fragile beauty. Mrs. Brueston, the widow of the descendent of the legendary Revolutionary War general after whom the village was named, lived in an elegant white country home with a wrap-around porch where she, a diabetic who owned her own candy store, lived in gentile grace. The small Methodist Church with its slender steeple was surrounded by an ancient wrought iron fence of elegant and refined beauty, and on the Main Street of Brueston, positioned directly on the street, stood a white brick home mounted with a plaque of gold beside its front door which read America's most proverbial words - *George Washington Slept Here*. The visiter who viewed Brueston from that street would assume that a more ideal and a more picturesque location could hardly be imagined, but to the residents and those living in that region, racial hatred and strict segregation were only a short distance away.

That Sunday evening, Elaine stood at the screen door and called down the short hallway toward the dining room -

"Sarah, are you ready to go?"

As Frank drove his car the short distance from the gas pump to the side door, Elaine once again shouted -

"Sarah, are you listening? Hurry up!"

I rushed breathlessly into the kitchen.

*"I'm sorry. I was waiting on the front porch.
There was a tiny little bird in the fir tree.
I wore my yellow dress with this pretty lace collar that -"*

*"I'm not blind, Sarah.
Why on earth do you have marigolds pinned all over your dress?"*

"Oh, I thought they looked pretty The color is so -"

"Take them off, every single one. Those old Nuns wouldn't let you pin marigolds everywhere. Looks ridiculous."

"Where are we going?"

"To a restaurant near the one where Bessie used to order
those rubbery old clams."

"The deer one?"

"Well, another one, but on the deer road."

"But what if those people like Mary come again into –"

"Then not a word from you. You hear? Not one word!
And none of your pointing either. We're not putting up
with your attitude anymore.
And I don't want any of your sassing about this either,
because before we drive there, we have to take this box
over to one of Colored Mary's relatives in Brueston.
And you do everything Frank and I say. Do you hear me?
None of your high and mighty. Frank's waiting. Run out to the –
And take off that silly marigold bracelet too.
And a marigold ring? Good Lord, take that off too.
Why on earth do we have to deal with such a kid as you?
Something new to cope with every damn day."

"Are Miss Bess and Mr. Clay –"

"They went to visit their friends in Jackson, but they'll meet us there."

Squeeeek

SLAM!

At the end of our lane, we turned right, drove down Rural Route 2 to the end of Greyson's cow pasture, then turned left onto a one-lane road which meandered its leisurely way past fields and farms toward the horizon where each evening Brueston's lights twinkled on one by one.

What massive trees grew along Brueston's Main Street, some as old as the country itself, huge ancient maples and oaks which provided abundant shade during the stifling temperatures of summer. When we came to the end of that village where the brick house stood where George Washington had spent the night, we drove off the pavement onto a muddy road which ran parallel to Main Street, a road I had never seen. Elaine told me to roll up the window on my side and to reach over and roll up the other, then to lock both doors. As Frank and Elaine rolled up their own windows and pushed down their own locks, Elaine once again reminded me that I was to ask no questions.

We passed shack after shack constructed of raw dark and dirty unpainted boards with short boards nailed around each window. Some homes were in such conspicuous disrepair that I originally thought they were chicken coops. A few had small porches with short boards serving as shallow steps, and all the houses were elevated off the ground by small piles of rocks placed at intervals. Some had narrow stone chimneys, while others had one metal pipe sticking out of its roof, and in only a few of the yards did I discern even a few blades of grass. They reminded me of my long lines of jelly jars holding roses in every conceivable stage of decomposition. Compared to our farm and to the brick buildings, wrought iron gates, and flourishing gardens of the Nuns, this back street of Brueston appeared to me as utter desolation.

One narrow wooden building painted white with a tall narrow steeple was the Baptist Church which Mary attended. To either side of that church, extending around the perimeter of the back of that property, stood a short picot fence, missing many of its vertical boards, which apparently surrounded a small cemetery. An arch defining the entrance to that graveyard interrupted that delapitated fence, over which a sign, badly in need of repainting, read -

Come to -e all ye wh- are weary a-- heavy la-en
and I wi-l give y-- rest.

As we passed, children playing jump rope stopped with the rope in their hands, and little children playing with silverware in the mud puddles stopped and stood up with their spoons in their hands, and the adults talking outside their homes stopped talking and stared at us. Both adults in the front seat talked quietly to each other, then Elaine leaned over the back seat and addressed me -

"Sarah, you do everything we tell you, no questions asked.
You stay in this car when we stop, and – well –
just don't get out, ever. You never know what those people will do
when they see – well, us. Do you hear me? Just don't get out."

Frank and Elaine opened their doors, then pushed their locks down again. Elaine picked up the box with her left hand, shook her right index finger at me as they closed their doors, then both adults walked toward a group of adults standing beside a narrow two-story shack which leaned as alarmingly toward the left as the Boogie Man house. On the right of that home too was a collection of armless kitchen chairs with various tears in the vinyl. I watched the adults for a while, speaking words I couldn't hear through the closed car windows, and noted that though their skin was the same black as Mary's, no one, neither the men nor the women, displayed her nearly constant barely discernable smile.

I wonder if any of them are saying "uuu huu" like Mary
always does. I wonder if when Elaine gave the box to that lady,

I wonder if she said "Uuu huu." I wonder if she said, 'I sure do thank you. It will be most appreciated' the way Mary always says that. She always says that to Mr. Carlson. That lady is wearing a white dress. Mary would like that! I wonder if she is the wife of the preacher at Mary's Baptist Church? I bet she is, and I bet she bought it in the Monkey Ward Catalog. I bet she did. The adults aren't looking at me, and over there, all the children are just standing and staring. Why aren't they playing like they were playing when we came? She's just standing there holding her muddy spoon, and those boys are just holding their jump rope, and she — she's just standing in the mud and staring. They all look like the statutes in St. Francis Chapel, just looking all the time, watching all the time, and they never move. Why are they staring at me? When I wave, they don't wave back, and when I say 'Hello' through the glass, no one says 'Hello' back. I know I did that right, because Sister Elizabeth says 'Hello' is for a formal introduction. Maybe they don't like my dress. Maybe they don't like yellow. But the little girl in the restaurant had a yellow dress just like mine, so some girls with Mary's skin like yellow. They're not even blinking! I don't know what I did wrong. Have I disobeyed any of 'The Rules of Christian Conduct'? I don't think Mr. Slain would say I did. I don't think I did anything I should be ashamed of. Frank and Elaine are still talking. I wish they would come back. It's getting hot in here with all the windows up, and I don't feel good anymore and — and those children don't like me. I'm getting scared, and — and it looks like they are scared of me. You don't have to be scared of me. I have friends at the orphanage who like me, and I'm nice to them. Kati and Mimi and I play together and we laugh and - I wish they were here, or Sister Catherine. Would she know why they don't like me? Why are those children just staring at me if they don't like me? Why don't they just pretend I'm not here and start playing again in the mud? I don't know why they don't like me and I – because if I did – if I knew why they – they - if I –

Feeling a shame and a confusion I could no longer bear,
I covered my face with both hands and fell down onto the seat.

Friday evening the following week, as Bessie, Frank, and Elaine
sat on the side porch, and I as usual sat in the glider trying yet again to
read *Moby Dick*, a parishioner from the Methodist Church drove up with
a box of clothing which he asked us to take to Mary's house. Since I had
never seen her house before, I was very excited.

"Where does she live, Elaine? Is it far away?
She lives in a trailer, but where is it, Elaine?
Is it in Brueston near her Baptist Church? Or is it far away?"

"You ask far too many questions for such a little thing.
Yes, she lives rather far away. Frank and I will take –"

"How long will it take us to get there? Will it be a long time?
Does she have a farm? Does she grow potatoes too?
Will it take long? Really long?
Because I really, *really* want to see where –"

"Chatterbox," was all Frank said.

"Land sakes, Elaine, it's that Catholic education
that makes her so mouthy.
Those Nuns are making her a little too assertive, if you ask –"

"Is it far away, Elaine? Will it take a long time?
I really want to see Mary's house!"

"You can see it, Sarah, but you can't go in."

"Can't go in? Why not? Mary comes into our house!
I really want to see if she has flowers.
But why can't I go in? Doesn't she want us in her house?"

"You can't go in, and that's final!"

"But why not? That's not fair. Mary comes into our -"

"Elaine, her mouth never stops! Runs like a faucet!"

"You can't go in, Sarah, because –
well - because niggers' houses smell funny."

How much I wanted to shout at her to stop saying that word,
that 'Mary's name is Mary!'
How much I wanted to scream at her at the top of my lungs –

'Mary and I smell the same! And – and sometimes -
sometimes, when you're not here,
when we wear Miss Bessie's lavender,
we – we smell – we smell like 'great ladies!'

Those were the things I wanted to scream,
but that last thought was a confidence I would never betray!

Mary and her husband lived in a blue-green trailer in a wooded area far from our farm, at an intersection of one road and one deserted railroad track called *Colored Corner*. Mary told me that she often gathered greens from between those rails, "'cause dey taste real good in my pots o'stew." The woods were so dense though that the other trailers

I presume were there were not visible. The pines, maples, and various other trees grew so close together that none filled out the way Bluebonnet's trees naturally grew. When I looked up at their tops swaying in the breeze, they looked like giant pencils writing on the clouds. A small oval of sunlit grass sufficed for Mary's front yard. Around the perimeter meandered a strange low fence, four short sticks in a square entwined with string, then a few feet away, four short sticks in a square entwined with string. This strange configuration progressed around the entire perimeter of her lawn. I couldn't imagine what that strange little fence could possibly be.

When we arrived, Frank and Elaine told me once again not to go near Mary's house, even if they themselves went up to the door. Mary and her husband walked toward our car. Then as Frank, Elaine, and Leonard walked back to the trailer, Mary came to me.

"Hi Mary. The Methodist Church brought you some – "

"I know! Dat's whut Laine jus' said.
Dem shirts fu' Leonard is most 'preciated."

"Mary, what's your little fence with the little sticks and that string?"

"O chil', come on over here. Lemme show you."

Mary pointed to the stick configuration nearby.
As she knelt in the grass, I knelt beside her.

"Dis is whut I done, Sarh. Miss Bess give'd me deez 'lil cuttin's frum her rose bushes. 'Lil cuttin's she call 'starts'. I planted 'em in de dirt all 'roun' my yard, den pulled out all de grass in dere. At furst dey din' look like nut'ing pokin' up out de grass, so I poked deez 'lil sticks in a 'lil square all 'round 'em, den wrapped dis string 'roun' de starts. Dat way I be sho' t'see'um an' not step on 'em by asksident."

"But they're so small, Mary, so – so tiny!"

"Dey sho' is, Sarh. Dey sho' is. Bu' dey's growin' chil', 'cause I watuh
dem evy day, an' I keep de grass 'way frum de cuttin's, an' someday,
Sarh, someday dey's gonna be great big like yo's is,
wid all dem purdy colors."

"But Bessie's roses are so big, right up to the bedroom windows!
It will take so long for yours to grow big. Can't they buy you –"

"Hush now, yung'in, hush. It's gonna be alright.
Someday dey's gonna be big too.
An' look Sarh, look way down dere. D'y'see way down in dere?
Dat's a 'lil tiny leaf! See dat?"

"Where Mary? I don't see any – Where is – Oh! There?"

"Yeah! See dat? Ain't dat somet'ing."

"Oh yeah, a tiny little triangle!"

"Yeah! Evy evenin' whin Leonard brings me home, I comes ou' shere,
an' b'fo' I goes intuh our home, I checks how my 'lil roses is growin'.
Ef'n Miss Bess brung me dooz big uns, I wudn't has de fun o'watchin'
deez 'lil uns growin' like I does."

"But they would already be big, Mary. You could cut real folded roses
for your own house. They would look so pretty in your –"

"O yeah, Sarh. Big uns 'ud be bloomin' alredy.
An' someday I's gonna has real roses in my trailer. Bu' wid deez
'lil uns, chil'? Dis way I kin see 'em growin' evy day.
'El I'll be! Look a'dat! Dere's 'nudder one way down in dere.
'Lil leaf's a'sproutin' dere too. See it?
An' look on dis here branch. Dere's one too.

O gracious chil'! Is – Is dat a tiny rose bud?"

The evening breeze rustled through those tall trees as Frank and Elaine talked quietly with Leonard. Mary and I crawled from tiny fence to tiny fence, admiring each and every new leaf and every promise of future buds as the safety pins on her sneakers occasionally caught on a fallen twig, and even more grass stains appeared on her canvas shoes.

As we were leaving, I finally understood why Sister Martha always said –

"Mary has a grateful heart, Sarah. She could be a lesson to us all.
More Christians should have grateful hearts like hers.
There would be much more happiness in this world if they did."

Though I never contradicted Sister's wisdom, I privately thought –

It's Bessie who should have a grateful heart!
It's Bessie who should be grateful for Mary!
Bessie's the one who should buy her a whole dozen big rose bushes!

If Brueston was famous for the American Revolution, Maysville was famous for the Civil War. Sir Jonathon White-Hall had sailed to America from England in 1784 with his wife and fourteen of their still living children. They built a one-story brick home near where the town of Maysville would one day stand. As the years progressed and their fortune increased, the family eventually added so many rooms and so many stories that the White-Hall home quickly multiplexed into a sizable mansion. Descendents of that family made history several times – during the battle of Antietum as well as at Gettysburg - miraculously emerging from both those brutal conflicts without so much as a scratch. Since Maysville had blossomed around his mansion, he was credited as being the father of that town. His sword was proudly displayed not in the family residence, but in the Town Hall.

Each September, Maysville celebrated the birthday not only of the town, but of Sir White-Hall himself. That day, everyone who appeared on the town streets was asked by the town council to wear Civil War dress. The women of the town made long skirts and bonnets which were as carefully preserved from year to year as Mr. Clay's fedora hat he kept wrapped in cellophane on top of Bessie's cedar closet. Since the high point of that celebration was the dance held at the armory, each woman also made one evening gown appropriate for that era.

On that festive day, hoop skirts and picture hats tied with long ribbons appeared on Maysville's sidewalks. Parasols with silk organza flowers appeared in the drug store, and baskets rather than shopping carts appeared in Sloane's. Everyone agreed that if the yardage in all the ruffles was placed end to end, the fabric would undoubtedly stretch for hundreds of miles through both battlefields. Family heirlooms were brought out of storage, with broaches appearing on bosoms and hat pins appearing on hats. That evening, all the ladies wore ropes of jewelry and dinner rings, and gracefully pinned their hand-made crocheted shawls over lace and ruffled bodices, dancing that magical night away with gallant men wearing brilliantly polished knee-high boots, long waist-coats with brass buttons, vests, and fringed sashes made of silk. Those who had heirloom top hats wore them poudly. The armoury itself was decorated with all the colors and flowers of fall, as was the White-Hall mansion. It was in that historic home where Mary held her first servant's position.

Long before Mary came to Bluebonnet, she was the head parlor maid at that mansion, the servant responsible for the four downstairs rooms bordering the center entrance hall.

One afternoon as Mary and I sat on the cactus window step, taking our rest because our knees were "plainin' just a bit," I asked –

"What did you do there, Mary? Were you the cook? Did you peel potatoes and make pies?"

"No, no chil', I warn't no cook, I was de downstairs parlor maid.
O chil', you wud o'loved dere 'brary! Gracious! Books clean up t'dat
ceilin' wid a ladder dat rolled back an' forth. I had t'keep dem books
dusted an' dem drapes shook out an' dem purdy carpets swept al'ys
in de same d'rection. My how dem rooms looked purdy.
An' evy day I had t'cut flowr's frum dere cuttin' garden
an' make big bouquets fu' dem tables."

"Were you allowed to cut the rose buds, Mary?
Did you cut the folded roses?"

"O yeah, chil'. De Missus tol' me to. Real purdy vases. Some was
plain, but some had flowr's painted right on de vase. Dere was so miny
'lil tables in dat big house, chil'. Seemed like evy chair had a 'lil table,
an' evy table had a 'lil vase. But in de hallway, dere was a big
roun' table, so fu' dat vase, I had t'cut a hol' basket o'flowr's.
Dey had a pond. I ain't ben back dere since den, bu' I 'spect it's still
dere. Wid geese, an' dem tall t'ings called cattails growin'
right in de watuh. I din' cut 'em t'ough, din' put 'em in no vases.
In de winter time dat pond was so purdy, wid snowflakes a'blowin'
an' shiny ice on dat dere watuh.
I had my own 'lil room right off de kitchen. Real nice. Real purdy.
I had a bed, an' one chair, an' one 'lil table. De Missus said I kud pick
one daisy fu' de vase on my table."

"Like the daisy you let me pick that day just for me?"

"Dat's right, Sarh.
Dat is whut I was t'inking 'bout whin I let y'pick dat flow'r.
An' I had one winduh dat looked out back toward dere fe'els.
An' on de wall was four pegs fo' my dresses."

"Did you wear this dress, Mary? The dress you wear now?"

"O gracious no, chil'. I wear'd a yun'form. Black wid real purdy

ball buttons an' a 'lil w'ite collar fo' de day."

"Like the Nuns?'

Mary chuckeled.
"Somet'ing like deres, yeah. Den at night whin dey had a party,
dey had a lot o'parties, I wear'd 'nudder black dress wid a 'lil lace collar.
Dat lace was so nice, real nice. I sho' looked purdy back den."

"If you had a pretty dress like the Monkey Ward Catalog,
and your own pretty room, and one pretty daisy,
why did you leave, Mary? Why?"

Mary slowly folded her hands in her lap.
After a pause, she looked deeply into my eyes and whispered -

"You stay 'way frum dat shed, Sarh. Is you hearin' me?
Jus' stay 'way.
Not evybody is es nice es dem fo'ks at dat orphage."

One morning I bounded into the kitchen, expecting to throw my
arms around Mary at the sink, but I glanced at the far corner and saw on
the top step Mary's brown paper bag.

"Is it today, Mary? Are we going today? Are we? Are we?"

"No chil', not tuhday. I's sor'y. T'ought we was, bu' Miss Bess wants
me t'shuck all dis here corn an' make dat relish Mistuh Clay likes,
bu' we kin go tuhmorrow."

"You brought both –"

"O yeah, both. Fo' us both. We doan want no bites.

Tuhmorrow mo'nin, b'fo' dat sun gits hot. Ain't pose'd t'rain nohow.
So tuhmorow early we's goin'. Bu' now, I got's t'shuck dis here corn.
Gracious! She must'a got me twelve dozen!
I's gonna be boilin' all day, an' it's pose'd t'be hot enyhow!
Den I got's ta —"

As Mary's voice trailed off about her daily litany of chores, I
retrieved from the pantry my two little yellow sand pails which by now
were stained a deep purply-blue, and placed them on the top step near
Mary's brown paper bag.

The next morning, after the men left for the fields, and Bessie,
Frank, and Elaine left for a sale at the Montgomery Ward Store in
Jamestown, and the remains of breakfast patiently waited on the table,
Mary took out of that bag two pair of her winter knee socks and yet
another box of safety pins. She took off her sneakers, pulled on her
socks, then replaced her sneakers and adjusted their pins.

"Alrigh' Sarh, hop up in dat rockin' chair an' take off yo' sandle shoes
an' unbuckle dem toe buckles too like las' year."

Mary knelt before me and took out of the bag another pair of socks.

"Mary, will there be snakes?"

"Chil', whut'd I say whin you was 'lil?"

"Dey woan bodder us none ef we doan bodder dem."

"Dat's right, An' whut'd I say las' year?"

"Dey woan bodder us none ef we doan bodder dem."

"An' whuts I gonna say tuhday?"

"Dey woan bodder us none ef we doan bodder dem."

"Dat's right. Now hol' still while I git deez – Stop swingin' yo' legs! I got's t'git deez socks on 'em!"

Mary's skin glowed as the faint light of morning filtered through the leaves of the philodendron window.

"Gracious Sarh, look how you's grow'd! Deez socks is still comin' up over yo' knee, bu' not es far!"

"I'm getting big! I'll be in the second grade!"

"Y'sho' is! Now hold dem 'lil legs still while I pin deez socks tight 'round yo' knees. Hol' still so I doan stick ya like I done las' year. 'Member dat?"

"It's all right, Mary. That was an asksident."

Mary pinned my socks tightly around my knees, folded up the toes of each sock, then replaced each shoe.

"Looks like I got's t'do whut I done last year. De top buckle fastens real nice, but dat toe buckle got's t'be pinned ag'in."

Mary placed one large safety pin through each buckle then through the first eyelet of my strap.

"Dere, Sarh. Dey still doan fit real good, bu' we's all set t'go."

Squeeeek

SLAM!

As Mary carried her buckets and I carried my pails, I wobbled across the wide gravel sea, wobbled past the gas pump, and wobbled past the weeping willow near that huge shed. Then we entered the narrow gravel tributary which flowed beyond the echo-bird barn, back towards Anderson's dairy farm where blackberry bushes scrambled over that split-rail fence in wild profusion and fantastic disarray.

"My legs are itching already, Mary."

"Now y'know whut I's gonna say t'dat, Sarh. Whut's I gonna say?"

"Dey doan itch es much es jiggers."

"Dat's 'xactly right. Dey doan itch es much es jiggers.
Sarh, while we's walkin' on dis here gravel, I wanna tell y'somet'ing I t'inks 'bout evy time we walks here. I's gonna tell y'bout dis while we's still on dis gravel, den whin we turn left ontuh dem two ruts, whin we step intuh dem two ruts, you's gonna know somet'ing dat's gonna make dat one step mo' 'potent. It's 'bout my great-granmama, an' dis 'il give you somet'ing else t't'ink 'bout dat's mo' 'potant den jiggers.

"My great-granmama was a slave, Sarh. Whin she come'd t'dis land, her name was frum Afrika. Her family called her Wawalla. Dat means 'beautiful.' I hear'd she really was beautiful too. Wawalla lived on a plantation way, way down yonder frum here, an' whin she come'd t'dat plantation, her Missus named her Mary, jus' like me. Walwalla was a slave in de big house. Dere she was called Mary, bu' in dem slave cabins, she was still called Wawalla. Her Missus was mean, Sarh, treat'n her bad, real bad all de time, so my granma wanted t'be free.

"So de blacksmith on dat plantation tol' her dere was a road dat de wagons travel'd, two ruts in de road jus' yonder past de t'ree corn fe'els she was a'seein' evy day. She din' know dat, bu' he know'd. He know'd dem ruts headed north, an' ef she stepped ontuh dem ruts t'her left, she was goin' t'be free. It'ud be a long, long way fo' sho', bu' dem ruts 'ud take her t'd'land o'de free.

"So she waited an' waited in her cabin 'til one night it was a'rainin' hard. Dem slaves al'ys said de Lord called t'dem in de thunder. She know'd de rain 'ud wash out her tracks. De plantation owner 'ud know she 'scaped, bu' he wudn't a'know'd which way she went. So whin it was rainin' real hard, she hur'ied thruu dem t'ree fe'els in de dark, 'cause corn fe'els hids fo'ks real good enyhow, den she come'd t'dem ruts, jus' like de blacksmith said. Den de moment come'd whin she know'd dat ef she stepped t'her left intuh one o'dem ruts, she'd be on her way t'freedom. So dis is whar we is now, Sarh. At de end o'dis here gravel, an' we's 'bout t'turn left ontuh deez two ruts jus' like she done."

"Headed toward the blackberries."

"Headed toward de land o'de free, Sarh.
So lets step tuhgether an' know whut we's doin'."

I didn't understand anything of what Mary was saying, but it did make that small movement seem very important when we stepped off the gravel...then into those ruts.

"Did Wawalla eat corn, Mary? Did she eat blackberries?"

"O I's sho' she did, chil'."

"I like corn and blackberries. So do you. We like the same things."

"Dat's righ', Sarh. We like de same t'ings.
An' we's both gonna like dis cobbler real good."

We finally arrived at that split-rail fence with its berried shrubs and the tall grasses where the hungry jiggers lived. The sun had not yet risen above the hill near Malcolm's place. Beyond that fence stretched a vast meadow where the Anderson herd grazed, but this early in the morning, they must have still been in the barn. The bees which forever hummed through those berried branches were mercifully sluggish in the cool morning air.

"You 'member de rules 'bout –"

"Only pick the black ones. The red ones don't taste good, and the green ones aren't ripe."

"An' d'odder rule? You 'member?"

"Yeah. Twist each berry a little, but don't pull down, or the branch will snap and stick me."

By the time we had filled all four containers, the golden fingers of the rising sun were glowing above Malcolm's hill. We knew that when the fingers came, it was time to walk back. We turned around on our narrow rut road and observed that the farm looked so much smaller at this distance.

"De mess on dat kitchen table doan seem so big frum back here. Doan seem so big a't'all, an' it doan seem like it's gonna be so hot tuhday."

As I wobbled along that rut with my purple-yellow pails and Mary walked behind me with her buckets, I asked over my shoulder –

"Mary, last night Elaine and I drove into Maysville. Is Washington Avenue named after George Washington because he slept there?"

Mary chuckled, "I 'pose so, Sarh."

"Well, we drove down that street and – Why do the two schools have different names? Why is the first one called White and the last one called Colored when both are made out of the same red brick? Do you know Mary? They're both made out of the same brick like we have

at the orphanage, but one is called White. Why is that?"

"Dis aftuhnoon we kin make us some nice ber'y cobbler."

"Yeah. And Mary – the glass! There's glass all over the sidewalk at that last school, because most of the windows are broken! It looked like somebody threw something through those windows, and nobody cleaned it up! There's even some cardboard in some of the windows. Isn't that principal worried the glass will hurt his children? Aren't the parent's worried to send their children there? Mother Agnes would have a fit if that happened at the orphanage. She's tell those janitors to clean that up right away, because she would be worried that –"

"An' den, ef we got's eny ber'ies left over, we kin jus' put 'em in a 'lil bowl jus' fu' us."

"Yeah. And why doesn't that last school have a real door? At the first school there are two doors that both open out, but at the last school, there's just a piece of metal, or just a board. I couldn't see from that far away. Why is that Mary? Why isn't there any door at that last school?"

"We kin jus' put a 'lil sugar on de rest an' eat 'em, an' nobody 'ud know."

"yeah. And why aren't there any pretty bushes at that last school? The first one has green bushes like we have at the orphanage, and there's even one hydrangea blooming that looks like the one blooming near our front porch. Why doesn't that last school have any pretty flowers like the first school when both the schools look the same? Why is that Mary?"

"Y'know, I do b'lieve it's gonna be es hot tuhday es yestuhday Sho' feels like it's gonna be."

"yeah. We have pretty grass at the orphanage where the boys play ball
and we run around, but there's no grass at that last school. The first
school has grass like we have at our farm, but that last school doesn't
have any! Where do the children play, Mary? Only in the dirt?
That's where they play in Brueston.
Do some children just like to play in the dirt?"

"Dem men's gonna has t'dig up dis mustard growin' in dis hedge row.
Mistuh Clay doan like dat durn stuff a't'all."

"No. And what does Colored Toilet mean, Mary? Are they pretty?
Are they different colors, or do they have flowers on them?
Can I have a Colored Toilet when I'm big? Can it be pink?"

"I doan know if dere's gonna be 'nough ber'ies fu' eny mo' trips
back dere. I's guessin' de birds' gonna git mos' o'de rest."

"Probably. And how does the wind know to blow all the trash toward
Colored Toilet? How does it know, Mary? There's no trash
at the other one. Why is that? And you know what else, Mary?
Elaine and I were walking down the street by the sub shop,
and we saw a field hand walking toward us.
The Sisters taught us that when a Nun is walking toward us,
children should step to the side to show respect.
So I tried to step off the sidewalk so that man could pass.
And you know what happened, Mary?
Elaine wouldn't let go of my hand!
She told me to keep holding her hand! And she kept holding it harder
and harder, squeezing my fingers so hard, and I still tried to step off
the sidewalk, and I finally told her that she was hurting me while that
man kept walking toward us, but she wouldn't let go of my hand
no matter how much I tried to pull away.
That man was coming closer and closer and Elaine kept saying,

'You stay right here by me! Stay right here by me!'
Why did she do that, Mary? She was so angry at me.
That wasn't nice."

Suddenly Mary's voice behind me sounded low and flat,
as though all her energy suddenly drained away.

"Den whut happened?"

"He had to step off the sidewalk.
There wasn't room for him.
There was only room for us."

Mary said nothing.

We walked for a while in silence.

Then Mary said –

"De barn is gittin' bigger now.
I know dat mess's still dere.
We's 'most home. We's mos' dere.
It's gonna be es hot es yestuhday. I know dat now."

"It feels strange not holding onto your dress.
I like holding your dress.
I don't like holding Elaine's hand."

"Dat's alright, yung'in.
You's holdin' dem pails, an' we got's a lot o'good ber'ies.
We's 'most home, chil', an' we's gonna make us a nice cobbler.
An' now we's back on dis here gravel.
We's 'most home."

*"It's a good thing, because my knee socks
always fall down when the barn gets big again.
My safety pins only last till the gravel."*

The migrant workers on Bluebonnet were the people upon whom Mr. Clay's farming success did utterly depend, but rather than their being deeply appreciated for their exhausting efforts, they were treated with as much indignity and as much disrespect as twentieth century slaves. A few summers in my childhood, the migrants were Spanish-speaking people who drove up from the Southwest, but during most summers, the migrants were from Mississippi, Louisiana, and the Deep South, their dialectical speech so broken and fragmented that they were very difficult for anyone but Clayton Clay to understand. They lived on Clifford's farm near MacPhearson's, the woods and its mirage, arriving at Bluebonnet each morning in a school bus which had obviously been painted and repainted a shocking shade of yellow so many times that the bus appeared to be very nearly an iridescent green.

Until I visited Clifford's farm later that summer, I would not know of the deplorable conditions in which the migrant workers lived, the men, their wives, and children forced to endure such oppression. I learned as an adult that the workers were miraculously grateful to Mr. Clay for treating them so well! – since their living conditions on other farms were much worse. It was through them that I learned that racism was not a unique and ugly characteristic of Bessie and Clayton, but was a systemic evil deliberately and forcefully passed down through the generations.

Mary sat at the table squeezing dough between her thumb
and index finger, forming perfectly uniform rolls
which she dropped into muffin tins.

Squeeeek

SLAM!

"Mary, where's the library? Where is it, Mary?
I've been looking all over this farm for the -"

"Whut's you talkin' 'bout, yung'in?
I got's t'git deez rolls in deez muffin tins, an' den I –
Whut's you talkin' 'bout?
Most evyday you's talkin' 'bout somet'ing I doan know.
Whut you ast me yestuhday – 'Whut's a Dairy Queen?'
Gracious! An' de odder day it was, 'Whut's a harpoon?'
Dere ain't no –
Whar's dat butter fu' deez rolls? Whar's de -"

"I looked in the big barn, and it isn't in the big room with all the
milkers, and it isn't in the little room where the milk swirls around
with all the spiders and bugs. That's so nasty!
I looked in the weighing room where the big scales are,
and it isn't in the stall where the calves are born, either,
and it isn't -"

"Whut's my gonna do wid shuu, Sarh. Dere ain't no –
Whut'd I do wid dat melted butter?
Dis heat is makin' me lose my mind!"

"I looked between the boards of the echo-bird barn, but all I could see in
there was straw. Is it in the silo? I hope it's not way up high
in the big barn, because - Oh Mary! There must be a thousand mice
in those walls! I hear clawing all the time in -"

"Sarh, dere ain't no 'brary nowhar on dis here farm.
De only books is de ones y'know 'bout."

"Only 'Farm Journals?' And only 'Potato' and 'Tomato' and -"

"Yeah, chil'.
Why's you t'inking somet'ing like dat is on dis here farm enyhow?"

*"Because the migrants have little children, Mary.
I see them in the fields, and they come every morning
in a school bus, so there must be a library in their school.
I just can't find their school, Mary. I've looked everywhere.
Do you know where it is? Is it in the shed?
If it's there, could you take me to the books?"*

Mary suddenly stopped her preoccupation with the rolls,
pushed the muffin tins away,
and turned sad eyes toward me -

"Chil', I's sor'y 'bout - 'bout - I really is -
I wish somebody 'ud take you t'dat big 'brary in Maysville,
'cause you's wantin' dat book learnin' an' all so bad.
Seems like somebody here otta. Bu' Sarh, dere ain't no – no –
I's sor'y, yung'in, bu' dere just ain't no 'brary here.
Bu' Sarh, dere is somet'ing we kin do."

"What?"

"Doc Dobson is gonna call soon 'bout whin he kin come
an' talk t'Mistuh Clay. An' whin he does, Sarh,
I got's t'go tell him down in dat shed!"

"Can I come? Can I come? Mary, please! Can I come?"

"You kin go wid me ef –"

*" – I hold onto your dress? I'll hold on, Mary, I promise.
I'll hold on real, real, real tight! Can I come? Can I come, please?"*

"Yeah, ef you hold onto my dress an' –"

"- don't talk to the field hands?"

Mary chuckled in her characteristic way
and once again shook her head from side to side.
"Yeah, ef you hold onto my skirt an' doan talk t'-"

Ring!.....Ring!....Ring!...Ring!...

Silence

"That's our farm, Mary! Did you hear that? That's only four rings!
I remember the hog farm is –"

"Hush chil'. I got's t'answer dis phone.
'Hullo. Dis is Bluebonnet...Yes, Doct'r Dobson...Aftuh y'goes
t'Baxter's you's gonna...Yes Suh. I be sho' t'tell Mistuh Clay.
Yes Suh."

Mary hung up the phone.

"Sarh, we got's t'tell Mistuh Clay dat – Lookee you, clappin'
yo' 'lil hands ag'in. You hast t'hold onta my dress an' –"

"- don't talk to the field hands."

"Dat's right. I's gonna take you in by dat side door
whar dat durn shelf fall'd off an' broke my arm."

Squeeeek

SLAM!

As Mary and I hurried across the wide gravel sea, I tugged at her dress in eager anticipation, just as I pushed my shoulders into the front seat of the car when we pulled onto Rural Route 2 for the first time each June. I was as fascinated by the interior of that enormous shed as I was fascinated by the interior of the echo-bird barn. All summer, both of the shed's wide front doors were pushed to the side, continuously revealing that great yawning black hole. Torrents of light from the blazing sun did nothing to illuminate the obscurity of that void.

We entered by the small side door near the weeping willow where bales of straw were stacked near that tree. Mary mentioned and apparently pointed to the new shelf where long ago the old shelf had fallen, but because my eyes were temporarily blinded by the abrupt reversal from harsh sunlight, I saw nothing but black. I clung to her dress with both hands and stumbled across the dirt floor in the direction of the voices I knew so well.

Since Mr. Clay was talking to various workers, Mary stopped a respectful distance away from the men. I slowly became aware that we were surrounded on all sides by huge towering presences, great dark forms looming over me. As my eyes little by little became accustomed to the dim interior, and the darkness diffused from black to foggy grey, I realized those huge forms were the mighty combines and various John Deere tractors which I had always seen from a distance. Laying in the dirt directly before me was the massive cultivator, whose huge metal coils unlocked Bluebonnet's chilled earth each spring. Near the wall beyond the men stood the green antique combine which had caught fire in the wheat field which stretched from the Boogie Man Road to our shed. Nearby was the plow which long ago had been drawn by Mr. Clay's original plow horse whose bridle hung proudly on the wall of the side porch.

"'Bou' hund'd, Suh," a migrant said.

"Only a hundred? No more than a hundred?" shouted Mr. Clay.

"Nawsuh. Hund'd's all we got's."

"What the hell have you lazy brutes been doing all morning?
There's four trucks headed here right now!"

"'El Suh, dis mawnin', Suh, our truk wuz brok', an' den
Massuh Clifurd kudn' fin' dem new bags dat –"

"What the Hell? Couldn't find the bags?
The printed ones were sent last week!"

"Ah knows, Suh, bu' he kudn' fin' 'em. Dey wuz d'liver'd t'Massuh
Winstun's, an' we kudn't fin' 'em. Massuh Clifurd wuz gwyne t'ast,
bu' den he got 'um. An' den, Suh, den dat bel' dun slipped 'gin, an'
Massuh Winstun has t'tak it 'part. An' den, Suh, dat fus' truk o'tattahs
wuz bad, Massuh Clay. Dey wuz bad sum'fin awhful. We den' git mo'n
a t'urd o'dem at de mostes'. Mos' o'dem we has t't'row down', kuz –"

"Damn it! I don't care what you – you -
There's four trucks headed this way!"

"Bu' affah dat, de las' truk, Suh, wuz bettah, Suh. It wuz bettah,
an' dis 'un heah is all gud. Dat's why we got's a hund'd now.
Dey's comin' hard now, Suh. Dey's real gud.
We's doin' bettah."

"Hank?"

"Yes Sir?"

"Is Clifford still plowing those eighty acres?"

"Yes Sir, but he's almost done."

"Has Palmer started the fields near Glacie's?"

"Yes Sir, just started, and - "

"Mr. Clay?"

"What d'you want, Paul?"

"The first truck just arrived, under the maple –"

"Damn! Only a hundred bags?
Good God, we need thousands!"

"An' Massuh Clay, Suh, I ain't meanin' t'b'no fuss, bu' in de bus
is a sik 'un, Suh – a 'lil un, Suh, dat's – dat's real bad off.
We wuz wonderin', Suh – we ain't meanin' t'b'no fuss.
Bu' kin a doct'r cum, 'cuz –"

"There's one truck here already,
and another three on the way, and only a hundred bags?
I don't care if you people have to work from now
straight through to sun-up,
you're filling four God-damned trucks!"

Mr. Clay stopped shouting and gesturing wildly, but continued to talk urgent business with two workers named Tom and Bill. Mary waited silently for his attention as patiently as she waited each and every Friday for Clayton's hands to pass into her weathered palm one solitary twenty dollar bill. As I became increasing accustomed to the dimness of the shed, my gaze wandered down to the building's opposite end.

Sparrows flitted about in that entrance. Though I had heard their chirping in the shadows where Mary and I were standing, I saw them now among the massive beams supporting that huge roof. There, silhouetted against the sunlight streaming through that wide opening, was the back end of a truck upon which men with skin like Mary's stood effortlessly hurling bushel basket after bushel basket down to other men standing with outstretched arms who were waiting on the ground. They swung their burdens with a steady measured cadence, elegant graceful arcs perfected over years, even decades of heavy muscular labor. Sometimes the men in the truck hurled bags onto the ground, and sometimes they tossed individual potatoes, but usually they swung down bushel after bushel in a continuous hypnotic rhythm which caused me to sway slightly from side to side as I clung to Mary's dress. Those potatoes had made their way from Bluebonnet's prolific fields to the processing shed where they would be sorted, bagged, and eventually sold to a hungry nation.

Inside that back door stood two long parallel lines of straw bales stretching from that door to the center of the shed. Between those bails stretched the rickety and rattley chains of Mr. Clay's infamous conveyor belt, its hard metal grinding sound punctuated by the chirping of those hovering sparrows. Upon those bales sat the women responsible for examining each and every potato as it meandered its way from the truck to the end of that belt where burlap bags, printed with *Clayton Clay* accompanied by a picture of the flower *Bluebonnet* waited for the bounty of his famous farm. As those potatoes jumped and jostled over those chains, clumps of dirt and mud fell through the metal links onto the dirt floor below.

The women's arms made continuous circular motions over that belt, movements which were as graceful and hypnotic as the movements of the men hurling bushel after bushel down from their sunlit truck. Each woman's hands patiently lifted, turned, and replaced each potato with rigorous scrutiny, removing those with the slightest blemish so none would rot or mold when lowered into the bags, discarding those unworthy of being an export from the domain of Clayton Clay. Because of the great clouds of dust hovering eternally over the scene, the hands and faces of all the migrants had regressed from black to various shades of beige. Viewed from the distance where I was standing, only Mary herself appeared to have black skin.

"It looks like a Mass at the orphanage, Mary, with all that dust like incense, and the priest and the altar boys moving the same way all the time, and –"

"Hush, chil'. We got's t'wait fu' Mistuh Clay
'til he's done talkin'."

Suddenly one man at the end of the shed slowly, powerfully sang out three notes of music, a simple rise of a minor third in a deep, low voice which sounded like the resonate baritone of Father Anthony at the orphanage. Only three notes, three tones hanging heavy in the dusty air, carrying with their resonance the absolutely authority of unshakable, unfailing faith.

"He
as the sparrows chirped in the rafters and flashed through shafts of light,
has
and the belts continued to rumble and rattle down their slope,
dun"
and the women made their graceful circular movements as their potatoes rolled by.

Then that powerful male voice ceased.

As though desperate to preserve such beauty and such richness in that environment of exhausting labor and chronic stress, the dust-filled air simply would not allow his final note to die away. After his last echo sadly reverberated off the rafters, a sudden unwelcomed hush fell upon that shed. Though the conveyor belt continued its metallic rattle, and the men's conversation with Mr. Clay continued in quiet tones, and the birds continued to sing their tiny cheerful songs, the atmosphere in that shed was plunged into a vacuum, a sonic void which silently screamed, silently implored his deep reassuring voice to pour forth once more.

Then as suddenly as it had mysteriously disappeared, that heavy baritone intoned again –

slowly…

solemnly…

piously…

"Whut - He – has – sed –"

After another pause of expectant silence in which the whole world seemed to wait in breathless anticipation for his masterful voice to return, he continued –

"Heal'd - de - sik - an' - ras'd - de -ded
Den - frum - sin - He - set - me - free."

I stood spellbound at the reverent atmosphere which had suddenly invaded that shed as swirls of incense spiraled ever upward toward the sparrows. The profound trust expressed in that simple melody had transformed the migrants' ceaseless activity into one almighty act of praise. Other male voices then joined his baritone, the exultant power of that combined chorus swelling with ever increasing strength, as the sparrows continued to flutter and the bushels continued to swing, and the chains continued to rumble as the women continued their chore, and the potatoes fell obediently into their bags one by one. Peace had been found in their exhausting existence because from sin they'd been set free.

"O one o' deez days
Though totally consumed in the white man's service,
It woan be long
no cruelty could ever extinguish their faith,
One o' deez days
no indifference could ever engender doubt,
It woan be long
no pain or agony had the power to overwhelm them,

Ah's gwyne home
no degradation could fill their spirit with darkness,
T'sing my song
no suffering however brutal would fail to stimulate hope.
Dat frum sin
Undaunted, fearless, intrepid, they labored on,
He's set me free."
knowing beyond a shadow of a doubt
that from sin they had been freed.

"He has dun
Never at the orphanage had I felt such power in the human voice,
Whut He has sed
never had I heard such a joyous hope,
He has dun
never had I perceived such a blatant refusal
Whut He has sed"
to acknowledge the petty concerns of this world as life's
ultimate goal.

Then the women contributed the freshness of their voices as they
spontaneously embroidered the rapturous tones of the men -

"Heal'd de sik,
"He helped de po' an' needy thruu dat Bible lan'
An' ras'd de ded
Go tell Mary dat He's sho'ly ris'n frum de ded
Den frum sin
Den frum sin O frum dem wages o'dat debil's sin
He set me free."
Hallelu O glory! O Hallelu! I's free!"

Their singing to me had become the resonance of eternity, as though one celestial choir had unexpectedly descended onto earth. Their voices ever rising and falling in that cloudy tabernacle, resounded through the darkness as though their song had been declared into existence on the first day with light itself! Each artful alteration in each new stanza was a fresh paean to the glory of God. As the men continued their mighty arcs, and the potatoes continued to fall, and the women continued their graceful movements, and the sparrows continued to flutter, and the dust continued to swirl…

I tugged at Mary's dress.

"Not now, Sarh. I got's t'keep my eyes on Mistuh Clay t'see whin he's done talkin'. Jus' a bit longer, Sarh. Y'got's t'be patient, chil'."

I tugged even harder at Mary's dress.

"Sarh, how miny times I got's t'tell you dat we got's t'be patient."

I tugged with both hands even harder at her dress.

"Mary, p - please - I - I have to find the - the stream."

"O Gracious! O Glory! Sarh, doan shuu faint on me! Doan faint!
O Mistuh Clay, Mistuh Clay! I's so sor'y t'trupt,
bu' dis chil' is a'faintin' on me.
O Gracious! Ef'n I doan git her outta -
I ain't meanin' t'be no truble, bu'- but de vet is comin' righ' quick.
Just es soon es he gits done at Mistuh Baxter's,
he's gonna be here. I doan mean t'be no truble, Suh.
O Sarh, I's gonna car'y you outta here 'cause you's –
O Gracious, chil', you's es w'ite es a sheet!
I's sor'y t'trupt, Suh. I doan mean no -
Chil', here, lemme gadder you up an' -
Lemme car'y you out t'dat willuh tree an' lay y'down.

O Sarh, you's gonna be alrigh', jus' keep breathin',
keep breathin'. Yo' lil' lungs is full o'dat dust an' dirt.
O Gracious! Keep breathin', Sarh!
'Member chil', al'ys, al'ys 'member, y'got's t' breathe.
'Member dat? Y'got's t'breathe."

Holding me in her arms, Mary rushed passed the tractors and combines and passed the new shelf on the wall, then stepped hurriedly over the threshold of the shed. Once again I was blinded, this time by the sudden brutal light. As the singing continued in ever louder choruses, Mary laid me down on the grass beneath the weeping willow and began to fan me furiously with her safety-pin apron.

"You's gotta git some blood in yo' lil' face, Sarh,
'cause you's lookin' mi'ty po'ly. Jus' keep a'breathin', chil'!"
"One o'deez days
"Dat's whut you's gotta do. Jus' keep breathin'!
You's all filled up wid dat dust an' dirt. Keep breathin'!"
It woan be long
"Lord, help dis chil'. Please help dis - She ain't –
Gracious, Sarh, I never knows whin you's gonna faint, er fall,
er go starin' intuh space."
One o'deez days
"We'l jus' stay righ' shere on dis here grass a bit
'til you's feelin' better, den we'l git back t'de house."
It woan be long
"I's gonna git y'some nice iced tea frum yestuhday,
er you kin has some o'dat lemonade we made tuhday."
I's gwyne home
"An' I's gonna git you some nice ice fo' yo' po' 'lil face."
T' sing my song
"An' in a bit, you be feelin' right es rain. Right es rain."
Dat frum sin
"I's sho' o'dat, Sarh. You's gonna be feelin' ag'in right es rain."

He's set me free."
"You soon be feelin' fine. I know dat, Sarh, real fine.
Dat's my promise."

It really was true, just as Mary promised. She helped me across the wide gravel sea, into the house, and into Bessie's rocking chair by the philodrendon window. Fluttering about the kitchen like a frantic mother bird over her young, Mary hurriedly gave me the last glass of yesterday's iced tea and a fresh glass of today's lemonade. After she knelt before me, wrapped an ice cube in a dish rag, and urgently stroked my face, I revived and felt considerably better.

"Mary?"

"I's righ' shere, chil'. Whut's you needin'? Whut's you needin'?
Tell me enyt'ing you's needin', chil', enyt'ing, just enyt'ing,
'cause I's gonna git enyt'ing you's –"

"Mary, they sound so happy."

"No, chil'. No, dey ain't no happy. Dey's sunk down in de misr'y."

"But Mary, they're singing so loud, they must be happy."

"No chil'. De louder dey sing, de deeper down dey's sunk.
Dey's crying out t'God 'cause dey's deep in de misr'y."

*"Then – then if they're crying out to God
because they feel so bad, then – then the shed isn't a shed, Mary.
No. It's a church."*

At midnight, I heard quiet voices in the lane. I carried my little chair away from the fir tree window and sat at the window facing the lane. One eighteen-wheeler still remained under the maple tree. Four trucks, as promised, had been sent that day by the broker, John Jeffers, and one truck still waited in the night for its load of fifty and one hundred pound bags. Mr. Clay was talking quietly to the driver, telling him, at long last, to "Pull around so we can start loadin' up." It was true, just as the Mississippi migrant had said, that every load since that morning had been good. Every light in the shed shone brightly that moonless night. Though the migrants had been allowed a short dinner break when we gathered around our own table, driving back to Clifford's farm to cook for themselves, they had effectively been working in that shed for eighteen hours straight.

I can't hear any more singing now in the shed. It must be very quiet in there. If Mr. Clay is saying that it's time for that truck to turn around, then all the potatoes have been bagged, and the conveyor belt has stopped, and the men on that back truck aren't swinging those bushels anymore. It must be quiet there now without that rattley belt moving all the time. I guess the sparrows are asleep in the rafters too. Mr. Clay is walking back toward the shed now and putting on his work hat again. I can see him in the light from that tall pole by the gas pump and the light from the shed. The driver is getting back into his truck. That sound is always so loud when that engine starts up, and it will be even louder in the night.

Last week, a truck came here in the middle of the night by mistake. It had come to the wrong farm. Mr. Clay went down to see what was hap-

Gracious! I was right!
That engine is so loud, I'm covering my ears.
I'm not listening to that anymore!

The driver that was lost needed to go to a farm called - I forget the name - but it was the name of another flower on Rural Route 20, but instead the driver had come to Bluebonnet on Rural Route 2.

Those drivers must know the names of lots of flowers. Even Clifford's farm is called Goldenrod. Well, that's not a flower, but it almost looks like one. The Nuns put bouquets of goldenrod on the altar in the fall. They grow by the wild asters near the back gate.

I was very surprised when Elaine came up to the attic that night when that driver was lost. She told me not to be afraid, that the truck had come here by mistake, and that I should go back to sleep. She didn't say to 'drift off' the way Sister Catherine does, but she told me everything was all right, and I didn't need to be afraid. Why was she nice to me then? She's usually not nice to me, but that night she was. And why was she nice to the mother of that sick little boy in the bus this morning? Why did she take that mother and her son to the doctor, and why did she pay for the medicine herself? The adults here are so hard to understand. I never know what they are going to do.

That driver is backing up to the shed, now. How can he drive that huge truck in the dark backwards? After the migrants load up all those bags, then they can go home.

All the adults at the orphanage are the same all the time. They even dress the same all the time. Mother Agnes is always serious, and Sister Martha always talks about gratitude, and Sister Catherine is always so quiet in the night room with her book with the pretty ribbons. Even Sister Alice always makes fun of Sister Grace, but the children aren't supposed to notice that.

All the adults here though are so different all the time. Sometimes Bessie is funny, but she can be so mean. Mr. Clay can laugh so loud when he talks about Adelina, but he can hiss like a snake and say all kinds of bad words too. When Sister Martha asks for stories, I don't say all those bad words that Mr. Clay says.

But Mary is always the same. Always looks the same.
She got mad at me once though, when I forgot the water in that cup,
but she was just scared of Bessie. That was just an asksident.

The migrants are always the same too. They all are tired and hungry,
and I guess they get sick a lot, just like the migrant at the pantry
door. He thought he was dying, and so did I in that shed today.
I couldn't breathe, just like in the corn field. Mary said my lungs
were full of dust and dirt. I felt like I was sick and dying too, just like
he did. Mary gave me cold drinks and then I felt better, but until then
I thought I was dying. That's why I kept pulling at Mary's dress.

How do the migrants ever feel better? Do they have lemonade and iced
tea in the shed? All I saw were tractors and farm machines.
I didn't see any refrigerator. I guess they don't have anything to
drink except water at the spicot by the rose-petunia patch,
or Mary would have given me some of their lemonade
when I was faint in the shed today.

Jesus always talked about giving "a cup of cold water in my Name."
He used to say, "I was thirsty and you gave me a drink."
When Mr. Slain asked me if I had memorized that verse,
I said that one right the very first time.

I wonder if the migrants would feel better if I gave them iced tea
and lemonade. I wonder if I gave them both, if they would feel better.
I sure felt better today when Mary gave me a glass of each one. Even
if we don't have any lemonade, we always have iced tea. Mary always
makes so much, we always have enough to share. She makes iced tea
in a spaghetti pan, really big! She uses fifteen whole tea bags!
That's what I'm going to do. I'm going to offer a drink
to make the migrants feel better.

I'm going to sit on that side porch in the morning. A few migrants
always come up to the spicot about the same time. I could ask them if
they'd like a glass, but I won't tell anyone in this family what I'm
doing though, because I know they always get mad at me for being
nice to anyone who looks like Mary. I don't know why they do that,
but they always do. Everything here is so upside down
from the orphanage. The people here get mad at me when I'm nice!
I can't imagine what Mother Agnes would say about that!
I'm going to give them lemonade or iced tea.
They can have either one. I guess what Mary said about me is true.
I was upset with her for saying that, but I guess it's true -
I'm a fox in a bad world trying to do good things.

I'm sure those migrants will say,
'I do t'ank you. Dis sho' is mos' 'preciated,' just like Mary does.
Then I would be offering a drink to Jesus. He was thirsty too.
I'm sure He would like that. It was so hot in that Bible land.
I'm sure it was as hot as here. So that's what I'll do tomorrow. Wait in
the glider like a fox in a bad world, and then I'll jump up like a fox
in the hen house and offer a drink to Jesus.
He and Mr. Slain would like that.

❧

O doan dat look like my brudder
Hallelu, O Hallelu!
O doan dat look like my sister,
Hallelu, O Hallelu!
O who's dat comin' yonder,
O who's dat comin' yonder,
Is dat Jesus comin' yonder?
Hallelu!

It seemed to be consistently between ten and eleven o'clock each morning that a group of mothers with their children, or a man or two, would walk from the shed toward our house seeking water. Since the spigot was to the right of the side porch where the tall roses climbed right up to the bedroom windows, that sole water source was positioned so deeply within those shrubs that it was effectively inaccessible. I was always scared that the migrants would get pricked by the thorns, or their turbans would get caught in the branches, or worse, that their little ones would get stabbed in the eyes. Since all my efforts to improve Mary's life had ended in abysmal failure, I attempted to improve the lives of the field hands by offering alternatives to that spigot.

The next morning, I sat on the side porch in the glider waiting for the moment when I could offer a drink to Jesus. A mother with two little boys walked up to the porch near the rose-petunia patch. I jumped up with eager antipation and sat on the side of the porch, my legs swinging over the edge. As Sister Elizabeth always instructed, I began as a formal introduction –

"Hello, I'm Sarah. Certainly is a nice day. Mary and I don't think it's going to be as hot as yesterday when I looked for the library in the barn and almost died in the shed."

The two boys looked at me with shocked expressions as their mother thrust both her hands over their hearts and drew her children close to her dirty skirts.

"I was wondering if you would like some lemonade. Mary and I made two big pitchers this morning, and we even remembered to add lots of water. Mary said it's just syrup if you forget the water."

The boys continued to stare at me, but their mother meekly looked at the ground as she shook her head slightly from side to side.

"You don't have to be scared of me, because I'm nice to everybody at the orphanage. If you've never had Mary's lemonade, you may not think it's good, but it really is. She puts –"

"Sarah?" Elaine called from the kitchen, "Who are you talking to out there?"

"Oh! I'm just talking to this lady and her boys. I was telling her that the weather today doesn't seem to be –"

Squeeeek

"Bessie, you'll never believe this. Sarah, what on earth do you think you're doing?"

"Oh! Hi Elaine. I was just worried that her boys would get stabbed in the eyes with those rose –"

"Get in here."

"But that spicot is so far into those bushes that –"

"Get in here, right now! Shew! This damn bee is always here. Frank, your patch on this screen is tearing away already."

"A new door," was all Frank said.

SLAM!

The next morning, I sat once again on the side of the porch near the rose-petunia patch and whispered to a mother wearing faded overalls and a blue work shirt, whose skin was patchy grey with dust from the shed. I spoke to her and her toddler very quietly because Elaine and Bessie and Frank were in the kitchen again, and I didn't want to be interrupted.

"Hello, I'm Sarah. Certainly is a nice day. Mary and I don't think it's going to be as hot as that day when I looked for the library in the barn and almost died in the shed."

The toddler became so scared that he scurried behind his mother while still holding her hand, grasping her overalls while peeking around her leg.

"Your little boy doesn't need to be scared of me, because I'm nice to everybody at the orphanage. I was wondering if you would like some iced tea. We don't have any lemonade today, because Mary ran out of lemons, and Bessie hasn't been to Sloane's yet, and Mary's not allowed in there. But she made a big pot of iced tea yesterday, and it's already cold too, because last night she left it in the –"

"Elaine," Bessie asked from the kitchen, are you hearing the same talk on that side porch? Go see if Sarah is –"

Squeeeek

"Sarah, how many times do Bessie and I have to to tell you not to –"

"Oh! Elaine, I was just telling this lady about looking for the library in the barn. I was just wondering if she had seen any books at their school in the –"

284

"Élaine, what's that crazy girl doing?"

"Bessie, do you really have to ask what she's doing? Really? Don't you and I already know? She's generously providing us with another ordeal to deal with, like she generously provided one yesterday, and I'm sure will generously provide us one tomorrow. Sarah, get in here!"

"But it's so hot in the shed, Elaine, and the migrants breathe all that dust and –"

"Get in here Sarah, before this damn bee buzzes into this house, and the flies."

"But I thought they would feel better if I gave them –"

"Land sakes, Laine, it's that Catholic education that makes her so mouthy."

"I know, Bess. They say she's a smart little girl at the orphanage, but I don't see any evidence of that!"

SLAM!

The next day was bi-weekly laundry day, when all the "clean dirt" the farm provided came out in Mary's "washin' 'sheen." The old hand-crank-ringer antique had been dragged into the kitchen to stand by the china cabinet and the sink. The combined smell of soap and bleach was overpowering. Frank and Elaine had driven to the Sears Store in

Jackson, Bessie had driven to Sanford's, and Mary had been sent upstairs to gather all the pillowcases and sheets. I had a brief window of opportunity to discuss the merits of lemonade and iced tea with any visiting migrants without any adults in the kitchen interrupting.

Just as I had hoped, one migrant wearing his work hat and overalls came out of the shed and walked across the wide gravel sea toward the farmhouse. I jumped out of the glider and sat down again on the side of the porch near the spicot, eagerly awaiting his approach. As he walked around the rose-petunia patch, his face was hidden under the brim of his hat, but when he came closer and raised his head, I could tell that we had met before. When he saw me, he stopped abruptly by the petunias and stared at me with a fixed, blank, expressionless stare. It was that migrant from Mississippi who had begged for food at our pantry door two summers before, who had spoken such strange words that I couldn't understand anything except *sick* and *hungry* and *dying*. I did remember our conversation though, and remembered that I had been hurt, because I had invited him in.

My opening words which the two previous days I had considered to be so grown-up, suddenly seemed immature and childish beneath his gaze so intensely concentrated and fixed. He appeared to be waiting, waiting for me to speak. Apparently he would not approach the spicot unless I spoke first. Gathering up all my courage beneath his rigid stare, I risked the only truthful words I could think of –

"Do - do you still like green beans?"

He said nothing.
I encouraged him to respond by volunteering –

*"Sometimes I like something, but the next year I don't.
I still like green beans, but I've never liked brussel sprouts."*

He moved not a muscle, displayed no indication that he had heard my words at all. His eyes seemed hollow in his expressionless face. I risked again –

286

"I was wondering if you would like some lemonade. Mary and I made two more pitchers this morning, and she remembered to add lots of water. She said it's just syrup if you forget the water."

He continued to stand utterly motionless near the petunias, studying me so intently, I wondered if he were breathing. If I had not seen him blink periodically, I would have wondered if he were alive at all. He was as still and mute as the statues in St. Francis Chapel. The last time I had seen him at the screen door, he had talked to me. Why was he just staring at me now? With some impatience, I risked his silence once again –

"If you'd rather have iced tea, we have a spaghetti pan full of that. The tea bags are still in it. Mary hasn't taken them out yet, because she's gathering up the laundry. But I could ladle out some and add some ice. I can reach the freezer now without a chair, if you would like some."

He said nothing. My impatience deepened. He seemed to be peering down to the very bottom of my soul, so intently were his dark eyes fixed on mine. I had never before experienced anyone who radiated absolutely nothing, a person who exhibited no life at all. Only his eyes were living because they blinked. With obvious impatience, I risked again –

"When I almost died in the shed, Mary gave me lemonade and iced tea, and they really helped me, because there was dust in my lungs. If there's dust in your lungs, you might like some too, because I didn't see any refrigerator by the conveyor belt."

When he refused my generosity by solemnly pointing toward the spicot, I exploded –

"Nobody in that shed likes lemonade or iced tea?

Then for goodness sakes, let me get you a glass
so the water doesn't taste like metal!"

With supreme frustration, I jumped up and rushed toward the screen. But by the time I reached for the handle, he had stooped down like all the others and drunk directly from the spicot. I watched as he backed out from under the roses, then stood up and resumed his expressionless stare. Then he did something I will never, ever forget. Gazing steadily at me, he backed slowly away from the roses, backed around the S curve of the rose-petunia patch where the hummingbirds hovered each evening, and backed slowly into the lane. When he came to the center of the lane, just before he turned to walk back to the shed, he took off his hat and bowed to me.

No words had passed between us this time, just a locking of our eyes and a gesture with his hat. Somehow though I knew I had impacted the black world. I had beaten my skinny body against a locked racial door so many times before, but this man had allowed me entrance. For one brief moment, both our skin tones met without that hatred so prevalent on that farm. That was enough for me. I don't remember being obsessed with that spigot ever again, because I had offered a glass of water to Jesus, and though He had refused, I had offered it just the same.

Frank, Elaine, and Bessie were leaving after dinner for another day trip. As much as I wanted to spend that afternoon with Mary, they insisted I had to spend the day at Clifford's farm, *Goldenrod.* Frank and Bessie were waiting by the car, but Elaine was still in the kitchen gathering up Bessie's things for the trip including her *charge-a-plate.* Though the kitchen table still stood littered with the remains of the noonday meal, Mary had mysteriously disappeared into the pantry.

"Elaine, why can't I just stay with Mary?
The other times you let –"

"Because we won't be back till late tonight, Sarah,
and Mary will have to go home."

"But can't I just – Please? I don't wanna go down to –"

"Sarah, you're a little too high and mighty. Always are.
You're going to Clifford's, and that's the last of it.
No arguing, no stiff-leg thing, no staring, no nothing.
I'm taking out Bessie's things to the car,
and you better follow."

"But I –"

"Get a move on!"

Elaine left the kitchen –

Squeeeek

SLAM!

But before I could follow her, Mary called to me in an urgent hoarse whisper from the pantry –

"Sarh!
Sarh, come on ou' shere, quick! I got's t'talk t'you!"

Feeling that powerful allegiance to Mary which on that farm overrode every other emotion, I ignored Elaine's demand and instead ran into the pantry. Mary was standing behind the washing machine, making urgent motions with both hands for me to hide behind that machine with her.

"Come on! Come on over here righ' quick, Sarh.
Hur'y, hur'y, hur'y!"

I rushed over to her
as she leaned down and looked directly into my eyes -

"W'ain't got's much time, Sarh,
so I need you t'listen t'me real good. Is you listenin'?"

"Yeah. Why are we -"

"Chil', ain't all chil'n nice es you.
Ain't all chil'n nice es yo' friends at dat orphage.
Dem kids at Clifford's farm? Well – dey – dey's rough, Sarh, real rough.
You keep yo' wits 'bout you."

"My what? What are -"

"Keep yo' wits 'bout you? Well – y'know how hard y'has t't'ink
whin you's readin' dat dead whale book?"

"Oh yeah! Those long words are so hard to -"

"An' y'hast t'keep t'inking an' t'inking an' t'inking all de time?"

"Yeah?"

"Dat's whut y'got's t'do tuhday down dere."

"Think like Moby Dick?"

"Yeah, 'member t't'ink like dat.
An' you be careful, Sarh. You know 'bout whut's fittin' an' whut ain't
fittin'. An' y'knows whut you's learn'd at dat orphage.
An' ef you see somet'ing y'know ain't fittin', dat's dang'rous –"

"Sarah? Get out here! We're waiting!"

"Chil', whin dere's somet'ing dang'rous, y'al'ys go stiff,
an' y'woan be able t'do dat dere. So you got's t'keep t'inking
an' t'inking an' t'inking - "

"Like Moby Dick?"

"Yeah. An' ef yo' legs lock up, an' y'go stiff, den you 'member
t'git dem 'lil legs movin' ag'in an' walk 'way.
Keep dem wits 'bout you, 'cause –"

"Sarah? Come on! How many times do I -"

"An' if dere ain't no big fok's dere tunight, you –"

"Keep your wits about me."

"Yeah, an' if yo' legs lock up, you –"

" - keep them moving and walk away."

"Yeah, an' al'ys do dat hard t'inking, 'cause – "

"Sarah, get out here now! Right now! I mean it!"

Mary hurridly lifted her apron, reached into her dress pocket,
took out that worn penny she said she always kept there,
and shoved it into the pocket of my shorts.

"You keep dis penny wid you all tuhday an' all tuhnight. Y'hear? Dat 'il
'mind you not t'go stiff, keep dem 'lil legs a'movin', walk 'way,
an' do dat hard t'inking. Y'hear me?"

"Yeah. Not t'go stiff, keep dem 'lil legs movin', walk 'way, an' do dat hard t'inking."

"Dat's 'xactly right, 'xactly right.
You run on, now. Doan touch dem dogs!
An' stay 'way frum dat barn. An' dat cabnit ain't no –"

"Sarah, if you don't get out here now,
I'll have to come in there and –"

"An' 'member, 'member, *'member*, keep yo' 'lil legs a'movin'!
An' ef you go stiff – "

Squeeeek

"- do dat hard t'inking –"

SLAM!

"- like Moby Dick! Like Moby Dick!"

"Sarah, Frank and I think
you are undoubtedly the most maddening child in the entire world!
Seems like I've been calling you all afternoon!"

"Mary was telling me about Moby –"

"Get in!" was all Frank said.

"Frank and I and everyone else get so tired of you, Missy.
You provide a new ordeal every damn day!"

As Frank drove out the lane, Mary called to me from behind the dirty screen –

"Be careful, Sarh!   Stay 'way frum dem dogs!
You got's t'be strong in dis world!"

When we came to the end of the lane, we turned left onto Rural Route 2, then drove past the hog farm, the Boogie Man Road, and the two farmhouses facing each other.   When we came to the little stone bridge, I noticed that a large piece of cardboard was propped against the trunk of that tree.   The words printed in crayon read simply - *Remember.* I wondered if that word meant that I should remember Mary's words, or if I should remember that the migrants had crashed.   Beyond that bridge, we turned right onto the winding country road which led to Clifford's farm where the migrants lived.

What a magnificent old farmhouse was Clifford's home at Goldenrod, another three-story house with a grand center hall.   A southern style columned veranda, which stretched around three of its exterior walls, offered shade and welcomed breezes from the fields during the stifling heat of those summer months.   Because Clifford's wife possessed none of the talent for growing the perennials and roses which flourished under Miss Bessie's vigilant care,   the deep front garden at Goldenrod was simply composed of various flowering trees and shrubs, punctuated by glorious maples and towering elms, which thrived in a gently rolling landscape of shallow valleys and diminutive hills.

Clifford's lane was very different from ours.   The mighty shed at Bluebonnet was where the farm machinery for Clayton's farms was kept. Tons of rolling combines, tractors, and eighteen-wheelers had packed down the gravel to the point that it was as hard and enduring as concrete. The lane at Goldenrod, though, was simply dirt with indentations of all shapes and sizes, which I'm sure served as mud puddles of glorious proportions.   The two purposes of Goldenrod were to provide Mr. Clay with additional acres for potatoes, as well as his one acre of sweet corn near the stream, and to provide housing for his busload of migrant workers.

"Sarah, you do everything JR tells you to do,"
demanded Elaine as our car stopped at the end of that dirt lane.
"He's five years older than you, and as everyone knows,
he's a whole lot smarter. You obey him today.
You hear me? Don't give anyone your now infamous grief.
We'll all be back after dark. There's JR coming now.
You behave yourself, Missy."

As I got out of the car, I heard Elaine remark to Frank -
"Just a couple more days, Frank,
then we can take her back to that orphanage."

"Come on Sarah. Hurry up!" JR shouted.
"We're all fishing in the irrigation pond out back,
but there's things I want to show you."

As JR and I walked up the lane, I saw that directly across from
their side porch was a two-story dirty-white house which leaned as
alarmingly to the left as the Boogie Man house.

"Why are you stopping, Sarah? Come on!
There's things I want to show -"

"Does a Boogie Man live here too?" I gasped.
"One lives in Brueston in a house just like that, and one lives on the
road to Jamestown. Does - does a Boogie Man live here too?"

"I don't know what you're talking about, Sarah.
That's where the migrants live – in that little house."

"All of them? All? A whole bus load of them?

How do they fit in that little house?"

"Oh Sarah, come on. I don't know. I've never been in there. Their house has to be close to our house so we can see what those migrants are doin', but at night it's too close in the dark. That's why we keep the dogs. Come on, Sarah. Why are you just standing there like a statue? *Come on.*"

I stepped only a few more steps, then stopped and watched JR walk toward a slab of concrete near the side porch. From out of that slab rose a three foot metal pipe with a hole at the top, through which were threaded the short metal chains of the attack dogs Three giant German shepherds continuously prowled round and round that concrete slab. When one saw JR approaching, that dog abruptly stopped, his legs rigid in the same stance. Then the other two looked toward our direction, and the low snarling began. As JR drew closer, the snarls grew louder, intensifying into growls, the scarlet eyes of those dogs riveted upon their aggressor. Then when JR stepped directly up to the slab, all three dogs reared back on their hind legs. straining desperately at their chains, their jaws snapping, their teeth flashing, straining higher and higher in a frenzied attempt to bite him.

"GET AWAY FROM THEM!" I screamed.
"GET AWAY, JR! THEY'RE TRYING TO HURT YOU!"

JR picked up a long stick which lay near the slab, and carefully, from the full length of that stick, began to savagely strike the legs of those dogs. Their frenzied cries rose in a cacophony so intense that I screamed again and slammed my hands over my ears.

"STOP IT! STOP THAT! JR, STOP!
THEY'RE TRYING TO HURT YOU,
BECAUSE YOU'RE HURTING THEM!"

"We have to keep 'em mean, Sarah.

GET DOWN, YOU DAMN DOGS!
Daddy says keep 'em mean. *Get down!*
We don't want those people comin' into our house at night,
so these dogs have t'stay mean. *Get back!* Filthy dogs!
And they'll stay mean if we hurt 'em."

I stood there gasping, unblinking, my heart hammering. The violence I had intuited and briefly witnessed at our farm materialized before me as prolonged, sustained, and brutal. JR continued to savagely strike them, shouting, **"I'm making their legs sing!"** Then just as suddenly as he had begun, JR threw down the stick in the same place where he had found it, as the frenzy of the dogs regressed from barks to growls to low continuous snarls.

"That was so mean! That's just mean!
You're just mean! That was so -
You should - you should not -"

"Daddy always says, 'Hit 'em for all their worth.
Then they'll always obey.'"

The irrigation pond where the other grandchildren were fishing lay behind a wide red doorless barn which stretched laterally before us beyond either side of the dirt lane. Though this barn was as large as the barn I knew so well, it had two openings which never closed, two identical openings on either side which allowed me to see through the building to the irrigation pond in the distance. I wondered why the barn needed to be so big, since all the farm equipment was kept at Bluebonnet. Maybe that's where - I thought with a sinking, sickening feeling - Do the migrants sleep in there, the ones who can't fit in that tiny house? Do they have to sleep - with - with the rats?

JR said he wanted to take me up to the second floor to show me something. I was so traumatized by the preceding scene, I could barely speak –

"Does – does the Boogie Man live up there?
Are there more dogs up there? Are – Are there rats?"

"Oh come on, Sarah," shouted JR.

"I don't wanna go!
There might be rats and – and snakes – those little green –"

"What a scardey-cat you are! Come on, I want to show you their – "

"Their what? Will there be rats, JR? I hate rats. I hate them!
And I don't like mice either. Mother Agnes says they're God's
creatures too, but I hate them. Sister Martha does too,
because she found one in her shoe, and Katie found one in her –"

"You're sure no farm girl! Rats and mice are here everywhere.
Snakes too. What a yellow-belly!
Come on, I want to show you this."

JR led me into that barn where the air hung hot, heavy, and motionless. My fears suddenly intensified as I struggled with the nauseating smell, a suffocating stench which made it difficult to breathe. JR, who apparently was oblivious to the odor, climbed a shaky wooden ladder up to the second floor with all the nimbleness of a monkey, while I clung to the rungs below him in sheer terror.

"Why does it stink so bad in here?
Mr. Clay's barn smells like straw and dust,
but it doesn't smell like this! This one makes me sick!
And this ladder looks so scary!
Isn't there some other way to get up there?"

"Oh Sarah, stop complaining. What a sissy!
You're sure no fun to play with. Just grab onto the sides,"
JR called down from the second floor.
"Climb on up. Even if you fall, you'll fall into straw!
City girls are such scaredy-pants!"

"I guess – I guess I can climb slowly,
like the steps at the farm with Mary.
I can be careful if I – if I –
my sandle shoes on one step and my hands on the next.
But I feel like I'm going to throw up!
My stomach keeps getting hard, like I'm going to –"

"You'll get used to the smell. Just breathe through your mouth.
We only smell it at the house when the wind changes.
Hurry up, Sarah! Come on, so I can show you!"

After what seemed an eternity of fear, I finally stepped off that rickety ladder into a vast expanse of straw studded with upstanding pitchforks positioned at intervals. The smell was overpowering! My urge to vomit was so strong that I clamped both hands over my nose and mouth and kept swallowing hard.

"I don't see anything but straw and pitchforks!"
I mumbled through my fingers.
"Why did you bring me here to see straw and pitchforks?
We have straw and pitchforks on our own farm.
And I'm going to vomit. I can't breathe!
I got's t'breathe!
I have to keep swallowing hard so I –"

JR stretched out his arms on either side
and turned around in a circle –

"This is the migrants' bathroom.
This is where they come – up here to –
Good God, Sarah! What are you doing kneeling in the straw?
Are you – Is she puking? Oh God, is she puking in the straw?
Sarah, get up! Stand up!
If you lean over that far, you'll get shit in your hair!
Jesus Christ, now you're vomiting in all this shit!
I'll grab this pitchfork here and shovel it under.
My God, Sarah, you look green.
You going to puke again? Good God almighty!
Heaving like there's no end to –
Are you done? You city girls. Are you done?
Lean back a'ways so I can turn it over into the –
Isn't there enough stink up here without you making it worse?
Oh stop your moaning! Sounds like you're dying.
Wipe your mouth on some straw. No! No, not your shirt! Jesus!
Some straw! There. It's turned over. Stink on stink."

JR hurled the pitchfork down with utter disgust -
"I'm getting out of here."

"H - help me, JR - pl - please."

"What? I can barely hear you, you sissy."

"Pl - please, could you - could you help me?"

"I can't hear you! What? Now you're crying too?"

"I can't - I - I just - just can't -"

"Sarah, you sound like some mangy kitten
whimpering in the straw, bothering everybody.
My God, what a cry-baby! Oh stop that bawling! Good God almighty.
You can sit up here and sob all day if you want to.

I'm going down. I don't have all day to cope with such a –
Oh cry all you want, cry-baby. Nobody cares if you stay up here all day.
Nobody will miss a city girl. I'm going down."

JR climbed down the rickedy ladder with all the nimbleness of a
monkey, as I cried feebly in the straw, the pitch fork standing before me.

The irrigation pond smelled horrible too, as bad as the second
floor of the barn, because huge bubbles burst lazily upon the surface
through an abominable layer of bluish-green scum. JR's five brothers
and sisters were lined up on that abysmal shore, each attempting to catch
whatever unfortunate creature lived in the bottom of those putrid waters.
Still feeling sick, faint, and shaking from the experience with the dogs
and the barn, and still worried that at any moment another Boogie Man
would mysteriously appear, I sat unobserved far back from the group,
trying my best to hide among the weeds behind all the children.

"How many catfish have you caught?" JR asked.

"Not a one," grumbled Billie. "We're just watching.
Maybe we already caught them all this summer.
Guess we'll have to have burgers for supper."

JR forcefully assumed the central position among his siblings
and grabbed a pole. Then with a violent backward motion of his wrist,
he snapped the line forward over his shoulder. I felt a sudden tightness
near my collar and a sting in my neck. Not realizing what had happened,
I was bewildered what that dual sensation could be. Then as the pain
began, I froze with fright as I realized his line had coiled around my neck
with his hook embedded in my vein. When JR noticed that his line was
stuck, he pulled it forward more forcibly. I cried out! Everyone turned
around, and when they saw blood streaming down into my collar, their
faces flushed with horror. They shouted toward me –

**"My God, JR, she's hurt! Good God, get it out!
Get the hook out, JR! She's bleeding!"**

As JR frantically attempted to dig out the hook without causing me to bleed further, his fingers trembled and fumbled. With a quivering voice filled with terror and profound dread, he pleaded with wild eyes —

**"Sarah! Don't ever, ever tell Daddy!
You must promise *never* to tell Daddy!
My God, Sarah, never tell, never,
'cause he'll beat me!
He'll beat me!
He'll beat me,
and – and then he'll beat us *all*!"**

*I wanna go home! I wanna go home!
Please, please somebody, take me home!*

Deep guttural cries and wracking sobs tore through my body, making my wound throb with every heartbeat, as I hid the remainder of that horrible afternoon near the end of the lane behind the largest shrub.

*Please, please somebody, take me home!
Please take me back to the orphanage!
Somebody, PLEASE! I WANNA GO HOME!
Everybody is mean here! I thought just Bessie and Clayton were mean. But now Clifford is mean to his children,*

and mean to the migrants, and JR is mean to the dogs, and everyone is mean to everybody. The whole family is mean – the grandparents and the children and – and now their children. Somebody, PLEASE! I WANNA GO HOME!

The wheat in that field is rolled into huge wheels.
The setting sun makes them look like they're on fire!
Maybe they're wheels of Ezekiel's chariot all yellow and red.
It's Ezekiel's fire and lightning!
Ezekiel come and take me home!
Ezekiel please! Please somebody take me home!
Somebody, PLEASE! I WANNA GO –

"Sarah! Are you out there hiding? Get in here now!"
JR called from the porch near the dogs.
"Sarah? Sarah! Where are you?"

"I don't wanna come! I don't wanna!"

"Stop that silliness right now, city girl, and get in this house!
It's getting dark. We had supper and washed up,
but you didn't come. Sarah, get in here right now!"

"But I don't wanna go into your –"

"Get in here *now*! We have a game to show you.
Come on! The fireflies are coming, and it's time to go in."

Feeling utter dread within a state of profound emotional, psychic, and physical exhaustion, my knees shaking, my body cold and shivering, I crept slowly with great effort up the yard and entered the house by the front door. All the children were standing around the

dining room table upon which a large book was positioned in the center. When they saw me, JR exclaimed –

"Where on earth have you been? Your face's all red and blotchy.
You city girls sure like to cry. Spend the whole damn day crying.
There's leaves in your hair, Sarh, and your shirt is all wet.
What a sissy! What a cry-baby! Glad I'm not a city girl.
There, stand there at that end of the table.
We're going to play a game,
but first, we've got something to show you."

The children began to snicker as JR opened the book to reveal pictures I had never seen.

"Look at that one! What do you think about that, Sarah?
Bet you never saw anything like that!"

I stood there incredulous…squirming…feeling horribly uncomfortable.

"W – what are those n - naked people doing to each other?"

The children exploded with laughter.

*"Are – are they being mean to each other too? Is – is everybody mean?
I don't think Mother Agnes would - would like me to see
these pictures, or –"*

"You're hopeless, Sarah, just hopeless.
I'm sure glad I'm not stupid!"

I stood there in shock, knowing beyond all doubt that I was hopelessly inadequate for this world – that I couldn't keep up with the adults, and now couldn't keep up with the children either. Since they had obviously studied those pictures many times and were intimately familiar with each photograph, JR closed the book. He pulled from the binding a long envelope, which apparently served as a bookmark, and removed from it a gold key, which looked so much like the key Mary used to open Bessie's cedar closet. All the children stood in a breathless hush as JR walked to the end of the dining room and inserted the key into a large cabinet. There inside the opened double doors stood six upright shotguns.

"Bet you've never seen one of these, Sarah! These are shotguns. They're kept always loaded for those migrants. They know they're here, and they know they're loaded. If they'd ever get past the dogs in the night, they know these shotguns are here."

JR removed one slowly, his forefinger on the trigger. Pointing it toward the ceiling, he explained -

"We're gonna play 'Chicken', Sarah. Everybody knows how to play this except you. We pass this shotgun from person to person, all around the table, but the trick is, each person has to keep his finger on the trigger until the gun is completely out of his hand. That means both fingers will be on the trigger at the same time, each finger pointing in the opposite direction. But that's what makes this game so fun."

If I felt hopelessly inadequate for life then, I feel totally inadequate to describe my emotional state then, because my terror had reached such an extremity that my feelings just came to their end. I felt nothing. It was as though I had died standing up, my consciousness mercifully erased. I lived no longer, but neither did I die.

I stood there frozen stiff, yet utterly weak. But when I saw JR lower the gun to a horizontal position, then pass the shotgun to Billie, both their forefingers on the trigger, I silently screamed to myself –

I'm not playing! You can't make me!

and I shoved my hands into my pockets and felt Mary's penny.

"Chil', whin dere's somet'ing dang'rous, you al'ys goes stiff, an' you woan be able t'do dat dere. So you got's t'keep t'inking an' t'inking an' t'inking...an' ef yo' legs lock up, an' y'goes stiff, den you 'member t'git dem 'lil legs movin' ag'in an' walk 'way.
Keep dem wits 'bout you."

Remembering Mary's words and drawing strength from her penny, I somehow found the presence of mind and the physical strength to leave the room. With a stiff and petrified body, I lurched with wooden legs down the two steps into the dark kitchen, fell down hard under the table, and buried my head in my hands.

Feeling then returned to me, the fear of the dogs so near the door, and my thoughts coiled together into a tight frenzied knot. While I waited for the gunshot, I tried frantically to *'think like Moby Dick. Think like Moby Dick.'*

No one except Mary remembers me, so Clifford's children won't be remembered either. Neither parent will notice if one of their six children suddenly disappears. I'm not worried if someone is killed, because children here aren't important anyway, but I am worried that if there is a mess, the parents will remember that child, so all the mess will have to be cleaned up very quickly before the adults came home.
But how can I clean up a bloody mess quickly?
It will have to be done quickly!

Still listening for the shot in what was by now the deathly quiet of that house, I rubbed Mary's penny as my mind raced –

How can I get blood out of the rug? Should I scrub it with a rag? If brains are on the ceiling, can I reach them if I stand on a chair? If blood is on the table, will it stain the wood? What about the curtains? Oh no! They're white! If I have to wash them, they won't dry in time, and if they are missing at the windows when Clifford comes home, he might notice that one of his children is missing too!"

Still listening for the shot, I panicked –

What do I do with a dead body? Will it have any head or chest?
If I drag it anywhere, will I make more mess in the other rooms?
How will I bury it? I'm too little to carry the pitch fork,
but can I lift a shovel?

Still listening for the shot, my ears straining in the silence…
when suddenly I heard low laughter and movement in the next room.
After a pause, I knew the gun had been put away.

The remainder of that evening the seven of us were alone is a
blank, a living death, a death in life. I remember nothing else because
my little consciousness was simply too exhausted to remain aware.

Frank and Elaine, and Clifford and his wife returned very late. I
do remember that the four adults and I stood in the darkness in the lane
between the two houses where I faced the open red barn. I remember
making a visual sweep around me. Clifford's house was to my left, with
its scary book and even more scary loaded guns. The dogs were now
awake and vigilant, roaming continually about that concrete slab. Ahead
of me in the distance was the migrants' bathroom, and beyond that, the
irrigation pond where I learned that all the children suffered. To my
right was the tiny migrant house where a woman stood at a window, her
baby strapped to her back. Two little children in the upstairs window
looked down, pointing their fingers at me. Beyond that house was that
wheat field I had studied all afternoon, with its enormous wheels of
wheat, the wheels of God's chariot, Ezekiel's flaming Chariot of God. I
suddenly realized that I was the only person standing exactly in the
center of the lane. Between the white world and the world of the
migrants, the dividing line was me. The connection between those two
worlds was me.

⚲

THE CHRISTMAS LIGHT

Dere's a star in de East on Crismus morn',
Rise up, shephud, an' follow
It'l lead t'de place whar de Christ was born,
Rise up, shephud an' follow

If y'take good heed t'de angel's wurds
Rise up, shephud, an' follow
You'l fugit yo' flocks, you'l fugit yo' hurds,
Rise up, shephud, an' follow

The windshield wipers of Frank's car swished softly in the night as lacy filaments of snow drifted diagonally across his headlights. It had gently showered the entire way across the turnpike. Though road conditions had never been treacherous, traffic had moved at a slower pace, the motorists around us mercifully mindful of the ways of Mother Nature. Five hours had been added to our customary travel time of seventeen hours, so it was nearly midnight when we saw at long last the foggy hallucinogenic glows of Maysville's wrought iron street lamps.

Frank and Elaine had offered to pick me up from the university to spend Christmas on the farm. I was thrilled for the opportunity to see for myself if all the legends I had heard over the years about that season on Bluebonnet were true. I sat in the back seat in a dream-like reverie, because I had never before approached the farm in total darkness, never before seen this farmland nestled under great sweeps of flannel-like white. How strange not to see the whispy billows of Sanford's asparagus farm. How strange to observe Porter's vegetable stand enclosed with snow-patched boards. As our headlights turned in a slow graceful arc onto Rural Route 2, how strange not to hear the customary conversation about diapers on Blackwell's clothesline, rain the previous evening, electrocuted cows, or swollen creeks. The entire world was silent. All passengers in our car were silent. The only sounds were the soft swish of the windshield wipers and the low hum of the heater of our car.

As we turned into the lane, I could plainly see that the first legend was true. Clayton truly did suspend enormous red and green lights from the flat roof of the house, bulbs so huge that I realized the walls of my attic bedroom truly would be hot to the touch. My fir tree, standing in majestic isolation, reflected the colors of the season on its branches of glittering white. Sometime recently, hard driving wind had obviously blasted so fiercely across those fields that snow indeed was banked up along the left side of the lane nearly to the utility lines. As our car crept past that long frozen wall and pulled up to the porch beyond the barren Rose of Sharon, I saw that Bessie's meek little blue pump as well as the tub of sleeping portulaca were topped with pointed snowy caps. The porch light illuminated Bessie's enormous evergreen wreath hanging on the kitchen door, and that wreath as well as the neighboring bridle of Mr. Clay's original plow horse sported huge red velvet bows.

Then through the dining room window, I saw another legend now proven verifiably true. I couldn't help but laugh. Bessie had always said that Clayton trudged into the woods every December to cut down a Christmas tree, but never in all their years on Bluebonnet did he bother to measure its height. Every season their tree was not too short, but rather far too tall even for the high ceilings of the farmhouse. Each one, she always said, bent downward from the ceiling a good three feet.

"Isn't that just like a man,"
she always grumbled,
"doing the same durn thing year after year after year and never learning that it wasn't right to begin with!"

So there in the corner of the dining room I saw an enormous pine, far too grand for the proportions of that room, its central stem turned away from the ceiling a good three feet, its star drooping forlornly downward, illuminating not the ceiling above, but the red velvet skirt beneath. Everything was as Bessie had promised. All the legends except one about Christmas on the farm had so far proven true.

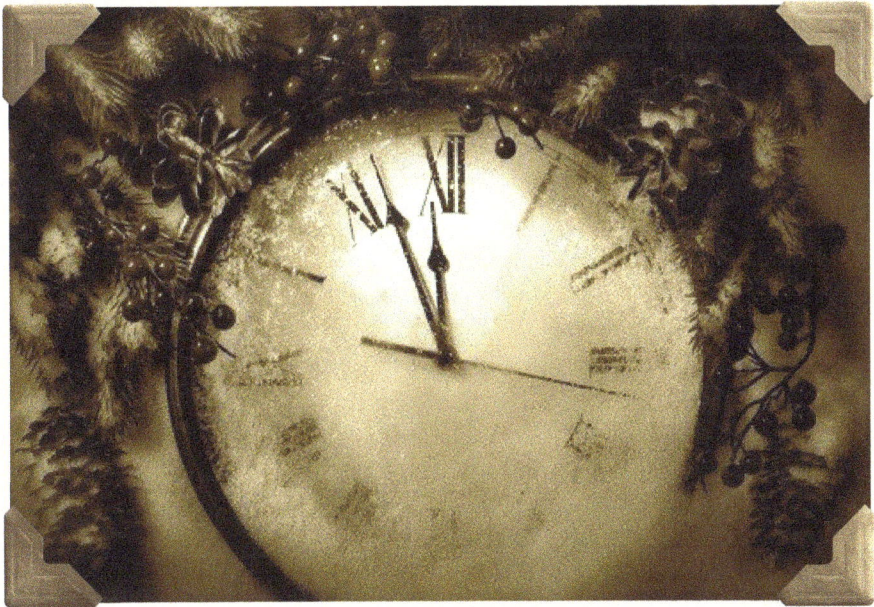

I stood at the kitchen door as every summer I always stood at the screen. Bessie and Clayton had obviously retired for the night, because on the table, an antique oil lamp had been left to cast its welcoming glow throughout the room, and the remains of a fire gently flickered in that cavernous void behind the old wood stove. Delicate triangles of snow glittered on each pane of the cactus window, and the glass of the blue-willow china cupboard shown pale yellow in that gentle light. The room was sunk in a stillness in striking contrast to the perpetual bustle of the summer.

When we entered that room, I proceeded as though by instinct into the pantry. As I lifted the lid of the silver cake-saver, I realized that of course there would be no vanilla cake with chocolate frosting waiting patiently there for me. But much to my surprise, much to my delight, I did find one meek little muffin standing on the same plate where my cake appeared each June. Propped up beside it was a scrap of lined paper which read in clear block letters - *For Sarah.* I smiled with a soft warmth in my heart as I shook my head from side to side as though I were saying 'No'.

Mary never forgets, I thought. *She always remembers.*

I heard Frank and Elaine whisper "Good night" before they tiptoed up the back stairway. Then that Christmas farmhouse kitchen was left *to darkness and to me.*

Though I was very tired and truly did look forward to snuggling beneath my two quilts, I also wanted to savor the enchantment of this rustic scene. I made a pot of tea in the blue-willow tea pot I had never used before, set it on the old wood stove, pulled over Bessie's rocking chair and positioned it near the fire and Mary's stool. A large tattered basket of twigs and kindling stood on the floor to the left of the fireplace, but to the right, just as Bessie had promised, stood a stack of those logs which had obviously once served as substantial tree trunks. All the legends I had ever heard in the infernal temperatures of summer had all been proven true this Christmas. I poked the remains of the fire then added some kindling as well as a few of the smaller logs. Flames shot upward with a pleasant heat and a merry glow. How right was Thoreau when he observed –

> *This is a delicious evening, when the whole body is one sense,*
> *and imbibes delight through every pore...*
> *all the elements unusually congenial to me.*

I felt enclosed in a warm embrace of happiness as I settled down in the rocking chair to drink tea, sample Mary's muffin, and reminisce.

I realized that night that I had never before noticed the mantle over that fireplace. Apparently my gaze had been so consistently absorbed in Mary that my vision had always terminated in her sitting on the stool by the stove. What a monstrous plank of ancient wood that mantle was, with great horizontal splits and rough places where tiny curly filaments, which glistened golden in the reflected flames, still promised splinters to the incautious. It hung there in striking contrast to the mantle in Bessie and Clayton's bedroom, with its delicate scroll carvings and dainty figurines. I marveled that this massive antique, which could easily be two centuries or more old, had no doubt been hoisted into position on the backs of many powerful men.

The bricks which lined the opening were scorched and bleached by the heat of thousands, if not tens of thousands of fires. Nearly every brick displayed every conceivable shade of beige and tan, as though each represented one migrant worker whose skin had been transformed by laboring long days sorting potatoes in Clayton's dust-filled shed What a remarkable history those tired old bricks could tell. I recalled that the fireplace in Dicken's *Christmas Carol* was lined with Dutch tiles depicting scenes from Old and New Testament Scripures. I doubted that any of the bricks in the fireplace of the Clay family would remind me of any scene from the Gospels except *the feeding of the five thousand,* but I did know that so many if not all of the images of the farm and of life itself were indissolubly wed to Bluebonnet's lowly house maid.

I would never again peel a potato or a tomato, or slice a cucumber or butter an ear of corn without remembering Mary. I would never see a pine tree or a hydrangea which did not remind me of her safety pins. From roses to screen doors, from flies to ringing phones, from dust to dinner plates, thousands of the most commonplace images of every human life were fused for me with the memory of Mary. I would never again witness the proud parade of expensive fur coats or smell the scent of lavender in a garden without remembering my dearest friend. Mary had been as elemental to my formation as earth, water, and air. No matter how long I lived or in what state of physical health, or how prolonged my aging and physical decline, I would remember her till my dying breath, because all God's children, all God's ducks, and every single one of God's cacti "got's t'breathe."

I didn't realize until I began classes at the university how much Mary's existence resembled the life of house slaves in America's antebellum South. In that era of fabled charm and grace so exaggerated by the idyllic whims of popular novels and Hollywood, the racial hatred of the slave owner dominated the plantation, a hatred clearly demonstrated to me at a very young age by the deplorable living conditions of the migrants on Goldenrod where savage attack dogs continually growled, and by Clayton and Bessie hissing like snakes at anyone with Mary's skin. But the plantation owner, like Clayton Clay, left domestic affairs and domestic stresses to the mistress of the home, just as Clayton left Bessie to tend to a deteriorating farmhouse and the duties of one slave. As long as bounteous feasts were presented three times each day upon his kitchen table and adequate hot water was available for his weekly bath, the common household concerns of Bessie and their children were extraneous to Clayton's domain.

It was common in plantation houses for tensions to run high between the mistress of the plantation and the house slave who knew the interior life of her mistress far better than the mistress knew the mind of her slave. It was not uncommon for house slaves to help raise white children and even serve as midwives to their mistresses, just as Mary had helped raise the children on Bluebonnet and delivered one child herself. This wild uncharted frontier between intimacy versus racial hatred, and companionship versus presumed inferiority, created a complexity of class relations which I as a child could never fathom. Apparently Mary sometimes unwittingly violated one of Bessie's vague unspecified boundaries, which always resulted in Bessie's directing physical violence toward her servant. As carefully as I had listened year after year to discern exactly when that invisible boundary was crossed, that subtle violation, which was always beyond my detection, resulted in terrible pain for Mary.

Like southern slaves of two centuries ago, Mary returned each evening to her own home to perform the same household chores she had provided each day for the Clays, just as house slaves and field hands had returned to their slave quarters to tend their own gardens and provide for themselves. Apparently Mary rejuvenated herself for her evening responsibilites by studying the teeny leaves on her fledging rose bushes, crawling around on her hands and knees to provide herself with a blessed moment of hope. It was no wonder she had no time to sew her work dress, no wonder that the quickest solution was a safety pin. She was a slave twenty-four hours a day.

Since slave mistresses traditionally did not kill their house slaves for disobedience, as some slave owners killed their field workers, house slaves sometimes tested the limit of their mistress' power. This dynamic was reenacted each summer during those delightful scenes of dress-up wearing Bessie's fancy clothes. The mistress was the keeper of the plantation's *keys,* since the intimacy of the mistress-slave relationship apparently did not include elemental trust, despite the close association of that relationship during the bearing and raising of children. But in the case of that relationship on Bluebonnet, the meager consciousness of the naïvely ignorant Bessie was no match for the keen intelligence and shrewd observations of her servant. Mary knew where the key to the cedar closet was kept and also understood the ways of her mistress. The profound distrust which Bessie had of Mary was equal to the absolute trust which Mary placed in me. We were perpetrators of two supposedly unspeakable crimes – of violating a racial boundary, and of violating the property of the slave owner. What horrendous consequences would have resulted if our delightful afternoons had ever been discovered, and the discipline which would have been directed toward me can only be imagined.

Though field slaves traditionally took the colossal risk of running permanently away, house slaves sometimes ran away for short distances apparently to prove a point. This dynamic was fulfilled each summer when Mary left the farmhouse with her buckets for the blackberry patch, consciously…thoughtfully…stepping into the narrow rut beyond the gravel, just as her great-grandmother stepped into that rut toward the Underground Railroad and the Freedom Train. After we turned around each time to return home, Mary always paused and commented that this farmhouse didn't look so big from back there. Apparently she was reliving a racial memory of seeing the plantation's big house from a restorative distance.

Sitting before that fire with Mary's stool standing to my right, what crushing regret I felt for that litany of questions I fired at her about the racial segregation in Maysville. What an callous trampelling of that sensitive heart which had suffered so much more than I would ever feel. The only excuse I could offer to console myself was that I was only seven, a little girl trying desperately to understand a world which was obviously outside the sheltering walls of the orphanage where the *Rules of Christian Conduct* were clearly presented and obeyed. My only excuse was youth. Apparently Mary understood that too, because that particular excursion did nothing to alter our relationship.

How easy it would have been for Mary to vent her frustration about her poverty and racial hatred on the only little person on that farm who would not have been believed, or even if I had been believed, the only person about whom no one cared. Those summer days could have easily become a ninety-day succession of lemonade scenes, retaliatory rages and vengeful outbursts behind closed doors which would have emotionally crippled me for life. Instead, she and I formed a bond with the same tensile strength as the bond I would have had with my own mother.

Year after year we had driven back to the farm, and it hadn't taken long for my physical frame to tower over Mary's. Year after year I had attended the same performance of *Bluebonnet* which I had attended the previous year. The characters and costumes were always the same, the staging consistently consistent, and with rare exceptions, notable exceptions, the extras were always mute. But primarily I had been studying our specie's greatest internal conflict - the stark opposition of good verses evil staring at each other with as much fixed determination as the two parents stared at each other across the restaurant table when I was only four. That snowy midnight by that fireside, I finally realized that the virtue I had seen each summer in Mary and the migrants had delineated the evil of racism, and the evil of racism had illuminated the good in its recipients. From the good I had directly learned love, and from the negative space surrounding the evil, I had studied love. From both directions, from both viewpoints, I had studied love.

Though I had attempted very early to establish the teachings of Christ on the farm, I had also learned very early that Christianity is a religion which has its greatest impact over extended periods of time. As hard as I had worked to break down racial barriers by simply setting a table, guarding a spigot, and opening one screen door, it could take centuries for the commandments of racism to be ultimately shattered, and that new tablet reading *All men are brothers* to be carved in stone. This meant that very nearly all my attempts to establish a permanent good would meet with personal defeat. Most of my Christian life, therefore, would be dealing with my own apparent failure.

Mercifully though, I realized too, largely from physical sensations, a feeling that my heart was swelling with love, that my soul was strong and struck dumb with awe, and that my mind was firm and resolute, that the ideal end for me was not my goal. Instead, the attempt alone to be Christ-like was of consummate importance, because the atmosphere on that farm was saturated with God. It was for Him that I had set that table, to Him I had offered that glass. By studying the photographic negative, I had discerned the positive; by observing the bad, I had intuited the good. By charting the contours of the negative space, I had abstracted the face of God. His Spirit was everywhere, in the distance between every thorn on every rosebush, *flam(ing) out, like shining from shook foil,* and from every wheel of wheat. It was Love Himself who hovered near that hallowed spigot, and His eyes were upon me, as my eyes were locked onto His. All this I had witnessed. All this I had treasured. All this I must write about one day.

As I finished the last drop of tea and ate the last crumb of Mary's muffin, and the fire gently crackled as it burned down to scarlet embers all aglow, I tried to find the words which would adequately convey what Mary herself meant to me. What exactly was the depth of love I felt for her, for the woman who had dared to break through the racial barrier to provide one little life for one little orphan? As tears flowed freely into my now empty cup, I realized that there simply were no words, no grand phrases, no epic poetic lines. The only adequate representation for my love for her could not be captured in words at all. The only adequate representation for my love for Mary was silence.

The next day was Christmas Eve when the entire Clay clan was scheduled to descend like locusts onto that dining room with its colossal pine for supper. All that morning, Mary and I made a dozen pies while looking absolutely ridiculous. Each of us was wearing an oversized university sweatshirt over which a university hooded sweatshirt jacket was neatly tied under our chins. We looked like two great power-blue bears lumbering around our den. By noon, every flat surface in that kitchen was covered with sweet potato peels, pumpkin skins, pecan shells, and lemon rinds, all dusted with flour as with a fine sprinkling of snow, while quart mason jars from canned cheeries and peaches soaked in sudsy water in the sink. The room smelled of all the exotic spices of the Far East, an intoxicating blend, an ethereal blend which made me want to eagerly eat the very air. As that dozen pies cooled on the old wood stove and Mary and I stood nearby admiring our handiwork, she articulated a thought I will never, ever forget –

"I jus' doan t'ink we's gonna has 'nough!"

I fell into a chair, dropped my head in both hands,
chuckled, then moaned -

"You have got to be kidding, Mary. Gracious!
Those twelve pies could feed the entire state of Rhode -"

"I do b'lieve I got's a few tatters left. I kud make a w'ite tatter pie too,
an' den maybe a po' man's cake."

"I've never heard of either of those,
but I don't think either is necessary.
Anyway, what is a white potato pie and a poor man's cake?"

"O huny, you'd love dat w'ite tatter pie.
It's jus' mashed tatters an' sugar, an' a 'lil 'nella.
I got t'ree mo' eggs too, so dat's jus' 'bout right.
An' dat po' man's cake is real, real good. Real good.
Jus' raisins an' flour an' dat's 'bout all."

"Well, I don't think either is necessary.
Besides I see two fruitcakes on Clayton's desk.
Who are those from?"

Mary sat down beside me and whispered her secret -

"You promise not t'tell nobody I told ya.
One is frum dat trailer down in Jamestown dat Miss Bess says –"

"Clayton's mystery woman on Saturday night!"

"Yeah, an' d'odder is frum dat barmaid at –"

"Clayton's bar! The one who apparently wears tight sweaters!"

320

"Shhh, now Miss Sarh, doan shuu tell nobody.
An' now I jus' 'membered deres a five pound box o'choclit in de bottom
drawer o'dat file cabnit. It's frum dat Brueston lady -"

*"The diabetic who owns her own candy store!
How hysterical! Absolutely hysterical. This is all so funny.
I'm so glad I came here this season, Mary. This is all so funny."*

Mary and I chuckled as we enjoyed a few moments of dearest
companionship. Then as though by intuitive understanding, I made
another pot of tea and placed a few more logs on the fire as she cleared a
portion of the table and set out two saucers and cups. We seemed to
realize that each of us needed a few moments of rest, because Mary's
continuous litany about supper would soon begin. We sat down at the
table, poured our tea, and luxuriated in the warmth of the fire and the
heavenly scents. As I swirled my tea with my spoon, she asked -

"Whut happened t'yo' slacks dere, Miss Sarh?"

*"Oh, I tore it here somehow. Luckily the tear is on the seam.
So I just pinned it together until I can get back to my sewing
machine. Carlson's safety pins sure come in handy."*

"Sho' do."

*"I was wondering about something, Mary.
In my American History course, we're studying
the Underground Railroad. Do you have more stories passed down
through your family about your relatives who escaped on —"*

Suddenly Mary stiffened. Her teaspoon stopped still in her cup. Her face bore an expression of piercing agony I had never seen before. I wondered if she had borne that same expression when we were walking back from gathering blackberries as she listened to my endless barrage of questions which simply could not be answered.

"Miss Sarh? I - O huny, I ain't meanin' t'be no fuss. I ain't meanin' ta - Bu' Miss Sarh, I cain't tell no stories 'bout my family tuhday. Dey al'ys make me cry, Sarh. 'Bout dem dogs runnin' - an' den Wawalla, she – Dem stories al'ys make me so sad, 'cause dey's terr'ble tales fu' me, an' – an' –"

"Oh Mary! Mary, please forgive me! I am so, so sorry. I was – well - so casual, that I wasn't remembering that, of course, those memories would bring up unbearable pain and –"

"But I know two stories 'bout w'ite fo'ks dat I hear'd at my church. My preacher tol' us 'bout 'em. E'fn y'want."

"Oh yes! Mary, please, I would love to hear stories, that is if it wouldn't be too hard for you or cause you any pain."

"Dere was a w'ite Missus who lived in a big mansion house way up on a hill near a river. Dat house, he said, was es big es dat mansion house I used t'work in. Real tall, t'ree stories lookin' down on dat river. Her daddy had made 'bout fifty wide stone steps intuh dat hill leadin' frum dat big house down t'de watuh. Nobody know'd whut she done in dat house in de night 'cept de sto'keeper. Evy mo'nin', she went t'his 'lil sto', like Miss Bess goes t'Sloane's, car'yin' her 'lil shoppin' basket. Sometimes dat sto'keeper 'ud jus' say, 'Mo'nin' Miss Suzanne. Hope you find evyt'ing you's needin'. Have a good ev'nin'.' Bu' some days he'd say somet'ing like dis – 'Mo'nin' Miss Suzanne. You jus' missed Flora Simpson. She said she's havin' company tuhnight 'bout eight

o'clock. A real nice 'lil family wid two 'lil 'uns an' a fine baby boy.'
Bu' Miss Sarh, whut he was really sayin' t'her was dat a slave family
was 'scapin' t'her house dat night, rowin' 'crost dat river in de dark,
an' she had t'git redy fu' two 'dults, an' two chil'n, an' one baby.
Sometimes dere was odder fo'ks in dat sto', so dat sto' man had t'be very
careful whin he was a'talkin' wid so miny fo'ks listenin',
loud 'nough so nobody 'ud think enyt'ing was wrong,
bu' quiet 'nough so es not t'tract eny 'tention.

"So she'd go home an' cook an' git ready fu' dem slaves. Den later dat
aftuhnoon, she'd go out an' sweep all fifty o'dem steps, evy single one,
'cause dem stones 'ud be slippery in de spring wid all dat rain.
Spring was whin mos' slaves come'd, an' it'd be dark whin dey come'd
enyhow, an' she din' want nobody slippin' on dem steps.

"Den whin de sun was goin' down b'hind dem hills, she went upstairs
an' put a lantern in dat upstairs hallway winduh. No odder candles was
lit up dere, only dat light. Dat was her sign dat her house was a station
an' was safe. 'Bout eight o'clock den, she blowed out all de candles on
her furst floor, an' closed all o'her drapes, so dere warn't no light bu' dat
lantern upstairs. Den she walked so careful down all dem steps in de
dark, 'cause she kudn't car'y no odder lantern, walkin' toward dat river
all by herse'f. An' dere she waited 'lone by de watuh.

"She listen'd an' listen'd t'all de night sounds, an' listen'd t'de 'lil
waves lappin' at de shore. An' she stood dere, an' stood dere 'til de
moment come'd whin all dem sounds warn't 'potant no mo', 'cause she
hear'd dere oars a'rowin'. Dat family was comin' t'her, jus' like dat sto'
man said. Dey was comin' t'her, trustin' her, an' she know'd dey was
trustin' her lantern, 'cause she hear'd dere oars a'rowin'.

"Dat family 'ud leave fu' de next station de next night. Dey was 'bout
twenty mile 'part. Den de next mo'nin', she'd go t'his 'lil sto' ag'in
wid her basket ag'in, an' dat man might say, 'Hullo Miss Suzanne.
Rainy weather we's havin', bu' looks like it's clearin' up.

Have a good ev'nin'.' Bu' dere was de days whin he might say, 'Mo'nin'
Miss Suzanne. I hear Miss Maybelle's havin' four guests tuhnight fu'
dinner at 'bout eight.' Den she know'd she need t'buy
fu' four 'dults, no chil'n, an' she'd have t'go home an' cook fo' dem.
Den she'd have t'go out an' sweep all dem steps ag'in. Den she'd light
dat lantern an' put it in dat upstairs hallway, an' close all o'her drapes,
an' whin dat sun was down, an' it was all dark, she'd walk real careful
like in de dark down all dem steps ag'in clear down t'dat watuh.
Den she'd stand dere 'lone ag'in waitin' fo' dem slaves. An' she'd listen
an' listen t'all dem night sounds, an' listen t'de lappin' o'dem 'lil waves
on de shore, an' she'd listen 'til dat moment come'd whin she know'd
dem sounds warn't 'potant no mo',
'cause she hear'd dere oars a'rowin'."

"Oh my! Oh Mary, I have chills!
The courage - the raw courage -
and - and the persistence and the strength
of those abolitionists just astound me!"

"Sho' do, Sarh. Sho' do.
Dere was 'nudder w'ite Missus who had a 'lil baby 'bout one year ol'.
She helped up on dat Lake Erie lake. She was guidin' a 'lil slave family
wid two yung'ins t'de sho' o'dat lake. She an' dat family was all
hur'yin' an' hidin' 'mong dem trees 'til dey found dere 'lil boat on dat
sho'. Dat boat was sent by w'ite fo'ks jus' fu' dem.
An' whin dey found it, Miss Sarh, dat wind was a'howlin'
an' dat sky was so low, an' dem waves was so angry, dey was grey.
An' dat w'ite Missus kept holdin' a w'ite blanket close 'round her
yung'in, holdin' him real close. Dat family an' dat Missus all gaddered
'roun' dat 'lil boat, an' dat man was so 'preciative, an' dat mudder
was a'cryin', bu' dat w'ite Missus kep' sayin' –

'Git in righ' quick! God be wid you.
No, no, doan t'ank me. T'ank God! Git in righ' quick.'

"Den dat family got intuh dat 'lil boat, an' dat slave started rowin'
'gainst dat wind, rowin' somet'ing fierce, an' dat mudder was holdin' her
'lil un's real close in dat 'lil boat. An' dat sky was so grey, Miss Sarh,
an' dat watuh was so grey, dat evyt'ing looked all de same. An' dere 'lil
boat kept goin' up 'an down so hard in dem waves, bu' dat slave
din' care, Sarh. He din' min' dem waves, 'cause he was rowin' hard
fo' freedom fo' his family. But on dat sho', dat w'ite Missus
mus' o't'ought, 'O gracious, is dey gonna make it?'

"Den whin she seen dere boat was so far, far 'way yonder
dat she know'd dat in a minit she'd never see 'em ag'in,
y'know whut she done, Sarh? Kin you guess whut she done?"

"Oh Mary, please, my heart is in my throat with worry.
What did she do, please say what she –"

"She took dat w'ite blanket off o'her own baby, Sarh, her own baby,
an' started wavin' dat blanket way up in de wind. Es high es she kud
reach, Sarh, es high es she kud reach, she was wavin', an' wavin', an'
wavin' dat blanket. An' dat wind was a'whippin', an' dem waves was
a'choppin', an' dere she was standin' on dat sho' jus' wavin', an' wavin'
dat blanket at dem slaves. An' es dat 'lil boat was disappearin', an' she
know'd she'd never see 'em ag'in, it's like dat blanket was callin' t'dem.
Dat blanket was tellin' 'em –"

" – God will protect you!"

"Dat blanket was sayin' –"

" – God will keep you safe!"

"Dat blanket was callin' t'dem –"

" - God will get you to the Promised Land!"

A breathless hush fell on that kitchen. There was no sound now except the soothing lapping of the flames on the logs of the fire. As I lifted my cup again, this time with trembling fingers, my tears fell freely onto my hands.

"Dere's somet'ing else you shud know, Sarh, fu' yo' class.
Y'know de road out by our mailbox?"

"Rural Route 2?"

"Yeah, whar Leonard drives me t'work? Well dat road comes up
frum way, way down yonder pas' Mistuh Clifford's farm,
hundreds o'mile yonder pas' Clifford's farm.
An' it comes up north thruu 'Fearson's land, an' passes Clifford's road,
an' thruu dat 'lil woods, den over dat 'lil stone bridge -"

" - where the migrants crashed?"

"Yeah, whar dey all died. Den is passes dem two houses,
an' den comes up dat 'lil rise –"

" – just before Baxter's hog farm?"

"Dat's right. Den it passes our farm, an' de side o'Zellner's strawber'y
patch, den Greyson's, den passes all dem odder farms,
Wilson's, an' Malcolm's, den Blackwell's,
'til it stops in Maysville."

"Yes?"

"Miss Sarh, b'fo de Civil War, dat road warn't nut'ing bu' two ruts

fu' wagon wheels. Rural Route 2 was jus' two ruts thruu all
dis farm land, bu' dey was famous ruts, fo' sho',
'cause dem two ruts was de main Freedom Trail thruu here."

"The main - the main Freedom - Oh Mary!
The Freedom Trail passed our farm?"

"Dat's righ', Miss Sarh. Dem slaves got on dem two ruts frum way, way
down yonder pas' Clifford's farm, hundreds o'mile 'way,
steppin' intuh dem two muddy ruts in de spring on dere way t'freedom."

"Like Wawalla and the blackberries!"

"Yeah, jus' like my great-granmamma. Jus' like Wawalla steppin' intuh
dem ruts. An' dey walked, an' walked, an' walked up here,
den dey pass'd dat side road dat leads t'Clifford's farm."

"Oh yes! Yes, I see!"

"Den dey hid in dat 'lil woods fu' de day."

"Oh yes, the stream, of course! Water and shelter and shade!"

"Den whin it was dark ag'in, dey crost dat 'lil stone bridge
an' pass'd dat big ol' tree."

"Oh Mary, those slaves knew that tree?
They recognized that tree?"

"Dat's right, Miss Sarh, dat's right.
Dat tree wid dat 'lil bridge was one o'de sign posts on dat road.
Keep breathin', Sarh. I kin see y'ain't breathin' too well."

*"Y - yes, I – I am feeling rather faint.
But please, please go on!"*

"Dey had t'git t'Maysville in one night, 'cause dere warn't no place
t'stop dat was safe 'tween dat bridge an' dat town. Dat's 'bout twelve
er fourteen mile, so dey had t'keep walkin' no madder whut, keep
walkin' in dem muddy ruts. An' den whin dey come'd up dat 'lil rise
b'fo Baxter's, guess whut was de next sign post on de Freedom Road?
Guess whut dey seen? Guess whut dey'd ben tol' t'look fo'?"

*"After Baxter's? Well - there's no distinguishing landmark there.
No trees, or – or stones – or -"*

"Chil', dey was tol' t'look fo' a big w'ite house wid t'ree stories
dat'd be shinin' in de night. Dey was tol' t'look fo' dis house!
Keep breathin', Sarh, keep breathin'. I know how y'git.
An' over dat 'lil rise, de furst t'ing dey wudda seen was yo' bedroom on
dat thurd floor. Yo' bedroom was a sign post on de Freedom Trail!
O chil', doan faint on me, ag'in. Gracious! Keep breathin', Sarh.
Bend over a'bit, git some blood in yo' face.
Keep breathin', chil', 'cause dere's mo'.

"De slaves dat'd come north den east thruu dat back street o'Brueston
met slaves on our Freedom Road, an' dey all walked all dat night toward
Maysville. Dere warn't lights back den, y'know. No lights standin' on
no poles by no gas pumps. No yard lanterns. An' ef dere warn't no
moon, dat was harder fo' dem slaves, 'cause dey kudn't see nut'ing bu'
dat rut b'fo dem. Bu' it was easier fu' dem too whin dere warn't no
moon, 'cause all dem black fo'ks kud disappear in dat black night.
De Lord sho' was a lamp unto dere feet, Sarh, jus' like de Good Book
says, jus' like my preacher says. An' dey had t'keep dere babies quiet in
de dark. An' dey kudn't sing t'keep demselves a'goin'. An' dey kudn't
talk t'courage each odder needer. Dey all had t'be quiet es de grave. An'

ef enybody got sick, he had t'keep walkin', an' ef somebody was too
tired t'keep goin', he had t'keep walkin'. An' ef it rained in de night,
dey all had t'keep walkin', 'cause –"

" – because, oh Mary, because Maysville was the next safe station!"

"Dat's right, 'cause de only safe place aftuh dat bridge
was dem Meth'dist houses in Maysville."

"I – I don't know what to say. I am – well, just speechless!"

"Y'know dem two quilts on yo' bed?"

"Yes, the Monkey Wrench? And the Nine Patch?"

"Yeah. Well Sarh, whin de Freedom Train was comin',
whin de slaves hear'd it was drawin' near,
dey hang'd a Monkey Wrench quilt out a winduh of a cabin,
er over a fence, er over a door, er ev'n spread it on a bush,
so dat quilt 'ud tell all d'odder slaves t'gadder up dere tools,
like dere wrenches, dat dey'd be needin' on de Freedom Trail.
Not jus' wrenches, but t'ings like a 'lil compass, an' odder tools
dey kud use on dere trip north.
Dat's de furst quilt dey hang'd out t'tell evybody t'git redy,
'cause de Freedom Train was a'comin'.
Dat quilt has ben on yo' bed since you was a 'lil chil',
an' you's jus' now findin' out whut dat mean'd.
Dis house was a sign post long ago, an' dat quilt is here now,
so dat Freedom Train mus' be a'comin'."

'Oh Mary, Mary, this is all so – so powerful!
Tremendously powerful! I never knew all this. So incredible."

"Bessie an' Clayton doan know dis needer, I 'spect,
bu' my people do."

"Now I'm almost afraid to ask about the Nine Patch."

"Miss Sarh, in plantation days, all dem 'lil squares was de fe'els
on de plantation. Dat quilt was a map o'de place whar dem slaves
was born. De 'lil green patches was fe'els, maybe woods,
an' blue patches was ponds, an' yelluh kud mean –"

"Oh Mary, I – I never thought of this before.
Slaves born onto a plantation wouldn't have known how to escape!
They had never seen the land beyond their own fields
and their own slave quarters!"

"Dat's right. Dat's 'xactly right. So dey needed a map o'dere home t'git
yonder off dere plantation, an' dat Nine Patch quilt was dere map."

"That's incredible, just incredible."

"My how dem slaves must'a studied dat quilt. An' dem Mastuhs din'
ev'n know whut dere slaves was doin'. Dey just t'ought dey was hangin'
out dere quilt t'air in de breeze. Dem Mastuhs din' know dat dere slaves
was plannin' t'scape, dat dey needed t'know how t'git yonder
off de place whar dey'd all ben born."

"Absolutely ingenious. It really is true, what I've always heard.
If you want to hide something, leave it out in the open.
Deliberately leave it out in the open,
like hanging those quilts over the clothesline."

"Ain't dat de truth. Jus' hang it over a fence.
De hand quiltin' on some Nine Patches looks strange, Sarh.
Sometimes t'ain't ev'n er straight.
Dat was part o'dere map too, tellin' dem slaves t'go 'roun' dis fe'el,
er go 'round a swamp, er go 'round a hill. So dat quiltin' was 'potant
too, tellin' 'em how t'git off dere plantation an' stay safe too.
An' y'know who tol' dem slaves how t'git off dat land?
You kin tell yo' teacher 'bout dis too.
Dere was a blacksmith on dem plantations. He wurked de bellows an'
hammered de iron. My mamma tol' me dat de smith kud hammer
a message in his hammerin', jus' like my people used –"

Like the drums in Africa? Oh Mary, the drums in -

"Dat's righ', Miss Sarh. Like dem drums whar my people come'd from.
An' dat smith kud blow dem bellows wid signals too, jus' like –"

*"- the drums in Africa. Astounding. The slaves heard through wind
and rhythm that the Train was coming. I can't believe I'm hearing
all this, Mary. This is absolutely astounding."*

"Dere's mo', ef ya –"

"Oh please, Mary, yes. Yes!"

"Sometimes a blacksmith was sent t'odder plantations t'do his
blacksmith wurk, so he learn'd 'bout de land 'round his own plantation.
My mamma tol' me he was know'd es *Monkey Wrench.* An' he's de one
who kud tell dem quilters whut de map on de Nine Patch shud be,
'cause he'd seen de land out yonder. Monkey Wrench was know'd
es de smartest man on de plantation –"

"Oh I'm sure, because he knew the land beyond his own,

plus he could deliver the signals through the sounds of his forge
that the Train –"

"- was comin'. Dat's right.
So dat's why dat furst quilt de slaves wudda hang'd out in de air
was de Monkey Wrench. His was de quilt dat said,
'De Freedom Train's a'comin'. Gadder up yo' tools an' git redy.
An' follow de quiltin' on dat Nine Patch, follow de quiltin' o'dem fe'els
an' ponds an' go 'roun' dem swamps
clean 'way frum dis hard land o'slavery."

"Oh Mary, good heavens. This is utterly, utterly fascinating.
I've noticed that on my Monkey Wrench the patches are just
outlined with stitches. There doesn't seem to be any particular pattern.
But on the Nine Patch, the entire quilting pattern is circles.
They're not even interlocking, Mary. Now that I think about it,
I can imagine fields and a pond or two in the color of the patches,
but the quilting is just circles inside circles.
Does that pattern have a meaning?"

Mary's voice suddenly dropped very low.
I leaned toward her so far that our faces were almost touching.

"Dem circles, chil'?" she whispered,
"Dem circles dat doan lead nowhar?
Miss Sarh, dat pattern mus' mean – I guess dat means -
dere ain't no way off dis here plantation."

The scene before me possessed all the charm of a painting of Norman Rockwell. A hoard of children was crowded around the kitchen table, an impressionistic blur of red velvet dresses, tartan vests, and smart little bowties. Four generations of the Clay family had descended upon Mary's kitchen early in the evening for Christmas dinner. It was now about seven o'clock. All the opulent aromas of the feast saturated the air, scents of pineapple and ham, turkey and stuffing, cinnamon and cloves. A cacophony of laughter and loud boisterous talk emanated from the dining room where all the adults were gathered in what little space remained near that colossal pine, devouring the elaborate dinner Mary had prepared that afternoon followed by all the pies we had baked that morning. I heard none of the forced and leaden laughter which I always associated with the Clay daughters. From this distance, it seemed that everyone in that dining room was experiencing all the joy of the season.

I sat in the rocking chair which I had returned to the corner near the window and watched the delicate snow flurries which had begun swirling mid-afternoon. They had never fallen forcefully enough or been large enough to accumulate however. Apparently they arrived in the spirit of the season, to graciously contribute to the soothing atmosphere of the ideal Yule Tide outside as well as inside the home.

Mary sat on her stool in the cactus corner watching the colorful pandemonium before her, patiently waiting to respond obediently to every need. No words had passed between us the remainder of that afternoon. While I had dressed earlier in the attic for dinner, I stood in the window overlooking the lane, gazing down the road toward the little rise beyond Baxter's, then further down the road to MacPhearson's. I was in shock, stunned, speechless, totally in awe that my bedroom, the very window where I was then standing, had long ago been a signpost on the Freedom Trail, that run-away slaves trudging up and over that little rise would have seen the third floor of our farmhouse as a white beacon in the night. Apparently, if not beyond all doubt, this home had never been a station for those fugitives, never been a safe harbor for the weary and destitute, but it had been a symbol of hope that safety was only a few more miles away. Keep walking in those ruts, Wawalla, keep trudging. Step off the gravel into your rut and keep going at all costs. Ignore the exhaustion in your legs; ignore the pain in your feet. Ignore the weather and the pelting spring rains. Ignore even the terror of the white man in your heart. Just keep walking in your rut, Wawalla. Just keep walking through the night, because safe harbor is only a few more weary miles away. After all my study of the greatest classics of world literature, after delving deeply into the grandest poetry of the Western world, after earnest exploration of some of the greatest minds humanity has ever produced, I could not label the emotion I was feeling about our conversation that morning. All I was feeling was dumb shock.

That evening in the kitchen though, my thoughts continued to flow about the Christmas customs our class had studied which had been practiced on the various plantations in antebellum days. Most slaves had no conception of what Christmas even meant in the white world. African religious traditions were predominantly oral rather than scriptural; Christmas though was based upon a written tradition. Besides, literacy was actively suppressed among slave populations, and indeed was even considered by slave owners to be a serious threat to their own safety. How dangerous it would have been for white owners to encourage their subjects to learn that in the very country where Africans had been enslaved, the Constitution guaranteed that *all men* without exception were indeed *created equal.*

So rather than a religious holiday, Christmas for millions of slaves was a period of rest, usually of three days, in which no work was demanded. Christmas Eve, Christmas day, and the day following were referred to simply as *the three days of Christmas*, without reference to their religious meaning. I realized then with yet another shock, that this custom of a century ago was not fulfilled in Mary's life. She had worked yesterday, worked today on Christmas Eve, and though she would undoubtedly spend Christmas Day in the company of her loved ones in Brueston, she would be back to work again on December 26. The three day cessation of labor for this slave simply did not apply.

It was also customary for slaves to receive from their owners new clothing and new shoes on Christmas Day. But not so for my dearest friend. I couldn't bear to think that on the other side of the wood stove sat a seventy year old woman still wearing the same safety-pin dress, the same blackberry-gathering knee socks, and the same dirty safety-pin sneakers she had worn when I was a child. The only new clothes for her were two hideously oversized sweatshirts. When I realized that not even the most rudimentary customs of compassion observed during the days of the antebellum South were fulfilled in Mary's life, my emotions resurrected.

Disgust welled up in me that there was no indication at all on Bluebonnet that the Civil Rights Movement was blasting through this country like a hurricane. Not one single eddy of that mighty gale had wafted over the domain of Clayton Clay. None of the greatest marches and none of the great leaders were even mentioned here. It was as though all the racial unrest of the sixties simply did not exist. Bluebonnet, north of the Mason-Dixon Line, was steadfastly immune to change, firmly anchored in the South's failed Reconstruction Era. Racism here was not only accepted as irrefutable truth, but was a comfortable and self-serving truth! It was almost as though the Emancipation Proclamation for Mary had never been signed. My disgust plunged into outrage.

At that moment, a strange silver-white light suddenly glared from the dining room, a blinding light which cast a brutal harshness onto the two steps and down the short hallway toward me. All talk in that room suddenly ceased as Frank switched on his home movie camera with multiple bulbs along each side of the lens.

"*Come on in here, Colored Mary,*" Elaine shouted.
"*Clayton has a Christmas bonus for you!*"

"Hurry on in here, Colored Mary," shouted Mr. Clay.

"*Hey, Colored Mary, come on in!*
Hurry up. Frank wants to take your picture.
Daddy has another twenty dollar bill for you!"

I went rigid as I always did as a child when the racial stressor was overwhelming. I stared mesmerized at that Christmas light, my eyes magnetized toward that light, my neck at one with my spine, my whole body one solid inflexible beam. What a crushing degradation, what a massive humiliation Mary would now be forced to endure at the hands of this hateful family. I was appalled once again, *horrified* once again at the shameful racism of these supreme bigots. There is no humiliation greater than that which is thinly disguised as generosity.

As ever louder demands emanated from the dining room, Mary did not stir from her stool. Even if I had been able to move, I could not have forced myself to turn in her direction. Both of us must have been staring toward that ugly garish light, both thinking similar thoughts.

"Come on, Colored Mary! Frank only has so much film!"

I suddenly realized that if I didn't leave that kitchen quickly, I'd be forced to witness yet another moment of shame in Mary's long history of humiliations. In an instant, a surge of energizing power shot up my spine. I kicked off my heels, picked them up, ran down the short hallway to the stairway, threw open the door, and ran up both flights of steps to the attic. In a shaking fit of murderous rage, I threw my heels across the room toward the window near the lane, fell down on my bed, pulled up both my quilts, and sobbed.

THE FREEDOM TRAIN

De Gospel's train's a'comin'!
I hear it just at hand!
I hear de car wheels rumblin'
An' rollin' thruu dis land!
De fare is cheap an' all kin go
De rich an' po' all dere
No secund class aboard dis train
No diffunce in de fare.

It was my twentieth summer on the farm. Though I was no longer legally obligated to spend three months each year on Bluebonnet, I asked Frank and Elaine if they could pick me up from the university to spend yet another summer with Mary. That was the year of prolonged spring rains. Fields which had been planted were waiting to be replanted, and others which were never planted were still bare. When we passed Sanford's wispy asparagus farm, it was sadly evident that many of those ethereal plants from long ago had rotted in their rows. I was delighted though to see the slightly altered sign on the outdoor market across the road, which now read *'Henry' Porter's Vegetable Stand.*

When we turned onto Rural Route 2, Elaine commented as always about the fresh diapers on Blackwell's line, but the new baby was a new grandchild added to their ever expanding collection, and when we passed Malcolm's place, Elaine commented as always about the cows electrocuted long ago in their pasture stream. It was true as always that it had rained the previous evening, and the stream near Wilson's was swollen, but as always, the late afternoon sun was aglow when we turned into the lane.

How much that paradise had deteriorated. Bessie's eyesight had increasingly faltered until now, it threatened to fail altogether, some degenerative condition which neither surgery nor glasses could correct. That increasing physical loss plus the disadvantage of age and advanced arthritis had brought her talents as a consummate perennial gardener to a full stop.   The iris near the mailbox which used to edge the western boundary had dwindled to the point that only three feeble leaves separated by great tall clumps of various weeds provided the only memory that their formal aristocracy had once reined proudly there. Three thin stems arising from those leaves had bravely attempted to bloom, but apparently those regal promises had rotted in the bud. The mimosa which had struggled with bag worms for over a decade had finally succumbed, and the wagon wheels upon which Bessie had twined her most prized yellow roses lay overturned, the canes bravely attempting to sprout upward through the spokes. The perennials had been left so long unattended that many had simply died out, and I noticed with a sudden pain in my heart that the tall purples, daisies, and little mounds of little yellows were no more.

When Frank parked the car as always near the spirea, Miss Bess was sitting as always in the same rocker in the same place on the side porch, her white hair, which was occasionally blue, still piled on top her head in a thinner, smaller bun.

"We made good time, Bessie.
Seventeen hours again. So much rain this spring!"

"Oh Laine, like nothing we've ever seen before!
Clayton said a few acres by Ben Glacie's took hold,
but all the others will need to be replanted late."

"What happened to the little red barn?
I see there it's just a pile of boards."

"Oh Laine, one night when Clayton was out ridin' the roads again,
I heard a sound like a tornado racing through here.

*I couldn't see anything from the bedroom window,
but the next morning, Colored Mary told me that barn
had given up the ghost. Just fell over after all these years.
Sure sounded like a great swoosh, Laine, so loud,
like a tornado was comin' through."*

Though there is no grief quite like the death of a garden, I felt an even deeper grief about the death of my echo-bird. Hopefully, I thought, as I would have reassured myself as a child long ago, he has flown far away to a better home.

As always I gave Bessie nothing more than a polite kiss, then stood at the screen door. It was evident that Frank had futilely repaired it ever so long ago, because two more holes now neighbored his original patch. Peering as always through that kitchen, I saw the tall cupboard upon which stood Mary's silver cake-saver. As Bessie and Elaine endlessly gossiped, and Frank as always sat mute, I reverently opened the door -

Squeeeek

and closed it silently.

Though the garden had succumbed to the ravishes of time and neglect, the farmhouse itself had stood so long precariously balanced on that cliff between deterioration and total collapse that it apparently had achieved a comfortable equilibrium there. The ragged dirty cellophane over the sink and stove and the battered linoleum, which Mary said displayed no difference between the good floor and the bad dirt, appeared in the same state as previous years. The cacti continued to struggle feebly in the shade of that colossal elm, and the philodrendon, which twined around the chipped frame of the window facing the lane, was now nothing more than an endless twining of stems. My cake with chocolate frosting was decorated with those pink sugar flowers from

Sloane's, and on the top step near the cacti, I noted that the new issue of the Montgomery Ward catalog was patiently waiting for Mary and me.

As I stood at that kitchen table cutting four slices of cake, pouring four glasses of iced tea, and listening to the conversation emanating from that side porch, I realized that Bessie had outgrown her status as a comic figure, and instead had evolved into a tragic character. Unable to see more than a few feet in front of her, she gazed down that long avenue of her front garden imagining it bloomed with all the effulgence of previous years. Despite the mixed feelings I had always had for that woman, my heart broke to hear the words wafting through that dirty screen -

"Oh Laine, I wish you could have seen my iris last month.
I didn't get a chance to go down there myself,
but Colored Mary said she was sorry the State Fair happened
in August, because this year, if it had been held in May,
my iris would have won a blue ribbon.
Oh yeah, Laine, she said first prize!
And when Detsie Sanford brought over my Avon last week,
she said my yellow roses on that wagon wheel were so pretty.
And even Ida Mae, when she brought over
some more of her macaroni salad –
Doesn't she make the best macaroni salad –
she said those tall purples were 'Glorious.'
That was the very word she used. She said, 'Glorious.'
I guess all the rain we've been having made everything bloom
even more. I wouldn't have thought that, but apparently it did.

So I'm sure my mimosa won't have those bag worms this year.

With all that rain, I'm sure they won't come back.

And to think that Colored Mary said a blue ribbon for those iris.

Just proves even niggers know beauty when they see it."

I realized then that this summer could very well be the most painful summer I had ever spent on Bluebonnet - the garden in conspicuous decay, Clayton's fields still barren, the old racial attitudes still pervasive, and a crippled woman now nearly blind living totally in the past. As I backed into the screen carrying that tray of plates and glasses, I had no idea that the pain in my heart was just beginning.

Squeeeek

SLAM!

"Miss Bess?

I couldn't help overhearing the conversation about your iris!"

"Oh yeah, Sarah. State Fair is what she said.

And Ida Mae – you know Ida – she said 'Glorious'

That was the very word she used. She said 'Glorious.'"

It was merciful that Bessie's vision was so limited that she couldn't see the tears in Elaine's and my eyes.

The next morning, I found to my great relief that Mary was still the same. When I rounded the bend by the stove, there she was, standing at her perennial place at the sink, her hair still coal black, her dress still gleaming with safety pins. She looked up with radiant eyes and said simply through a broad smile, "Mo'nin', Miss Sarh." I answered through an equally broad smile, *"Nice to see you too, Miss Mary."*

All that morning, Bessie sat in that huge rocker by the window, viciously swatting any fly which landed close enough for her to see. Conversation focused as always on the latest gossip, about who had married, who was having babies, who had died, and about the guests we were about to receive. Henry and Florencie were bringing Henrietta and Little Ike for dinner.

As the noon hour approached, and Mary, Elaine, and I prepared the meal, Elaine asked –

"Bessie, how old is Henrietta by now?"

"Land sakes, Laine, let me think.
Sarah, how old were you when Henrietta was born?"

"Oh, let me see. That was so long ago.
I think – Was that - Yes. That was the year after the –
and the year before the – I was six then. Yes, I was six.
So that would make Henrietta fourteen or fifteen?
Gracious Bessie, how that time has flown!"

"You know, Sarah," Bessie continued, *"Florencie set up a real nice*
beauty shop on that nice piece of land that Ike Porter gave them.
Nice piece of land those five acres. You remember Grace,
her mother? Well, she doesn't do hair anymore.
I begged her to keep her shop open. I said, 'Grace, can't you do just
one head?' But she said she had given all her hair stuff to Florencie.

So now they just use that old trailer for storage. Florencie has a real
nice little business, so close to Maysville and all.
Clayton drives me there once a month to get that rinse put on my hair.
She does a real nice job, Florencie does. A real nice job."

"Miss Bess, I'm glad to hear they are doing so well.
Seeing the new sign on the outdoor market made me feel so good.
It will be nice to see them again."

"Laine, how are we going to fit so many people round this table?
How many will there be? I'm thinking thirteen."

"Well Bessie, that sounds about right.
You and Clayton, Frank and me, then Sarah, then the four of them,
and Palmer, Winston, Marvin, and that new one –
I can never remember his name.
Well, doesn't that make thirteen?"

"Land sakes, Laine, we'll just have to squeeze us all in, I guess.
Oh Sarah, could you take these bills down to the mailbox?
I almost forgot. Clayton wanted them mailed today.
Early this morning, he said, while we were still upstairs, he said,
'Bess, make sure somebody mails these bills today.'
One's for the broker and another for Doc Dobson.
He was here last week. One of Clayton's cows has mastitis again.
so Doc came over after he gave those shots to Anderson's herd.

Guess I was thinking more about this dinner than about his bills. If you could do that, Sarah? Those right there on Clayton's desk."

On my way to the mailbox, how desolate the garden appeared. I couldn't bear walking through the weedy grass, so I walked down the wide gravel lane. Memories of the effulgence and glorious scents of previous summers mercifully lightened my heart, because the present scene of exhausted perennials and barren fields was decidedly bleak. When I returned to the porch, I stepped up the two concrete steps and over the still-slanted floorboard. Then when I opened the screen -

Squeeeek

I stopped abruptly and stared!

Mary rushed over to me and whispered -

"Sarh? Sarh, close de screen. Close it.
Here, lemme close it fu' you."

Squeeeek

"You was lettin' in dem flies,
an' you 'member how dem bees jus' live on dat screen."

"Wh – What? Wh -Why is –"

Mary took hold of my sleeve and ushered me into the short hall between the kitchen and the dining room, then whispered –

"She cain't do no mo'en dat, Sarh.
So Laine an' I t'ought dis ud be good.
It ain't safe fu' her t'be in dis here kitchen nohow,
so she cain't cook no mo'.

346

She cain't see very far in front o'her, y'know,
an' her hands is so crippled,
she cain't car'y not'ing heavier den one plate at a time.
So dat's whut she's doin', Sarh,
settin' de table jus' car'yin' one plate at a time.
O my, ain't dat sad. She's got ol' so quick.
Look, she's jus' shufflin' back an' forth
'tween de table an' dat blue-willuh china cupboard.
Jus' shufflin', Sarh – so careful – jus' like a 'lil chil'.
I know, Sarh, I know dis is hard fu' you t'see.
Real hard fo' you t'see, but it's gonna all be right. It really is.
You 'member dat, Miss Sarh. You jus' keep dat in yo' heart –
it's all gonna be alright. I kin 'mos' hear her t'inking -
'Dis un is fu' Winston. I's gonna put dis un here,
an' whin I gits done, I's gonna –' O look, Sarh, ain't dat somet'ing.
Now she's shufflin' over t'de silverware drawer.
She knows she's safe ef she kin car'y one settin' at a time.
Jus' one t'ing at a time. She's gittin' mo' crippled evy day.
O Miss Sarh, po' Sarh. I kin tell y'ain't doin' too well,
An' – O no - Henry's car is pullin' up.
Why doan y'go intuh dat frunt parlor an' jus' cry fo' a time.
Dat 'ud do y'good. You doan has t'wor'y 'bout nut'ing, Miss Sarh.
It's gonna be alright. Doan shuu wor'y. It's gonna be alright."

"She – she's only set twelve, Mary.
There's – there's only twelve plates on the table."

"O yeah, I kin see dat now. She must a'fugot we was –"

"Don't bother her, Mary. Please. Please don't.
I - I'll just grab a plate and sit at the old wood stove with you."

Mary and I were sitting on that little step playing Preacher's Wife. The new Montgomery Ward catalog lay open in Mary's lap. The style of dress then was the minimalism of the sixties, but for the sake of the comfort that innocent ritual provided, I was planning to choose the gaudiest prints, and of course, sparkle buttons and bows.

"I remember the rules about this game, Mary.
Only one dress from my own page,
and I have to remember, because I can't look back."

Mary chuckled and said, "Dat's right, Miss Sarh. You 'membered."

"I remember the rules about Preacher's Wife,
and now I can carry the pitchfork,
but I still can't peel a potato in one long elegant spiral."

I chuckled too,
then shook my head from side to side as though I were saying 'No.'

"Frankly Mary, I think that metal rod in your arm
gives you an unfair advantage."

Mary laughed.
"Maybe you's righ', Sarh. Maybe you's right.
Dere ain't miny 'vantages in dis world. Dat's fo' sho'.
But dere is some, Miss Sarh. Dere is some."

"There's something I've always wanted to ask you.
Oh that's an unusual collar, buttoning off to the side.
Don't like that subdued print though. Maybe in a brighter color.
When did I first come here, Mary? I don't –"

"You was only one year ol'. Jus' a 'lil t'ing you was.
You stayed righ' shere dat summer fo' de furst time.
Frank an' Laine brung you, an' I stayed righ' shere all dat summer."

"You? You stayed with me? But I would have thought –"

"Frank an' Laine went 'way dat summer. I fugit whar.
Dey dropped you off an' left aftuh a few days. So I stayed righ' shere.
O ain't dat a purdy dress. All dem ruffles an' lace. Gracious!
Whar wud enybody git t'wear somet'ing like dat?"

*"Good heavens, Mary, I don't know. Buckingham Palace?
Certainly nowhere you and I would go."*

"You know in dat sto'room 'crost frum yo' room,
dere's dat ol' playpen? Y'ever seen dat?"

"Oh many times. Near those stacks of magazines."

"Yeah. I set dat up righ' shere by deez here steps in dis cactus corner
righ' shere, an' you played in dat, chewin' on dem slats,
an' chewin' on yo' po' doll, an' bangin' wid my wooden spoon.
Den whin it got too hot in dis kitchen, you'd start mo'nin' jus' like
de kittens o'Miss Bessie's ol' tabbie cat, an' den I'd car'y y'down
t'de end o'dat lane, down whar de iris ust t'be,
an' we'd sit in de grass in de shade an' let you feel all dem breezes
blowin' off o'dem fields. I'd car'y you over t'smell dem roses,
an' hol' you up so you kud see dem cows.
Gracious, how you loved t'talk t'dem cows!
We had an' ol' high chair back den. T'ink one o'dem Clay girls took it.
Bu' back den you sat in dat, jus' like you b'longed at de big table
wid all de big fo'ks, bangin' yo' spoon on de tray an' puttin' mashed
tatters in yo' hair. I t'ink you kud eat mashed tatters evy day
ev'n back den."

"Isn't that funny. Some things never change.
Who stayed with me at night?
Did Bessie and Clayton – were they –"

"I stayed righ' shere all dat summer."

"You? You did? That – that entire summer?"

"O yeah, Miss Sarh. You an' me was righ' shere all summer long,
evy day. Dat ol' washin' 'sheen got a wurkout, dat's fo' sho'."

"I bet! And where did I sleep?"

"O you was in dat double bed whar Frank an' Laine is now."

"And where did you sleep?"

"O dere's 'nudder prudy un, Sarh,
an' it has dem buttons y'al'ys liked. An' –"

"Where did you sleep, Mary?"

"You al'ys called 'em 'sparkle buttons.' You used t'say –"

"Mary? Where – where did you –"

"I – well - I – I slept on de floor, Miss Sarh."

"The floor? Every night on the – the floor?
Why?
Why on earth did you sleep on the floor?"

"Sarh?"
she whispered, as though hoping her words would not be heard –

"Sarh, you know– you know, hun, dat you is my chil'.
But t'ain't fittin' fu' no w'ite chil' t'git too close to a nigger.
Well, I got's t'git back ta – ta – Sarh?...Sarh?...
Chil', is you alright? Y'ain't lookin' too good ag'in.
Sarh, whar's y'goin'? You doan wanna play no mo'?
You doan wanna play Preacher's -
Careful, chil'! You's 'bout t'back intuh de –
You's 'bout t'trip over dat – **Sarh!** Did you hurt yuse'f?
Is you alright? *SARH!* Did you hurt –
You doan has t'run down dat lane. You ain't 'lil no mo'.
Chil', please doan run down dat lane no –"

Squeeeek
"MIND DAT FLOORBOARD!"

SLAM!

Mary rushed to the battered door, and called to me -

"Sarh, dere y'go runnin' jus' like a 'lil girl ag'in?
Chil', you's ol' 'nough not t'be runnin' 'way no mo.'
O chil', doan fall on dem stones.
Some stones in dat lane is sharp! O Sarh! – **SARH!**
O no, y'done fall'd ag'in?
DID YOU HURT YUSE'F?
SARH? *SARH!* **DID YOU HURT YUSE'F?**
STOP DAT RUNNIN' CHIL'! STOP DAT!
STOP, ER YOU'S GONNA HURT YUSE'F AG'IN!"

I didn't just run down the lane. I ran down to the mailbox, then back up through the dying perennials, then back down to the mailbox, then back up by the cow pasture, then back down to the weedy iris, crisscrossing that garden up and down and left and right, passing and circling every shrub I had loved for so long.

When my raw rage was too exhausted to run anymore, I fell down under the fir tree and shouted upward through those indomitable boughs -

"WHY ARE THE ONLY POINTS OF COLOR IN THIS WHOLE DAMN GARDEN THESE HOLLYS' DROPS OF BLOOD?"

De hammer keeps a'ringin' on somebody's coffin
De hammer keeps a'ringin' on somebody's coffin
De hammer keeps a'ringin' on somebody's coffin
Makes me know dat my time ain't long

De hearse wheel's rollin' somebody t'de graveyard
De hearse wheel's rollin' somebody t'de graveyard
De hearse wheel's rollin' somebody t'de graveyard
Makes me know dat my time ain't long

For the remainder of that summer, a strange quiet descended upon Bluebonnet. The men worked far from the house, replowing and replanting the fields. Bessie always slept late, always went to bed early, and after dinner took a long nap on her new antique sofa. Frank and Elaine took several sight-seeing trips to various historic landmarks, and as much as I would have loved to see battlefields from the Civil War and the homes of the Early American Fathers, I spent most of my time on that front porch of columns studying the complete Greek tragedies which were required for my world literature classes in the fall. No jelly jars holding roses in every conceivable stage of decomposition lined up like soldiers on every flat surface of the house, and I noted that the Mongomery Ward catalog had mysteriously disappeared. I continued to correspond with my childhood friends, Katie and Mimi, and sent long letters to Mother Agnes and Sister Martha who always loved to hear stories about the farm. The latest one though was filled with exclamation marks and underlines, and began with these inflammatory sentences –

Dear Sister,

It is my understanding that this planet holds billions of acres. How then can these meager one-thousand be so <u>insular</u>! so <u>arrogantly immune</u>! so <u>steadfastly anchored</u> in the past as to resist such a massive movement as racial equality sweeping the land! The only things that change on Bluebonnet are weather and more safety pins!

After dinner that day, I mailed my letter then walked back to the side porch. I could see through the screen that all the men had returned to the fields, Frank and Elaine had left for the week, and Bessie had apparently shuffled to her front parlor for her nap. The kitchen table still stood littered with the remains of lunch, and Mary, quite to my surprise, was still sitting on her stool. I opened the screen and closed it silently. The expression on her face startled me! Her eyes were staring wide open as though she were an image from an ancient mystery cult, and she sat as still as stone.

I was almost afraid to address her, since she seemed as riveted as the Nuns in prayer. But after a moment, I dared to whisper –

"Mary?"

When I received no answer, I said somewhat louder –

"Mary, is – is something wrong? Is something wrong?"

She continued to stare into space as though her gaze were fastened upon another dimension. Though I wanted to respect her meditation, I risked a third –

"Mary, are you all right?"

She slowly pulled herself away from that psychic state and focused her gaze upon me. Her voice was so low, it was very nearly inaudible, and her words were articulated with great effort -

"I's finely – finely piecin' dis all – all tuhgether.
Yeah. Yeah. I's finely seein' whut I kudn't see b'fo'."

Her voice was hushed, every word carefully chosen, each conveying a dark meaning far beyond my comprehension.

"What?"

I whispered, moving slowly closer to her –

"What are - What are you seeing?
Mary, you look so – so - Are you sure you're all right?"

"It was dat dog, Sarh. It was dat dog. I din' see dat b'fo'.
Yeah. Ain't dat somet'ing! It all begun wid dat dog.
Now – now I see. Yeah, I finely see. Yeah."

"What are you talking about, Mary? What dog?"

I eagerly pulled up a chair and sat down beside her at the old wood stove. She turned again toward me, and spoke in a slow solemn whisper –

"Dem daffodils, yeah, at dat daffodil time.
It was whin dem daffodils was a'bloomin', Sarh.

354

I come'd outta my trailer, an' dere was a dog
jus' layin' dere on his back."

"Oh dear, was it dead? Mary, was it dead?"

"No, no. O no, he warn't no dead, Sarh. He was just a'laying dere."

"He was probably just scratching his back.
You know how dogs like to –"

"An' den – Yeah, now I see. In de baffroom it was.
I was a'washin' dat 'lil mirror I keep in our baffroom,
an' dat slipped outta my hand an' den fall'd in de sink."

"Oh that's so easy to do in the bathroom.
When my hands get wet, they –"

"An' den whin I picked it up, Sarh, I kudn't see myse'f no mo'."

"Oh the back probably broke, Mary, when it hit the floor.
It's the back that makes mirrors able to reflect an image."

Her hushed voice continued with increasing wonder –

"An' den I planted collards right aftuh de las' snow,
an' dey all got wash'd 'way b'fo' we kud eat 'em."

"Yes, I know how hard it rained here this spring. Elaine told me.
I know even where I live, it rained so –"

"An' now – jus' now, whin I picked up dat dere glass,

it done broke'd in my hand."

"Oh Mary! Did it cut your –"

"It was just in my hand. I was jus' holdin' it in my –
an' it done broke'd.
My skin here ain't ev'n broke, bu' dat glass dere is in pieces."

"Oh my! I see. Well, I'll clean that up.
I'm glad you didn't cut your -"

"An' now, jus' sittin' here now, my righ' foot is a'itchin'.
Just a'itchin'.
So – so yeah. Yeah. Now I know. I know now.
Yeah. I know now. Yeah, I see."

"Mary, you're – you're scaring me.
Know what, Mary? What do you know?"

I leaned forward toward her as though hoping the lessening of
that meager physical distance would enable me to understand her words
whispered from an ethereal world far away -

"Dey's gittin' redy fu' me, Sarh. I knows dat now.
Dey's gittin' redy. Yeah, now I see.
Shud a'know'd, Sarh. Shud a'knowed dat b'fo', but I jus' din' see it.
But I see it now. Now I does. Dey's a'comin'."

Though I intuited the meaning of her enigmatic speech, I
shuddered to believe. I *refused* to believe! So I whispered as though in
total ignorance –

"Who - Who's getting ready, Mary? Who's coming?"

"Listen, Sarh…Listen…Is you hearin' dat?…
Listen, chil'…O listen…Dere it is ag'in.
Comin'…yeah, comin' frum so far 'way…Listen…
Kin y'hear dat breeze?…Kin y'hear dat breeze thruu dat fir tree?
O Sarh…O chil', dey's callin' me.
Dey's callin' me in dat wind, chil', an' I got's t'git redy too."

"Oh Mary, please, please don't. That - that's just superstition.
Putting two plus two together and coming up with five –
the meaning always totaling more that the sum of its parts.
They're just superstitions, Mary. Like that painting falling off
the wall when those Mexicans crashed.
Surely you don't believe those old wives' tales.
Everything you listed can be explained by –"

"I's de one dat tol' Miss Bess whut dat fallin' mean'd.
I's de one dat know'd dey all died. I's de one dat know'd."

Then I remembered Mary's face as she stood at that dirty screen
door fourteen years ago, gazing across those fields toward the mirage
where the crash had taken place. Her face then, I remembered, bore the
same haunted expression as today.

"My people knows t'ings w'ite fo'ks doan know.
My people knows de truth. Dey's al'ys done know'd de truth.
Dat's de truth mos' w'ite foks doan never know'd.
Bu' my people knows de truth."

My heart firmly resistant to the thought of her death, my mind
attempting to dispell the cloud of gloom that had pervaded the kitchen,
I announced rather brusquely –

"I'm cleaning up that glass."

Mary resumed her far away look,
and spoke once again in hushed tones –

"You gadder up dem pieces, Sarh, an' put'em in a bag fo' me."

"The glass? Pieces of glass? Gracious!
What on earth for, Mary? This is all so strange."

"So dey know whar t'find me, chil'. So dey know.
My people cain't 'ford no grave stones. Broke t'ings is all we got's.
You save dem broke pieces fu' me, chil'.
Den dey knows whar t'find me.
Whin dey comes, dey kin see."

The following morning as I was cleaning up after breakfast, a
blue-willow plate slipped out of my hand and broke in half on the floor.

"Gracious! This crockery is so old.
After all these years of repeated use, it simply needs to be replaced.
When Frank and Elaine get back, I'm going to suggest –"

"Dat's good, Sarh," Mary whispered once again.
"Dat's real, real good."

As we both knelt down,
I noted that the plate had broken into two perfect halves.

"Look, Mary. It's almost – almost as if we could –
Well, with a little bit of glue, it would be one whole again."

"Keep dat plate in pieces, Sarh, jus' es dey is.
Dat's good. Dat's real, real good.
I kin see dat on my – my – wid dem odder –
Yeah, dat's good. Dat's real, real good.
You gadder up both dem pieces too, an' put 'em wid dat glass."

I stifled my feelings for the first time in my life, because I knew that Mary was standing at *the very sill of the door of death.* Words from Melville's *Moby Dick* haunted me, because Queequeg, sensing death was near, appeared to Ishmael as Mary appeared to me now.

And like circles on the water, which, as they grow fainter, expand; so his eyes seemed rounding and rounding, like the rings of Eternity. An awe that cannot be named would steal over you as you sat by the side of this waning savage, and saw...strange things in his face... For whatever is truly wondrous and fearful in man, never yet was put into words or books. And the drawing near of Death, which alike levels all, alike impresses all with a last revelation.

It was the last week of August. I was to return to the university in four days. The temperature had climbed so high that heat lightning once again seared the sky in fantastic displays above the pasture's lonely chimney and the ruins of the echo-bird barn. I sat once again on that front porch of columns studying Sophocles' *Oedipus at Colonus.* Despite the heat, an eerie chill crept up my spine when I realized the parallels between Mary's life and what I read on the pages before me, parallels which were to be further fulfilled as the afternoon progressed. Oedipus, after his excruciating life of shame, persecution, and profound disgrace, had been summoned *to die by long continued thunder, the massive lightning hurled from the hand that never knew defeat.* Called by that *pressing summons* to which Oedipus could *delay no more,* he came to *the steep road, rooted in earth by brazen steps,* then in his *filthy robes,* finally sat down to die. The sense of impending death pervading the last few weeks, now mirrored in this required reading, so upset me that I put that play down on the porch and walked into the kitchen for more tea, lemon slices, and ice.

Mary was sitting alone on her stool, her eyes wide and staring again, as though she had seen *some deadly terror* her sight could not endure.

"Mary? Mary!

I was wondering if you would like to join me on the side porch.

We could have some tea and – and just talk about –

well, just old times when you and I used to -"

But she interrupted me in that same distant voice
which was beginning to unnerve me -

"We got's 'nough cold roast fu' supper."

"Oh certainly, Mary. There's plenty left from –"

"Doan need t'work no mo'."

"No. No need. I'll just slice some tomatoes at the last min –"

"So we kin go up in dat attic an' play wid dat train."

"Play with Palmer's train? Now? In this heat?

Mary, at this time of day, my bedroom is an oven!

And the thought of your climbing three flights of steps is –

Please, couldn't we just have some tea on the side porch,

and maybe talk about long ago when we used to –"

But before I finished my question, she rose from her stool soundless as a shade, passed silently through the kitchen, and entered the short hallway near where I was standing by the stove. I followed her as she unexpectedly passed the door to the back stairway which before today, we had always climbed together. She proceeded up the two steps, glided across the dining room, and entered that grand central hallway. Slanting shafts of light from the late afternoon sun, piercing the fir tree's solemn boughs, glittered through the hexagonal cut-glass facets of those panels framing that massive front door, casting hundreds of shimmering miniature rainbows of hope onto the staircase and walls. The walnut wood shown in polished gleam in that benevolent light.

Mary grasped that massive wooden coil at the base of that banister, and despite my protestations, began slowly, carefully, to pull herself up each step, spindle by spindle. Her safety pins flashed forth iridescent sparkles, and I heard her speaking as in a dream -

"Stay close t'me, chil'. Jus' drag dat basket an' stay close t'me.
Dey's al'ys be snakes, yung'in. Snakes all o'er dis here place.
Bu' doan shuu mind none, Sarh. Doan shuu mind."

I instinctively reached out and took hold of Mary's hem
as we climbed the white folks steps together.

Bowed by the weight of centuries he leans
Upon his hoe and gazes on the ground,
The emptiness of ages in his face,
And on his back the burden of the world.
Who made him dead to rapture and despair,
A thing that grieves not and that never hopes.
Stolid and stunned, a brother to the ox?
Who loosened and let down this brutal jaw?
Whose was the hand that slanted back this brow?
Whose breath blew out the light within his brain?

"Miss Bess was upset wid me dis mo'nin',

'cause I done fugot we doan has no mo' bread."

"Please – please don't worry about anything, Mary, please.
I'm right here. I'm holding your dress. Can you feel that?"

"I kin feel dat, chil'. I kin. Jus' hold ontuh me."

Is this the Thing the Lord God made and gave
To have dominion over sea and land;
To trace the stars and search the heavens for power;
To feel the passion of Eternity?
Is this the dream He dreamed who shaped the suns
And marked their ways upon the ancient deep?
Down all the caverns of Hell to their last gulf
There is no shape more terrible than this-
More tongued with cries against the world's blind greed-
More filled with signs and portents for the soul –
More packed with danger to the universe.

Her voice so etheral, almost disembodied -
"O chil', I hear you's cryin' ag'in. Whut's my gonna do wid shuu?"

"D - Don't - don't you mind, Mary, please.
Please - I - I just have something in my eye."

"You kin be happy, Miss Sarh. You kin be happy.
You's gittin' all dat book learnin' in yo' sparkle dresses."

What gulfs between him and the seraphim!
Slave of the wheel of labor, what to him
Are Plato and the swing of the Pleiades?
What the long reaches of the peaks of song,
The rift of dawn, the redding of the rose?

Through this dead shape the suffering ages look;
Time's tragedy is in that aching stoop;
Through this dread shape humanity betrayed,
Plundered, profaned and disinherited,
Cries protest to the Powers that made the world,
A protest that is also a prophecy.

"I still ain't hearin' no smiles, yung'in.
Y'got's such a purdy smile whin you's happy."

"I – I'll be all right Mary, if I – if I hold onto –"

"You watch dat floorboard, y'hear?
I doan know why Mistuh Clay doan nail dat durn t'ing down,
by all dem purdy roses an' dem 'lil hummin' birds."

O masters, lords and rulers in all lands,
Is this the handiwork you give to God,
This monstrous thing distorted and soul quenched?
How will you ever straighten up this shape;
Touch it again with immortality;
Rebuild in it the music and the dream;
Make right the immortal infamies,
Perfidious wrongs, immedicable woes?

"Sarh, t'ain't fittin' t'hear such cryin' frum a purdy w'ite chil'.
You ain't 'lil no mo'. How's we gonna pick dis cotton ef you's cryin'?
Mistuh Clay, he be so mad ef we doan cut dis sugar cane."

O masters, lords and rulers of all lands,
How will the future reckon with this man?
How answer his brute question in that hour
When whirlwinds of rebellion shake all shores?
How will it be with kingdoms and with kings–

With those who shaped him to the thing he is-
When this dumb Terror shall rise to judge the world,
After the silence of the centuries?

We entered my attic room. My childhood chair still sat meekly by the fir tree window where I had observed Leonard's headlights approach through the fog. My cardboard altar box still stood in the corner with an empty jelly jar waiting for its faded rose. My Monkey Wrench and Nine Patch were still folded at the foot of my bed. Mary sat down on the floor by Palmer's childhood train. Her gnarled hands began to move that little engine slowly around its miniature track…past the tiny pine trees…past the tiny maples…and her voice softly…slowly hummed the tune –

"Git on board…'lil chil'n…
Git on board…'lil chil'n…
Git on board…'lil chil'n…
Dere's room fo' miny a'mo'."

I stood at the window overlooking the lane and through my tears saw the heat sizzling up off the tin roof of the side porch. I watched the Mexican migrants in the potato field across the lane, their colorful clothing gracing those ruts as brushstrokes of paint on a canvas of green. Despite the late planting, Bluebonnet had once again produced a bountiful crop, as though that dirt had long ago forgotten such a thing as *crop failure*. I remembered the migrants' tiny leaning house, and I remembered those vicious attack dogs. I remembered those pitch forks standing in that great expanse of straw, and I remembered their rosary tree. And I realized once again, as I realized long ago, that I was the dividing line between two racial worlds. Between the migrants in that field and Mary with her train, the dividing line was me.

Oh God, such lives of misery for the benefit of whites! Good God, centuries of oppression for filthy gain! Your safety pins, Mary, are chains in the shackles of a slavery that has thrived in this nation for centuries! How could such shining virtue flourish under the lashings of such tyrannical whips?

> *Look down, turn usward, bow thine head;*
> *O thou that wast of God forsaken,*
> *Look on thine household here, and see*
> *These that have not forsaken thee.*

The merciful breeze which had wafted through the fir tree window suddenly ceased, and a heavy stifling stillness hung in the air. Mary continued to pull her little freedom train slowly round its track as I gazed down Rural Route 2, past the little rise beyond Baxter's, down toward where the woods came together. The heat from those fields and the humidity from that stream shimmered upward into that mirage which long ago, I perceived as rain - always raining down at MacPhearson's. MacPhearson's. MacPhearson's. Am I perceiving what I think I -? Is that - Am I – Can it be?

> *Listen, Mary...Listen...Are you hearing that?...*
> *Listen...Oh Mary...There it is again...*
> *Coming...coming from so far away...*
> *Listen...Can you hear it?...*
> *From way beyond MacPhearson's? Way down toward the South?*
> *That sound?...Mary? Can you hear that sound?*
> *Oh Mary...They're coming. I hear that now.*
> *Thousands and thousands are shaking the air!*
> *And now I see them, Mary! I see them, and they're coming this way!*
> ***They're coming this way!*** *Now I see!*
> *They're marching, marching through Selma, Alabama,*
> *and they're marching, marching through Louisiana.*
> *No matter how many ball bats crack their skulls,*
> *no matter how many hurled bricks break their backs,*
> *they're going to march and march and march and march*
> *till this whole damn country is a Promised Land.*
> *That clean dirt is coming, Mary. I see it coming,*

an' dey ain't gonna 'plain none whin dey git whut dey git!
The Freedom Train's coming for you, Mary. I can see that now,
and - and I see too it's coming for me.
I ain't comin' back here no mo', Miss Mary,
'cause I's so 'shamed o'myse'f.
I tried t'make yu' life better, bu' nobody 'ud let me.
Dey took yo' plate, an' dey took yo' corn, an' I kudn't do no mo'.
I jus' kudn't do no mo'.
Dat pain in my heart is so deep an' so achin',
dat I cain't breathe no mo', an' all God's chil'n got's t'breathe.
So I's leavin', Mary. I's goin' far, far 'way,
an' you's never gonna see me ag'in.
Bu' next summer - next June - whin you's makin' my cake,
I doan want 'nella no mo'. Not no mo'.
I want dat cake t'be choclit thruu an' thruu.
You make dat cake black thruu an' thruu.
An' whin you's makin' dat cake, Mary,
an' whin you's swirlin' dat frostin',
an' whin you's puttin' on dem purdy 'lil flowr's,
please, please 'member me.
Please 'member me, Mary,
an' please 'member dat I tried.

I left the farm that August. There was no formal good-bye. Mary, the migrants, and all the Clay family suddenly winked out of my existence, like a star, once of the first magnitude, slipping through the event horizon into the forever of a black hole.

In a Christmas card that December,
Frank and Elaine notified me that Mary died
the day before Thanksgiving.

Neither they nor any member of the Clay family
attended her funeral.

She was laid to rest in the Negro cemetery behind her Baptist Church.

The only markers on her grave are a small wooden cross,
fragments of broken glass,
and two perfect halves of one blue-willow plate.

COMPASSION

Kum bay ya, my Lord, Kum bay ya
Kum bay ya, my Lord, Kum bay ya
Kum bay ya, my Lord, Kum bay ya
O Lord, Kum bay ya.

Someone's cryin', Lord, Kum bay ya;
Somone's cryin', Lord, Kum bay ya;
Somone's cryin', Lord, Kum bay ya;
O Lord, Kum bay ya.

Dr. Watts was known as the most challenging and thought-provoking professor on campus, though he appeared at first glance to be the most absent-minded. The knots of his ties were often far left or right of center, and sometimes one lonely brown sock was paired with one lonely blue. He often conveyed an attitude of sheer boredom, which to the uninitiated seemed to indicate that his class would be an *easy A*, but students soon learned that his habit of staring out the window and focusing upon nature was simply a coping skill for bearing his philosophical ponderings when they were the most intense. That spring, he asked in that distant, dreamy voice which was in striking contradiction to his being a low baritone -

"What is mercifulness?"
as he gazed out the window apparently studying
the faint movements of emerging leaves
in the dewy breeze.

"Do unto others as you would have them do unto you,"
shouted Gregory, a musician who later became a priest.

"Y - Yes," Dr. Watts responded simply, almost in a whisper,
his eyes apparently tracking whatever birds were in flight.
Then he added in that characteristic tone of deliberate challenge –

"But is there not at least a *hint* of self-seeking
within that noble line?"

The entire class was stunned once again,
Dr. Watts' thoughts always so profoundly and endlessly disturbing.

"Is it mercifulness," he continued, "true mercifulness,
if the concealed intention is even *remotely* focused on self?"

After a pause
during which he apparently mustered all his courage,
Gregory ventured forth again-

"The Good Samaritan wasn't at all focused on himself.
His intent was solely the needs of that beaten man on that road.
He poured disinfectant in his wounds and bandaged them
and took that man to an inn where he would be continuously cared for.
He even was willing to pay for the care of a man
whom he didn't even know!"

"You're right, Gregory," said Dr. Watts slowly once again,
gazing at a fluttering kite which a bored student must have been flying
out the window at least two floors below.
"Indeed it was an act of mercifulness for a Samaritan to even *stop* for a
Jew beside the road, since the animosity between them was so systemic.
The Samaritan gave quite a grand display of mercifulness,
and is it not true that if he had been able to do more,
he would have displayed more compassion?"

"Absolutely," Gregory shouted out.

"Class, Gregory has articulated the common understanding –
that the grander the gesture, the greater the generosity.
Do you agree that this is the common understanding?"

"Yes, of course. Absolutely."

"So ladies and gentlemen, let's continue this line of inquiry.
If our hypothetical Samaritan could have stayed at that hypothetical inn
himself, would you say that implies more mercifulness?"

"Yes, of course," the class responded in unison.

"And if our hypothetical Samaritan
were a hypothetical medical professional,
who could have further cared for the victim's wounds himself,
would you say that implies even more mercifulness?"

"Yes, certainly. May we ask where you are going with -"

"But what if that Samaritan could do nothing?"
I blurted out. "What if he could offer nothing?"

The entire class turned toward my outburst,
all eyes riveted on me.

"What if – well - What if he had no wine?"
I shouted out, shocked at my own aggression.
"And – and what if he had no bandages?"

Dr. Watts no longer gazed out the window,
but turned his entire attention toward me.
"Please continue, Miss Winfield. Please."

"And – and what if that Samaritan had no money himself?
What if he was poor and couldn't afford anything?
What if he had no money at all for that inn?"

"Please, Miss Winfield, please proceed."

My emotions rising to feverish intensity –

*"And oh! – What if that Samaritan had no donkey,
and – and what if he couldn't stop the bleeding?
What if that man in that ditch got worse?
What if that Samaritan could do absolutely nothing, just nothing?
What if he couldn't do anything for him but – but hold him in his –
Is that not mercifulness?"*

"Miss Winfield?"
Dr. Watts eagerly leaned forward into my gaze.
"Sarah? Hold him in his – his – what, Sarah?
Hold him in – in – "

A breathless hush fell upon that room,
but all my emotions swirled in one devouring vortex.

"Miss Winfield? Are you able to continue?
Are you able to – able to - Mary Emory?"

"Sir?"

"Could you please assist Miss Winfield. Offer her a tissue, perhaps.
Our discussion seems to have triggered a deep response in her.
Yes, Mary, thank you. Sarah, when you are able,
I'd like you to finish your question."

The entire class was mesmorized
at the emotional display unfolding before them.

"Class, this is such an important point

that I'd like to pause here to give Miss Winfield some space.
She apparently is suffering - a memory perhaps?"

A moment later –

"When you are able, Sarah. When you are able."

The eyes of all were fastened upon me.

"Sir, I – I'm sorry, I don't remember the -"

You be alrigh' Sarh, jus' hold ontuh me.
Jus' hol' ontuh my dress, chil'. You be alright.

"You had asked,
'But what if that Samaritan could do nothing for that man,
except hold him in his –'"

"Hold him in his -?"

"Yes. Hold him in his -?"

Feeling faint and unable to breathe, the room spinning around me,
I whispered -

"What if – What if he could do - do - nothing
for that man - except -"

"Yes, Sarah? Except? Please, when you are ready, go on."

" - except hold him in his arms until he died?"

What if I can do nothing for Mary

except hold her in my heart until I die?

"Thank you, Miss Winfield. Thank you.
Thank you for ushering us into that utterly expansive
yet simultaneously constrictive universe of that existential master,
Søren Kierkegaard.
Mary Emory? Please usher Miss Winfield out into the hall, please.
She seems to be undergoing some sort of crisis.
Yes, just take her out into the hall. She could benefit from some -
yes, she definitely needs some air.
That bench in the hall around the corner?
Do you know which one I mean?
You do? Yes, then take her there. You'll have privacy there at this hour.
Take her there and give her some air.
Class, let's pause until Sarah and Mary leave the room."

"Hang onto me, Sarah. Just hold onto me. You look so grey,
like you're about to faint. Just around this corner, you can sit down
and —and - Sit down here, right here. Yes, sit down.
Sarah, you're not breathing. Oh no, you're about to faint.
Please don't faint. Please, please don't faint.
Sarah, you have to breathe! You've got to breathe.
Bend over and put your head between your knees. Lean over, Sarah -
Breathe! Breathe! Breathe!
There's no blood in your face, Sarah. Lean over farther.
You have to breathe! I'm going to put my hands on your back.
Can you feel them? Can you feel my hands there, Sarah? Yes?
Then breathe in and push up against my hands.
Just breathe in and push up — yes, that's right.

*Just breathe, Sarah. Yeah, that's right. Just breathe.
I don't know what you're remembering, Sarah, but you don't ever have
to go back there. You can't ever go back. Just stay here with me now
and know that you don't ever have to go back. And now you're crying.
Oh that's good. You're breathing now. There's nobody in this
hallway - nobody here but us. Just cry all you want, Sarah.
Just cry your little fill. Cry here all afternoon if you want to.
I'll stay with you as long as you need me. I'll be right here.
That's my promise. Just cry all you want,
and I'll stay right here."*

The remainder of that afternoon and evening will forever remain an impressionistic blur. I remember nothing of how we left that hallway, where we spent the evening, or how Mary returned me to my room. I remember only a torrent of images of wonder, grief, and love pouring out of my heart to my friend.

*"And she used to say 'clean dirt' and 'dirty dirt'. And guess what I
learned to say? I said 'clean dirt' and 'dirty dirt' too, just like she
did. And oh! 'Don't go down in that shed!' And she used to wonder,
'Are you running into that coop and scaring those chickens half to
death? They sure aren't laying like they should.' She had a light
brown scar on her arm, but she didn't get tired. And oh! 'Can I
carry the pitch fork?' And she'd say, 'Just hold onto my dress. Don't
be afraid of those snakes.' I really, really tried to peel a potato in
one piece, I really did, but she always – And the blue-willow plate!*

And then I said, 'She's sitting there by me!' We used to cut weed
bouquets, those tall weeds down by the wagon wheel.
And oh, I watered her cactus! Can you believe it?
I watered her cactus three days in a row! 'Only Arizona,' she used
to say, 'only Arizona.' And how could I forget! I used to take
lemon skins and hide…and she said 'I'm not dropping your teeth into
a glass by the time you're seven years old!' And she used to say
'Gracious!' 'All the time, 'Gracious!' And I thought,
'Is my fox head going to bite me?' Isn't that funny,
I thought that fox head would bite me."

I remember talking on and on, crying on and on, and sometimes
sobbing. I remember tissue after tissue, cup after cup of heavenly
scented tea, and crying and laughing at the same time. I remember
climbing into bed with profound exhaustion and marveling at the moon
rising slowly over Gardner Hall as it rose so long ago over the shed. And
I thought, *This moonrise is more glorious than I can bear.*

Mercifulness is a work of love,
even if it can give nothing and is capable of doing nothing.
Søren Kierkegaard.
Works of Love

What I was able to give to Mary, I had freely given.
What she was able to give to me, she had freely given.

We had given to each other compassion,
and in the end, that's the greatest gift of all.

I fell asleep in a massive peace and a mighty benediction. I
dreamt all night of great clouds of glittering fireflies swirling over alfalfa
fields under the shimmering glow of a cresent moon. Have you ever

seen great clouds of glittering fireflies swirling over alfalfa fields under the shimmering glow of a cresent moon? I have, and they are so, so beautiful.

I woke the next morning at 10:30 in my single room in Harper Hall. The sun was glistening off the windows of Gardner across the way. I had slept right through geology, and slept through western civ. As I hurried out the door to my world literature class, I saw a faded plant sitting on the floor next to my door. The card safety-pinned inside its crinkled pink foil read -

To Sarah, my dearest friend – I wanted so badly to buy you an armful of roses, tall purples, daisies, and some sort of little yellows, but being the poor college student that I am, I could afford only this flower labeled, 'Reduced for Quick Sale.'
Please accept this Easter lily with my deepest hopes that you are feeling better, and that you have found lasting peace about your experiences on your farm.
With affection always,
Mary

LOVE'S WEDDING DRESS

Well, my 'lil doney gal, doan you guess
Better be makin' yo' weddin' dress
Weddin' dress, weddin 'dress,
Better be makin' yo' weddin' dress

Well, it's alredy made an' trimmed in brown
Stitched all 'roun' wid a golden crown
Golden crown, golden crown
Stitched all 'roun' wid a golden crown.

I don't grieve for Mary now. She has attained the status of archetypal and simply cannot die. There is no way I could shrink her stature into the spare cubic footage of a commoner's grave. Sometimes the greatest gestures of generiosity are viewed by others as the most selfish. She was a combination of Earth Mother, Black Madonna, Suffering Servant, and Wisdom Teacher. She has always been my role model, and will continue to be for as long as I live.

I can't fathom what plane of being Mary inhabits today, what depth of the Mystic Sea inundates her soul. But in my romantic imagination, she is dressed forever in Mongomery Ward white, with matching shoes and gloves, singing in Heaven's Baptist choir as the Great Preacher's wife. And on her head is a merited crown of a weight I will never know, because she had lived her life as *a filthy nigger*, and had nobly borne that title on her cross with dignity, strength, and peace.

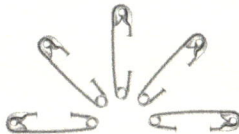

Dialect

One of the great accomplishments of the African-American people centuries ago was their learning English as a second language without formal instruction. Relying solely upon their intelligence and sense of hearing, these men, women, and children who had been captured with nets and forced across the Atlantic Ocean in shackles on slave ships in conditions of unimaginable squalor, were then required to obey the unintelligible sounds of the white man's language under penalty of death.

Two dialects are presented in *One Little Life.* Mary's vocabulary, which obviously had more northern nuance, was fairly easy for me as a child to understand and fairly easy for the contemporary reader to read. For those unfamiliar with dialect, a dictionary of her vocabulary has been provided in the following pages.

However, the speech patterns of the migrant workers who journeyed to the farm from the Deep South were very difficult for me to understand and for the contemporary reader to read, because their language combined both Negro dialect and southern nuance. Rather than provide a separate dictionary for them, their portion of each conversation found in Chapters Two and Seven has been translated into standard English in the appendix following Mary's Dictionary. Their unique spellings were gleaned largely from the poetry of Paul Lawrence Dunbar and from Mark Twain's *Huckleberry Finn.*

The reader is invited to read aloud portions of both Mary's dialogue and those of the Mississippi migrant for two reasons. This process will enable the reader to feel, vicariously, the actual effort slaves exerted to imitate the white man's sounds before fully comprehending the white man's meaning. Reading aloud the passages of the Mississippi migrant will enable the reader, to whatever degree the heart of the reader is open, to enter that man's despair.

Many in the contemporary world consider the presentation of any form of dialect to be subtly offensive to African-Americans. In this book, however, these two forms are presented without apology as a tribute to the intelligence, courage, and strength of a people who learned the most difficult of all languages under the greatest possible duress, and who exhibited the highest possible virtue while enduring the deepest possible deprivation.

Mary's Dictionary

A

afear'd	afraid
aftuh	after
aftuhnoon	afternoon
ag'in	again
alredy	already
al'ys	always
an'	and
ast	asked

B

b'hind	behind
b'fo'	before
b'neath	beneath
ben	been
bodder	bother
'bout	about
brudder	brother
bu'	but

C

car'y	carry
'cause	because
choclit	chocolate
color'd	colored
come'd	came
'crost	across

D

deez	these
dem ('em)	them
den	then
dere	their or they're
dey'd	they'd
din'	didn't
dooz	those
diffunce	difference

doan	don't
do'	door
d'rection	direction
d'odder	the other
durn	damn

E

edder	either
ef ef'n	if
eny	any
enyt'ing	anything
er	or
ev'n	even
ev'nin'	evening
evy	every
evyt'ing	everything
es	as

F

fas'n	fasten
fasn'd	fastened
fe'el	field
flowr's	flowr's
fo' or fu'	for
fo'ks	folks
foever fuever	forever
fugit	forget
fugot	forgot
furst	first

G

gadder	gather
gonna	going to
got's	have to

H

Heav'n	Heaven
hisse'f	himself
hullo	hello

huny   honey
hur'y   hurry
hurse'f   herself

I
'il   will
intuh   into
isn't   ain't

K
kin   can
know'd   knew
kud   could

L
land sakes   as in 'goodness sake'
lemme   let me
lif'   lift

M
madders   tomatoes
madder   as in 'no matter what'
min'   mind
miny   many
misr'y   misery
Missus   Mrs. or mistress of the house or plantation
Mistuh   Mr.
mi'ty   mighty
mo'   more
mo'nin'   morning
mos'ly   mostly
mos'   most   almost
mudder   mother
mus'   must
must'a   must have

N
needer   neither

'nella   vanilla
nut'ing   nothing
'nough   enough
'nudder   another
nowhar   nowhere

O
odder   other
on 'em   on them
ontuh   on to
outta   out of
overwid   overwith

P
po'   poor
po'ly   poorly
pow'ful   powerful
'posed   supposed
'preciate   appreciate
'preciative   appreciative
purdy   pretty
purtect   protect

R
reck'n   reckon
redy   ready
righ' shere   right here
roun'   round   around

S
shephud   shepherd
shere   here
sho'   sure
sho't   short
shu'ly   surely
shud   should
shuu   you   as in 'doan shuu' don't you
Suh   Sir
somet'ing   something

T

tuhday	today
t'aint	it ain't it isn't
t'ank	thank
tatters	potatoes
terr'ble	terrible
thruu	through
thurds	thirds
t'ings	things
t'ink	think
tol'	told
t'ought	thought
t'ree	three
truble	trouble
tuhgether	together
tuhnight	tonight

U

ud	would
undur	under
'lil un	little one
uns	ones
ust	used

W

whar	where
warn't	weren't wasn't
watuh	water
whin	when
whut	what
wid or wif	with
widout	without
widout shuu	without you
wil'	wild
willuh	willow
winduh	window
wisht	wished
w'ite	white

woan	won't
wurk	work
wud or wudda	would
wudda	would have
wunder	wonder
wunst	once
wurd	word
wurst	worse

X

'xactly	exactly

Y

y'	you, your
yelluh	yellow
yestuhday	yesterday
yit	yet
yo'	your
yung'in	young one
yuse'f	yourself

Responses of Mississippi Migrant in Chapter Two:
Introduction to Racism

"Ma'am, I'm no gentleman, but I'm more than just swamp trash.
I haven't had anything to eat for three days
and I'm powerful hungry after all that work.
Even swamp trash needs more than water to work.
I'm not meaning to bother you, I'm not meaning to be trouble.
I was just wondering –"

"This morning here, I was scared I was dying,
scared and feeling hungry and sick with no more than water
and because I'm all worn out with work. I am dying. I know that.
I am sick and dying, and I don't care anymore what old Mister Clay does
to me. Or his Mrs. I don't care what his family does to me.
I'm going to take that chance.
'What is the worst thing that can happen at the big house?' I thought.
Haven't I already had the worst thing? I'm dying anyhow. I know that.
They're going to lay me soon beneath that willow anyhow."

"Would you happen to have anything to eat?
Never mind it's not possum and greens. Never mind it's not corn pone.
Even if I have to ask them twice, I'm going to take that chance.
Even if these are the last words out of my mouth,
I'm going to take chance, or else I'll be dying in those fields today."

"I'm more than swamp trash, but even trash needs something to eat.
You are about to eat yourself, because I can hear that.
I'm no different, Miss, no different. I'm almost as good."

Responses of Mississippi Migrant in Chapter 7:
Introduction to the Demonic.

"About a hundred, Sir"

"No sir. Hundred is all we got."

"Well Sir, this morning, Sir, our truck was broke, and then Master Clifford couldn't find those new bags that –"

"I know, Sir, but he couldn't find them. They were delivered to Master Winston's, and we couldn't find them. Master Clifford was going to ask, but then he got them. And then, Sir, then that belt done slipped again, and Master Winston had to take it apart. And then, Sir, that first truck of potatoes was bad, Master Clay. They were bad something awful. We didn't get more than a third of them at the most. Most of them we had to throw down, cause –"

"But after that, the last truck, Sir, was better, Sir. It was better, and this one here is all good. That's why we got a hundred now. They're coming hard now, Sir. They're real good. We are doing better."

"And Master Clay, Sir, I'm not meaning to be a fuss, but in the bus is a sick one, Sir – a little one, Sir that's – that's real bad off. We were wondering, Sir. We aren't meaning to be a fuss, but can a doctor come, because –"

Acknowledgments

My gratitude to Miss Mina Marie Brown
for posing so patiently as little Sarah Winfield.

My gratitude to Scott and Karen Hammond
for graciously granting permission to photograph
their beautiful properties –
Hydebrook Farms,
Yellow Springs, Ohio.

Photo Credits

Images from the author's collection:
Cover photo; Page 137 (top); Page 167: (bottom); Page 197: (bottom);
Page 303 (bottom)

Images courtesy of Scott and Karen Hammond:
Page xi; Page 13 (top); Page 143 (top); Page 331 (bottom); Page 369 (top)

Image from istockphoto.com:
photo corners: copyright: hanibaram

Images from Shutterstock.com:
Cover background: watin; safety pins: microvector;
Page 13: Ramon grosso dolarea (bottom);
Page 35: Benoit Daoust (top); JÃÂ¶rg Unfried (bottom);
Page 59: sunlover (top); igor kisselev (bottom);
Page 77: Elena Dijour (top); Dustie (bottom);
Page 111: Sentimental Photos (top); Sharon Day (bottom);
Page 123: Mark Skalny (top); Dima Sobko (bottom);
Page 137: dmvphotos (bottom);
Page 143: symbiot (bottom);
Page 167: Gianna Stadelmyer (top);
Page 197: Jeff Feverston (top);
Page 209: Jeanne Provost (top); Flegere (bottom);
Page 233: Alex Sun (top); TTstudio (bottom);
Page 249: mongione (top); Cindy Haggerty (bottom);
Page 255: Everett Historical (top); Arina P Habich (bottom);
Page 267: val lawless (top); Lost Mountain Studio (bottom);
Page 303: Elena Schweitzer (top);
Page 311: Elena Elisseeva (top); Konstanttin (bottom);
Page 331: Everett Historical (top);
Page 369: Pete Spiro (bottom)

Endnotes

The lyrics of the Spirituals in this book have been adapted
to approximate Mary's speech.

v. William Faulkner. Knight's Gambit. "Tomorrow."
New York: Random House, 1939. 104.

ix. Harry Dixon Loes. "This Little Light of Mine."

1. *Richard Smallwood Lyrics.* "Calvary."
www.azlyrics.com/lyrics/richardsmallwood/calvary.html.

   John Milton Milton's Paradise Lost. Complete and Unabridged.
   Illustrations by Gustave Doré. London: Arcturus Publishing
   Limited, 2005. 111.

2. Milton. 113. 113. 113.

3. Milton. 113. 113.

5. Sterling Brown.
   *Modern American Poetry. Negro Folk Expression:
   Spirituals, Seculars, Ballads and Work Songs.*
   "Our Father Who is in Heaven."
   www.english.illinois.edu/maps/pottis/
   a-f/brown/folkexpression/.htm.

15. Seymour-Winfield. "Dere's a Promise Land a'Comin'."

23. Seymour-Winfield. "O, Whut's y'Gonna Eat."

32. These lyrics, which were found on the web years ago,
    have apparently been mercifully deleted. They are included
    here solely because they perfectly reflect the utter hatred I
    witnessed as a child for every skin tone other than white.

42. Gen 3:8

47. John W. Work. "Somebody's Knocking At Your Door." <u>American Negro Songs: 230 Folk Songs and Spirituals, Religious and Secular</u>. New York: Dover Publications, Inc., 1998. 192.

64. Seymour-Winfield. "Las' Night I Was a'Dreamin'."

67. "We'll Understand It Better Bye And Bye." cyberhymnal.org/htm/w/e/welunder.htm.

75. Work. "Where Shall I Go?" 118.

88. *Richard Smallwood Lyrics.* "Angels Watching Over Me."

95. Work. "Daniel Saw The Stone." 120.

110. Work. "God Is A God." 51.

116. Work. "All Over This World." 167.

122. Work. "Sometimes I Feel Like A Motherless Chile." 146.

139. Work. "Tryin' To Get Home." 55.

154. *Richard Smallwood Lyrics.* "My Ol' Misses Promise Me."

176. Work. "Give Me Your Hand." 170.

188. Work. "There's A Great Camp Meeting." 143.

222-223. https://answers.yahoo.com/question/indes?qid=20080116112847AAkbJIE. ghouly05.

Adaptation of "Ladies do and the gents you know
It's right by right by wrong you go,
And you can't go to heaven while you carry on so
And it's home little gal and do-si-do."

Remainder of lyrics by Sarah Seymour-Winfield
with traditional square dance calls.

224. "This World Is Not My Home.".
arnet.pair.com/RedEllis/lyr/worldnotmyhome.htm.

235. Loes. Refrain from "This Little Light of Mine."

272-277. Work. "My Sins Been Taken Away." 158.

281. Eileen Southern and Josephine Wright. "Oh Who's That Coming
Over Yonder, Hallelujah." African-American Traditions in
Song, Sermons, Tales, and Dance, 1605-1920. An Annotated
Bibliography of Literature, Collections, and Artwork.
Connecticut: Greenwood Publishing Group, Inc., 1990. 1312.

309. "Rise Up, Shepherd, And Follow."
cyberhymnal.org.htm/r/i/riseupsh.htm.

314. Henry David Thoreau. 'Solitude.' The Writings of Henry David
Thoreau: Walden. With an Introduction by John Updike. New
Jersey: Princeton University Press, 2004. 129.

318. Gerard Manly Hopkins. 'God's Grandeur.' The Oxford Book of
Christian Verse. Lord David Cecil, ed. London: Oxford
University Press, 1951. 495.

339. Slavery in Canada. "The Gospel Train's a'Comin'."
www.canadachannel.ca/slavery/index.php.

352. Work. "The Hammers Keep Ringing." 116.

359. Herman Melville. Melville: Redburn, White-Jacket, Moby Dick.
With Notes and Chronology by G. Thomas Tanselle. The
Library of America. New York: Literary Classics of the United
States, Inc., 1983. 1303. 1303.

Sophocles. 'Oedipus at Colonus.' David Grene, trans. The
Complete Greek Tragedies Volume II. David Grene and
Richmond Lattimore, ed. Chicago: The University of Chicago
Press, 1992. 146. 147. 147. 149. 149.

360. Grene. 151.

361-364. Edwin Markham. 'The Man with the Hoe.' The Cry for Social Justice: An Anthology of the Literature of Social Protest. Upton Sinclair, ed. Philadelphia: The John C. Winston Co., 1915; Bartleby.com, 2010. www.bartleby.com/71/

364. *Slavery in Canada.* "The Gospel's Train a'Comin'."

365. Algernon Swinburne. 'Before a Crucifix.' The Works of Algernon Charles Swinburne. With an introduction by Laurence Binyon. The Wordsworth Poetry Library. Denmark: Nøhaven, 1995. 145.

371. "Kum Bay Ya." www.scoutsongs.com/lyrics/kumbayah.html.

378. Søren Kiekegaard. Works of Love: Some Christian Reflections in the Form of Discourses. Trans. Howard and Edna Hong. New York: Harper Torchbooks, 1962. 305.

381. "Wedding Dress." (My Doney Gal.) www.trewamusic.net/files/trewa1.pdf.

Bibliography

Brown, Sterling. *"Modern American Poetry. Negro Folk Expression: Spirituals, Seculars, Ballads and Work Songs."* www.english.illinois.edu/maps/pottis/ a-f/brown/folkexpression/.htm.

Cecil, Lord David, ed. The Oxford Book of Christian Verse. London: Oxford University Press, 1951.

DeYanni, Robert. Literature: Reading Fiction, Poetry, and Essay. Third Edition. New York: McGraw-Hill, Inc., 1994.

Faulkner, William. Knight's Gambit. New York: Random House, 1939.

Fox-Genovese, Elizabeth. Within the Plantation Household: Black and White Women of the Old South. Chapel Hill: The University of North Carolina Press, 1988.

Grene, David and Richmond Lattimore, ed. The Complete Greek Tragedies: Sophocles. Volume II. Chicago: The University of Chicago Press, 1992.

Kierkegaard, Søren. Works of Love: Some Christian Reflections in the Form of Discourses. Trans. Howard and Edna Hong. New York: Harper Torchbooks, 1962.

Melville, Herman. Melville: Redburn, White-Jacket, Moby Dick. With Notes and Chronology by G. Thomas Tanselle. The Library of America. New York: Literary Classics of the United States, Inc., 1983.

Milton, John. Milton's Paradise Lost: Complete and Unabridged. Illustrations by Gustave Doré. London: Arcturus Publishing Limited, 2005.

Sinclair, Upton, ed. The Cry for Social Justice: An Anthology of The Literature of Social Protest. Philadelphia: The John C. Winston Co., 1915; Bartleby.com, 2010. www.bartleby.com/71/.

Smallwood, Richard. *Richard Smallwood Lyrics.* www.azlyrics.com/lyrics/richardsmallwood/calvary.html.

Southern, Eileen, and Josephine Wright. African – American Traditions in Song, Sermons, Tales, and Dance, 1605-1920. An annotated Bibliography of Literature, Collections, and Artwork. Connecticut: Greenwood Publishing Group, Inc., 1990.

Swinburne, Algernon. The Works of Algernon Charles Swinburne. With an Introduction by Laurence Binyon. Wordsworth Poetry Library. Denmark: Nøhaven, 1995.

Thoreau, Henry D. The Writings of Henry D. Thoreau: Walden. With an Introduction by John Updike. New Jersey: Princeton University Press, 2004.

Tobin, Jacqueline L. and Raymond G, Dobard, Ph. D. Hidden In Plain View: The Secret Story of Quilts and the Underground Railroad. New York: Doubleday, 1950.

Work, John W. American Negro Songs: 230 Folk Songs and Spirituals, Religious and Secular. New York: Dover Publications, Inc., 1998.

www.ingramcontent.com/pod-product-compliance
Lightning Source LLC
Chambersburg PA
CBHW050806270326
41926CB00026B/4570